The Great Silver Bubble

By the same author

THE ZINOVIEV LETTER
(with Lewis Chester and Hugo Young)

MEASURE FOR MEASURE

HOAX
(with Lewis Chester and Magnus Linklater)

THE DEATH OF VENICE
(with Phillip Knightley)

The Great Silver Bubble

Stephen Fay

HODDER AND STOUGHTON
LONDON SYDNEY AUCKLAND TORONTO

British Library Cataloguing in Publication Data

Fay, Stephen
The great silver bubble.
1. Hunt, Nelson Bunker
2. Hunt, William Herbert
3. Silver—United States 4. Speculation
I. Title
332.63'28 HG6047.S/

ISBN 0 340 28370 X

 Printed in Great Britain for Hodder and Stoughton Limited, Mill Road, Dunton Green, Sevenoaks, Kent by St Edmundsbury Press, Bury St Edmunds, Suffolk. Photoset by Rowland Phototypesetting Limited, Bury St Edmunds, Suffolk. Hodder and Stoughton Editorial Office: 47 Bedford Square, London WC1B 3DP

To Prudence

People of the same trade seldom meet together, even for merriment and diversion, but the conversation ends in a conspiracy against the public, or in some contrivance to raise prices. It is impossible indeed to prevent such meetings, by any law which either could be executed, or would be consistent with liberty and justice. But though the law cannot hinder people of the same trade from sometimes assembling together, it ought to do nothing to facilitate such assemblies; much less to render them necessary.

– Adam Smith, *An Inquiry into the Nature and Causes of the Wealth of Nations*

His watchmen are blind: they are all ignorant, they are all dumb dogs, they cannot bark; sleeping, lying down, loving to slumber.

Yea, they are greedy dogs which can never have enough, and they are shepherds that cannot understand: they all look to their own way, every one for his gain, from his quarter.

Come ye, say they, I will fetch wine, and we will fill ourselves with strong drink; and to morrow shall be as this day, and much more abundant.

– Isaiah 56:10–12

Contents

Illustrations

ACKNOWLEDGMENTS

1 Wide World Photos
2 Herbie Knott
3 Thierry Gayet,
4 Courtesy of Jerome Smith
5 Courtesy of the Federal Reserve

Prologue

The rich have always been with us, even if they are, as Scott Fitzgerald put it, simply 'different from you and me'. In the 1970s, however, for a small number of the rich, the difference was no longer that they had more money. Their wealth swelled so hugely that the English language was scarcely capable of defining it. There is no superlative of 'rich' adequate to describe the billions of dollars accumulated by members of this select group in a few places such as Texas and Saudi Arabia.

This exclusive bonanza was paid for largely by consumers of oil after OPEC ruthlessly quadrupled the price late in 1973. The benefits of that convulsion were immediately apparent in Arabia, but they trickled down through the economies of the West hardly at all. Instead, the new oil price helped create inflation, severe recession, and unemployment. The international economy, from Britain to Brazil, and from Upper Volta to the United States, was more vulnerable to unexpected shocks than at any time since the 1930s.

Of the three consequences of their bonanza, only inflation obsessed the new billionaires. Unlike the old rich, who confidently invested their money in blue-chip stocks and securities, the new rich were afraid that inflation and taxation would erode their fortunes. So they preferred to gamble rather than to save. They were still greedy for more, preferably in a form that was immune to inflation. They bought *things* that, unlike money, they believed, must increase in value. Some bought corporations, whole; a few bought silver.

Those who bought silver are the subjects of this story: Nelson Bunker Hunt, and his brother William Herbert, along with a couple of remarkably wealthy princes of the kingdom of Saudi Arabia, and their front men. As new billionaires, people with more money than other generations had ever dreamed of, they could buy on a scale that had never been contemplated before. Individuals – people whose faces could be spotted at a football game in Dallas, a camel race in Riyadh, or the unsaddling enclosure at Longchamp in Paris – controlled 280 million ounces of silver. Much of this was bullion, of a minimum fineness of .999, each bar impressed with its weight, serial number, and assay mark, and deposited in secure warehouses in New York, London, Chicago, and Geneva. The rest of this unique hoard was in the form of contracts to buy silver, known in commodity markets as futures contracts.

If the silver nominated in those contracts had actually been purchased (as it could have been) and added to the bullion, these few individuals would have owned a stockpile equivalent to four out of every five ounces of silver mined throughout the world in 1979, or, alternatively, nearly twice as much silver as is used in the United States in a year. Two hundred and eighty thousand 1,000-ounce bars of bullion, measuring 12½ × 5½ × 3½ inches would, piled on top of each other, have risen into the stratosphere, to 81,666 feet – almost double the cruising altitude of *Concorde*. Laid end to end, the bars would have stretched about 55 miles, roughly the distance from London to Oxford, or Boston to Providence.

Those were the physical dimensions of the hoard; its value was even more astonishing. When the silver price peaked at $50 an ounce in January 1980, that silver hoard was worth $14 billion, a sum which would have financed all the United States government's spending on medical care in 1980 or the cost of Britain's old-age pensions; and which was bigger than the gross national products of Kenya, Tanzania, and Zimbabwe combined. Although the specific object of the group of buyers was not economic power, they owned so much silver that they almost achieved it, for they were on the brink of controlling the world price.

Such rich men prefer to gamble with other people's money, of course, and since they appeared to be impeccable credit risks, much of their buying was done on credit lavished upon them by the biggest banks in the United States and Switzerland, and by the world's largest brokerage houses on Wall Street. But when the price began to fall away from that high of $50, brokers needed cash to cover the diminishing value of the futures contracts – cash that is called for daily in commodity markets and is known as margin. Because of the scale of the group's buying, their debts, as the price fell, were counted in billions of dollars, too.

The Hunts and the Saudis created a bubble in the silver market, and when it burst, their speculation endangered those brokerage houses, and some of the banks that had been such generous creditors. Wall Street teetered on the edge of a panic, and since all the financial communities of the West are now interdependent, a shock in one sector travels through the whole network with the speed of a telex message; the impact can shatter links anywhere along the chain. The day the bubble burst was so nerve-racking and frenetic that it was named 'Silver Thursday' on Wall Street, the first day singled out for the award of an adjective since 'Black Thursday' in 1929, an augury of the Great Depression.

The most alarming thing about the crisis caused by the silver bubble was that no one in the markets, or in the banks in the United States and Europe, or among the men running government agencies in Washington, could predict how it would work itself out or what the consequences would be. Anything could have happened, and the policymakers felt powerless to control events.

Because everyone, in fact, survived the episode in one way or another, many of the participants now adopt a more nonchalant attitude than they did at the time. It is almost as though they are trying to erase the memory of the awful threat that hung over them all, perhaps in the belief that if they forget about it, nothing like it will ever happen again. Others cling to the fashionable belief that it is only the great multinational corporations, not individuals, who are the captains of our fate. But to ignore the greed and eccentric motivations of the stupendously rich is an error. This story is about the head of a family that wanted to become the richest in the world, not for political power but because that was the way the Hunts always 'kept the score'. In the attempt, one member of that family single-handedly inspired the events that culminated in Silver Thursday.

Chapter 1

An Accident-prone Billionaire

It all began, as it ended, with an astounding gamble. I started by trying to understand the end; but, like most stories, the saga of Bunker Hunt's pursuit of riches beyond the dreams of avarice makes no sense until you go back to the beginning – to the Libyan desert in the 1950s.

Gambling comes naturally to wildcatters, the real oilmen who do the exploring and leave the marketing to smooth city men in collars and ties. The gamble is an instinct, and either it is in the blood or it is not. Bunker Hunt inherited that instinct from his father, H. L. Hunt, who was the archetype of a Texas oil billionaire – arrogant, prejudiced, mean, eccentric and secretive. Bunker wanted to prove to his daddy that he was just as good an oilman as old H.L. himself had been. When Bunker was in his twenties, H.L. might well have been the richest man in the world, so that was some ambition, and it needed some money. Bunker had both, but the scale of his ambition set him apart from other rich boys. To achieve the standard set by his father, Bunker's oil find would simply have to be one of the biggest in the world.

Bunker Hunt first drilled for oil in Texas in the late 1940s, and he found some, too; but it was a trial run, to familiarize himself with the basics. What he wanted no longer existed in America, where all the big fields had been discovered. He knew he would have to go abroad, to some place that had been ignored by the giant oil corporations – Exxon, Shell, British Petroleum, Texaco, Mobil, Gulf, and Standard Oil of California – which are known collectively as 'the Seven Sisters'.

Bunker chose Pakistan, where no substantial oil discoveries had been made before – or since, for that matter. He had the optimism of a real oilman, the hubris of a real Hunt, and the misfortune of a real beginner. His arrival in Karachi in 1953 caused a stir; he was a Hunt, he announced grandly, and the Hunts found oil wherever they looked for it. Bunker looked on the Makran coast, but he omitted to build proper roads, and when the rains came – nobody had told him about the rains – his supply trucks could not get through to the rigs. Supplies had to be parachuted in. The comedy had an unhappy ending: there was a decent gas field, but no oil; and nobody wanted the gas.

His colleagues told Bunker that the experience had not been entirely a waste of time and money, although it had consumed both in generous quantities. He had learned about the austere, lonely life on the rigs, had taken his first lessons in the perils of an independent oilman's relations with foreign governments, had established a reputation for cutting costs to the minimum. This was making a virtue out of necessity, but older oilmen than himself admired his ability to get a well dug far less expensively than the big exploration teams. Even so, his first foreign adventure was an expensive education. Pakistan cost him $30 million, and he had nothing tangible to show for it.

Bunker Hunt arrived in Libya from Pakistan in 1955. Libya was an inhospitable North African desert, whose most familiar features were World War II battlefields, but it did promise oil. Geologists were fairly sure that an old field discovered in Algeria would spill over into Libya, and the oil rush that began in the late 1950s was not confined to independents like Bunker; the vast multinationals were interested, too.

Libya had recently been given its independence, and the power to grant oil-exploration concessions belonged to King Idris, the first and last, who was able to finance a life-style to which he had not always been accustomed, with bribes paid for the best concessions – those in the west, by the Algerian border. Bunker did not like paying bribes. They offended his sense of morality, and they were expensive.

His reluctance did not rule him out, but the concession granted to him was just about as far from the Algerian border as you can get, in the province of Cyrenaica, toward Libya's border with Egypt. A further disadvantage was its location in the middle of minefields laid by the advancing and retreating British and German armies during World War II. But it was better than nothing, and the concession had been granted to Bunker personally. (His absolute independence was difficult to grasp at the time. He was not even a company, although commentators would refer to his operation as *The* Nelson Bunker Hunt, as if to invest it with the proper corporate status.)

The story could have ended right there, in the minefields, except for Bunker's instinct. As a gambling man, he believed that the more cards he could draw on, the better his chances would be, even if the cards were those which no one else thought worth picking up. He had observed a profound lack of interest among the Seven Sisters in vast stretches of the Sahara desert hundreds of miles inland from the Mediterranean. These were so unpromising that the king did not even expect bribes for them, so the concession was a bargain. Bunker ordered his geologists to draw up a claim. There was nothing to lose.

There was not much to go on, either. Geologists did not have the time to drive deep into the desert, and had to rely on old Italian maps. The area was some three hundred miles south of Tobruk, beyond the oasis of Jarabub, in the Calansho Sand Sea. There did appear to be a few promising structures in the sand, and the claim was drawn up to embrace as many as possible. Looking like a big T – for Texas, Bunker said – it was registered as Block 65 in the area known as Sarir. When the concession had been filed, Bunker flew down to look it over, and what he saw pleased him not at all. The geologist had misread the maps, and one whole limb of the T was right in the sea of sand.

His luck was no better in the minefields of Cyrenaica. One of his geologists was badly hurt when his jeep touched off an unexploded mine, and none of the wells produced commercial quantities of oil. Exploration meant time, frustration, and even more money, but Bunker was no quitter. In Dallas he borrowed from his brothers, Herbert and Lamar, to stay in the game. But his luck did not change, and by 1960 his money had all but dried up.

The Seven Sisters had not done much better in Libya. The oil in the sands near Algeria had proved illusory, so they began to look inland, and they discovered that one of the concessions that seemed worth a gamble belonged to Bunker Hunt. He does not like joint ventures, but when British Petroleum came along and offered to drill in Block 65 in return for half of any oil they found, Bunker had virtually no choice.

The deal did not at first appear to change Bunker's luck. In 1961 BP's experienced drilling teams struck out into the desert and drilled one well in Block 65. They reported that it was dry. So was the second well, and the third. With the bit still deep in the sand, the rig superintendent transmitted the bad news back to base. There seemed no need to mull it over; he was told to cut his losses and come home. It looked as though Bunker would be going home, too.

Then, just for luck, the rig superintendent drilled another ten feet into the sand before withdrawing the bit from the third hole, and, in doing so, uncovered Bunker's ace. That ten feet was enough to pierce the cap of one of the world's largest oil fields. It was the gusher Bunker had always sought – maybe not the biggest in the world, but certainly one of the Top Ten. It was a pity, of course, that he had not actually drilled it himself. Never mind; he owned half of it, it would do.

By 1965 the geologists had done their calculations and come up with a sum of the oil reserves in the Sarir Field: they amounted to between 8 and 10 billion barrels of oil, at least half of it recoverable. While the engineers studied methods of getting it to the sea at Tobruk, the economists worked out that Bunker's half share must be worth something around $4 billion, even at the depressed price oil sold for then. Although he had sold off 15 per cent of his share to Herbert and Lamar when he desperately needed cash, Bunker now had more oil in the ground than any one individual in the world, including his father.

In the summer of 1966, when the oil from the Sarir Field was almost ready to flow through the 350-mile-long, 34-inch pipeline to the Mediterranean, Bunker did something quite out of character. He phoned his man in London and said that he believed he would like to give a dance. He had something to celebrate – and it might even give an anonymous Texan a pleasing image.

The venue was the ballroom of Claridge's, one of London's deservedly fashionable hotels. Bunker gave a dinner for fifty before the dancing began, and a minor sprig of the aristocracy organized no fewer than twenty-two more dinner parties for the six hundred and fifty guests who were drawn from the British political establishment, the diplomatic corps, and the upper reaches of the oil industry. There were Hermès scarves for the women (Bunker worried that this might appear vulgar, but none of the recipients seemed to think so). The music was by Woody Herman and Humphrey Lyttelton, and the ballroom was transformed into a scene from the South Seas. A good time was had by all, including Bunker, who really enjoyed it, and his name did appear in the gossip columns.

There was no doubt among the guests that Bunker could afford it. His gamble had paid off magnificently. His share of the Sarir Field made him, notionally at least, the richest man in the world, and he was only forty. There was almost nothing he could not buy.

Only one man thought Bunker's dance was ostentatious, and he expressed his displeasure in Dallas. Old H.L. was decidedly crusty about the whole affair; he thought it a bad thing that young oilmen should parade their new wealth. So Bunker did what his daddy told him, returned to anonymity, and from then on let his image take care of itself.

Within six short years Bunker had lost his lovely Libyan oil field, but not before he had extracted many tens of millions of dollars' profit from his share of it. He thought the loss unjust, nonetheless. He is a religious man, but one Biblical text that he has never been able to adjust to is the one that acknowledges that the Lord giveth and the Lord taketh away.

Nelson Bunker Hunt was given plenty to start with. He was born in 1926 with a silver spoon in his mouth in a town at the epicentre of the Arkansas oil rush, appropriately named El Dorado. His financial inheritance was secured at the age of nine, when H. L. Hunt established a trust for each of his children; and since there are no riches like oil riches, Bunker grew up a very wealthy young man. He shared the family's physical characteristics, notably the small eyes that can narrow, in a blink, into suspicious slits, and he had a tendency to jowliness in the cheeks from boyhood. (No one in the family grew quite so large, however. Despite efforts to control his girth by jogging from time to time, Bunker weighs in at between 280 and 300 pounds.) But Bunker's inheritance was not confined to money and looks. To become better acquainted with Bunker, we have to know more about his daddy.

The story of H. L. Hunt is told in his autobiography, called *Hunt Heritage*. The volume is what booksellers describe as rare, and this is an apt description of a full-blooded *apologia pro vita sua*. It nestles, along with a collection of his newspaper columns, titled *Hunt for Truth*, in the Texas Collection of the Dallas Public Library, an admirable institution on Commerce Street. Although the two volumes do not tell us the whole story of old H.L., they are useful corroborative evidence for a tale that sounds suspiciously like a plot for a television series – *Dallas*, for example.

Hunt Heritage traces the family history all the way back to a chaplain who left Blackwall, on the River Thames, in 1606 and arrived in America on April 27, 1607, beating the Pilgrim Fathers by some years. Evidence for this is not documented; nor are the claims that H.L.'s ancestors included the first governor of Georgia and officers in the Continental Army. The Hunts were Southerners, who moved from Georgia to Arkansas, and lived there until the end of the Civil War, when Haroldson Lafayette Hunt moved north to Illinois to escape the turmoil of Reconstruction. There he married Ella Rose Myers, the granddaughter of Huguenot immigrants, and they had eight children. The last of these, christened Haroldson Lafayette Hunt, Jr., was born on February 17, 1889.

H.L.'s recollections of his childhood flatter him somewhat. He recalled an uncommon precocity in financial matters, dispensing advice that he would appear to have omitted subsequently to pass on directly to his sons. 'My father and elder brothers often traded in the futures commodity and provisions markets, sometimes in the stock market. When a little kid, I told them that trading in futures, for farmers and cattle raisers, was a gamble with people who shuffled out, and dealt, and telegraphed them what their hand was. Nevertheless, I have made a few stock market ventures, which, without exception, bore out the childish warning I gave my elders.'

H.L.'s mother, Ella Rose, was a teacher, but she was unable to persuade her youngest son of the virtue of education. In one of his articles, H.L. states firmly: 'I am asked if education is a requisite for success. My answer is that education is highly desirable in achieving refinement and culture, but for making money it is a liability. To accumulate wealth the money maker must be lucky and have his good fortune occur at a critical time. He must be of an acquisitive nature and should be energetic. Foresight may be stressed, but I look upon financial success as the result of accurate timing.'

So H.L. left school at fifteen and, apart from a couple of terms at Valparaiso University in Indiana, educated himself further in what is sometimes called the University of Life. If he majored in anything, it was poker. He took the jobs common among young men in the West and South in the early years of the twentieth century, working on farms and ranches, in lumber camps and kitchens; and wherever he went, a card game went along with him. Eventually he settled in Greenville, Mississippi, and soon he was, he reports in *Hunt Heritage*, 'one of the best players in that neck of the Delta'. Later that qualification was to be dropped, and he told an English reporter, Brian Hitchen, of the *Daily Mirror*: 'I never came up against a better poker player than myself. I don't believe there ever was one anywhere in the world.' And when he crystallized his business philosophy, he made it sound just like a poker game. 'Most business transactions are a gamble,' he wrote, 'some good, while in others the odds are bad. The percentage of success must be calculated and the deal made only if the reward will justify the danger of the loss. No deal should be made if the occurrence of a loss would be catastrophic, for a better time will come.'

In fact, the young H.L. was nothing less than a professional gambler – not just playing poker, but in real estate and the cotton market, using as his stake $5,000 inherited from his father. By 1914 he had been successful enough to persuade the daughter of a respectable merchant in the small Arkansas town of Lake Village to marry him. Like H.L.'s mother, Lyda Bunker was a schoolteacher, and there is persuasive evidence that he regarded Lyda as a mother substitute. In *Hunt Heritage* he praised her extravagantly, crediting her with 'about 90 per cent of our financial success'.

Blame for failure H.L. took himself, including a spectacular example only six years after his marriage. 'In 1920 the cotton market went tumbling,' he wrote. 'I told my factors to sell cotton, and when they failed to do so I decided the price was fictitious and sold the futures market short. When the price increased I posted margins until my cash was gone and I was closed out.' In other words, H.L. was broke. The only benefit he derived from the experience was the discovery that 'probabilities are not always dependable'.

Two years later, in 1922, H.L. discovered the oil business. When first he went to El Dorado, Arkansas, a year after oil was discovered, H.L. started by doing what he knew best – running a gambling saloon. But he quickly grasped that the real money was under the ground. Although his first well, known as Hunt-Pickering No. 1, was a disappointment, he struck lucky soon afterward. 'For a while I was so lucky,' he wrote, 'that the word got around to "follow Hunt and make a fortune", until I had a period of hitting dry holes, so the saying changed to "follow Hunt and go broke".'

H.L. brought his family from Lake Village to El Dorado. The first two children of H.L. and Lyda Hunt were born in Lake Village, Margaret in 1915 and the third Haroldson Lafayette Hunt, known more conveniently as Hassie, in 1917. The third child, Caroline, was born in El Dorado in 1923; a fourth, named after her mother, died in infancy in 1925. Nelson Bunker, a second son, was born on February 20, 1926. William Herbert came next, on March 6, 1929.

H.L. was still restless. His dry holes in El Dorado persuaded him to look for another game to play, and in 1925 he found the Florida land boom. But oil was in his blood now, and by the end of the decade he was in Texas, where, in 1930, H.L. founded his real fortune. Like Bunker in Libya, H.L. did not actually make the strike that put him among the super-rich. That had been made by a wily old prospector named C. M. (Dad) Joiner, and the circumstances in which H.L. purchased the leases in the richest oil field in Texas have remained ambigious. Dad Joiner always said that he had been cheated by H.L.; but Joiner was short of money, and H.L. made him an offer he could not refuse. Acting on another commercial rule of his own, H.L. established enough credit at the bank to enable him to buy out Joiner for $1.3 million – a fortune then, but only a trifle compared to the $100 million H.L. eventually made out of the East Texas oil field. 'In my business,' he wrote later, 'I always wanted to be the borrower, but succeeded in paying my indebtedness when due, and establishing excellent credit. Wherever I was I quickly sought to establish excellent sources of credit.' When H.L. became the largest independent operator in the East Texas oil field, he moved the family to Tyler, and his last son, Lamar, was born there in 1933.

But Tyler was too small for a man making as much money as H.L. In the 1930s he consolidated his fortune and bought a mansion in the expensive White Rock Lake area of Dallas, cheap then because of the Depression. Modelled on George Washington's house on the Potomac, it was actually named Mount Vernon, but was somewhat larger than the original. By 1945 H.L. was a big enough producer to be able to claim that he had produced more oil for the Allied forces than all the Axis powers put together. Since the one thing Germany, Italy, and Japan have in common is that they produce no oil, the statement does not bear much examination, but it was an impressionistic way of announcing to the world that H.L. was the biggest league. There was physical evidence of it in Dallas: at his offices one room was devoted entirely to his oil leases – they lined it, from floor to ceiling. H.L. did not own oil wells; he owned oil fields.

Judging by what H.L. put on the record, it might seem safe enough to assume that the Hunt boys and girls had an enviably secure childhood, cushioned against the unhappiness of the Depression and growing up graciously. But there were serious omissions in the record – how Bunker became the head of the family, for example.

Hassie, the eldest son, who had been named after H.L., was his favourite, and H.L.'s way of showing it was to impose his philosophy relentlessly on the boy. Like his father, Hassie was intrigued by oil, and he was very lucky. But by his early twenties, when Hassie was already rich by virtue of his own oil discoveries, he was becoming increasingly disturbed. Harry Hurt, the most assiduous student of H.L.'s life in Texas, quotes an associate of the old man's: 'I remember one time when Mr Hunt was taking him through the oil fields, Hassie jumped out of the car, and started rolling around in the oil pits. He got oil and grease all over. It was really a mess.' Hassie's behaviour turned from the odd to the insane and, aged only twenty-six, Haroldson Lafayette Hunt III went to hospital. He was suffering from severe manic depression at least, and there was a common treatment for it then that was not thought quite so horrible as it is now. H.L. agreed that Hassie should be lobotomized; the section of his brain responsible for his tantrums was removed.

H.L. sought other cures, but unsuccessfully, while Hassie lived on, first in a cottage in the garden of the Mount Vernon estate, and then in the mansion next door. He was seen occasionally in Dallas going to a game of one kind or another, and the sadness of his plight was heightened by the rumours that filtered into conversations about the family: it was said that his libido had been in no way impaired by the lobotomy, that one of the duties of Hunt employees was to find young girls to satisfy it – virgins from the Middle West, so the stories claimed. Hassie grew increasingly rich, and had less and less to spend his money on. The sight of him made Bunker and his brothers and sisters feel anger as well as pity. Margaret told an interviewer, after H.L. had died: 'My father destroyed Hassie.'

The sins of the father were not confined to his treatment of Hassie. The family was close, and although his children saw little of their father, they were genuinely devoted to their mother. One reason why H.L. was such a regular absentee from Mount Vernon was that Bunker and his brothers and sisters were not H.L.'s only family. They were the first, not of two families, which would have been remarkable enough, but of three. H.L., as they say, could not keep his prick in his pants. His own private explanation was that he had a 'genius gene', and that he was performing an inestimable service by passing it on as often as possible.

In Florida in 1925 H.L. had met a glamorous young Polish American named Frania Tyburski, and in the next eight years she bore him four children, two sons and two daughters. H.L. thought he had settled the problem of this second family when he paid Frania off in 1942 with a cheque for $1 million. But he did so only to repeat the experience with a new friend. He had met Ruth Ray, a pretty legal secretary, in Shreveport, Louisiana, and at the age of fifty-four began his third family. A son, Ray, was born in 1943, and a daughter, June, in 1944. Five years later there was another daughter, Helen, and by the time H.L.'s last child, Swanee, a girl, was born in 1950, H.L. was sixty-one. His eldest child, Margaret, was thirty-five, and his live progeny numbered no less than fourteen.

Lyda Hunt, who – as can easily be imagined – was a lonely woman for much of her life, died in 1955 of cancer. A couple of years later Lyda was replaced at Mount Vernon by Ruth Ray and her children, who had lived under the name of Wright; but Ruth Ray now married Hunt, which legitimized the children, and they became Hunts officially.

Their paternity was the only thing the children of the three families had in common. By the time Ruth moved into Mount Vernon, Lyda's children were grown up, and Frania's children lived anonymously in Atlanta. But the second and third families haunted Bunker Hunt.

The third family was a source of some irritation, especially when H.L.'s will made Ruth's son, Ray, his sole executor, but at least had the virtue of being a relatively private family affair. The second family, on the other hand, was an acute embarrassment when in 1977 Frania claimed a share of the spoils from H.L.'s will for herself and her surviving children (two had died, one of them in an air crash in Brussels that had destroyed a large slice of Atlanta's upper crust). After four days of hearings in a Shreveport courtroom, in which much of H.L.'s dirty linen was thoroughly washed, the first and second families settled out of court: the price was $7.5 million, a modest inheritance for a Hunt family. Bunker did not begrudge Frania's children the money; what he did mind was exposure of his late father to scrutiny and not a little ridicule. He would have preferred that the whole business had never come to court. 'He hated it,' his lawyer says.

Bunker Hunt's loyalty was not limited to the family name. He was proud of his father's acumen, and hoped to emulate it. He embraced many of H.L.'s attitudes, too, no matter how eccentric they were. When the behaviour of Bunker, and of his brothers, appears unlikely or even incredible, its roots can usually be traced back to the old man.

By the end of World War II, H.L. had become a legend in Texas, though he shrugged it aside with uncommon modesty. 'If I am a fabulous figure it is simply because I have never said anything about myself,' he claimed. He became a subject for national speculation in 1948 when *Life* magazine ran a cover story entitled 'Is This the Richest Man in the United States?' Only in 1952, when he was approaching the age at which most men retire, did he finally allow that he probably *was* America's richest man: his wealth was estimated at $2 billion, and his annual income at $54 million, after taxes (though he never paid much tax). H.L. discovered he liked publicity. Far from retiring, he then became a public figure, and took every opportunity to spread his philosophy. 'I'm a notoriety seeker now,' he announced.

H.L. was a great patriot in the peculiar mould of the Texas super-rich. He said, and no doubt believed: 'Our Republic is the best system ever devised earthwise, and it offers opportunities for all of us.' By the early 1950s he was, however, increasingly dubious about the way the system was being run, earthwise. The last president to have done a decent job, he said, was Calvin Coolidge. Franklin Delano Roosevelt was, for want of a better word, a fascist, and the trouble with his successors was that they had made America grievously susceptible to Communism. When his libido diminished, H.L. transferred his passion to anti-Communism, and one of his more mordant employees was exaggerating only mildly when he said: 'H.L. thinks that Communism began in this country when the government took over the distribution of the mails.'

H.L. was convinced that the Communists would take over America from within. 'That's where the danger lies. That's what we've got to guard against.' To ensure the guard stayed up, H.L.'s views were broadcast on 550 radio stations, in a programme called *Lifeline*, and repeated in newspaper columns that were literally advertisements for himself. He started a movement called Youth Freedom, a collection of pretty young women and handsome young men who could, like robots, recite the Hunt philosophy in a rehearsed speech lasting just three minutes. These activities were financed by a foundation, which was tax-deductible, of course, and was H.L.'s only charity. Despising the great institutions of the Eastern establishment, H.L. was convinced the Ford and Rockefeller foundations were trying to destroy the Republic. He was, of course, an uncritical admirer of Senator Joe McCarthy.

Surprisingly, he did not join the John Birch Society; he thought it was unnecessary competition. 'I don't think they're very effective. *Lifeline* does far more good,' H.L. told Max Hastings of the *Evening Standard* in London. Though he confessed doubts to Hastings about his own effectiveness: 'I'm not a very good anti-Communist, not well enough informed. I don't have any files or anything. I just get a lot of information from former FBI agents.' And the good fight was not to be carried as far as war with Russia. 'It would be a little too fatal,' he commented sagely.

At one time H.L. thought there was only one person fit to inhabit the White House. He hoped that General Douglas MacArthur would be nominated in 1952, and when he was not, H.L. hoped he would succeed President Eisenhower, but by 1960 H.L. had been converted to the Kennedy camp – indeed, he was in Kennedy's tent, successfully pleading the case that the vice-presidential nomination should go to a fellow Texan, Lyndon Johnson. 'I knew Kennedy's father was pretty much to the right, and I thought Jack would go as far to the right as his father wanted him to,' he explained; it was, perhaps, how he would have expected Bunker to react to parental advice.

He was still running his business on his eightieth birthday, when public attention was increasingly focused on his eccentricities, like his passion for health foods, some of which were manufactured – under such brand names as Gastro-Majic – at a food plant he owned, called HLH Products. He was notable as the billionaire who took a nut-and-prune cutlet in a brown paper bag for his office lunch. ('Get me out of the office before lunch,' employees pleaded with the secretaries as they went into H.L.'s office. But they could never escape H.L.'s health lectures – he thought it a mistake to change underwear too often, for example.) A last, memorable newspaper photograph shows H.L. crawling on his hands and knees, claiming that it is the best exercise in the world.

The one thing H.L. did not talk about was the size of his fortune, although he could not help hinting at it, as when he explained in 1968: 'I used to smoke cigars all the time. Then twenty years ago someone reckoned my time was worth four thousand dollars an hour. I knew my time was worth forty thousand an hour and I reckoned I couldn't waste time as valuable as that looking for matches, so I quit smoking.' (Assuming he worked ten hours a day, that amounts to $96 million a year. H.L. might not have been exaggerating.)

He quit gambling, too. In his fifties and sixties he bet such large sums on weekend football games that his staff had to help him distribute his stakes around various bookmakers, since there was none in Dallas large enough to absorb all of them. Ruth, his second wife, stopped all that, and prodded H.L. gently in the direction of the Baptist Church, of which he became a rather frail pillar.

H.L. ran his business almost to the end, long after his grip had become enfeebled. His sons were worried that he was being cheated by some of the employees, and they grew increasingly humiliated by evidence of his senility. Long after Lyndon Johnson left the White House, H.L. would tell them to call the President when they had a problem. When it sank in that LBJ was no longer there, H.L. announced that his youngest son, Lamar, must replace the president. Lamar was scheduled by H.L. to run for the White House in 1972. The only thing Lamar wanted to run for was the ownership of a football team. The children were not amused.

H.L. died on November 29, 1974, at the age of eighty-five. If he had wanted an epitaph, he might have been satisfied with the observation of a fellow oilman, J. Paul Getty: 'The corporations in which I own shares are rich enterprises, but I am not wealthy. They hold the property. They control me. In terms of independent wealth, there is only one man, H. L. Hunt.' His was a hard act to follow.

Bunker Hunt cannot be faulted for failing to try. His Libyan oil made him rich, but by the mid-1970s that was merely caviar on the bread and butter. Although H.L.'s will left the largest share of the Hunt Oil Company to his second family, the first family's Placid Oil Company was no mean producer of revenue, especially after the oil price rose dramatically in 1973. There was also the Penrod Drilling Company, which owns countless drilling platforms and rigs, and many others. Bunker was never sure what the companies were all worth; he just knew they were worth enough. 'Money has never meant anything to me,' he says. 'It was just something that if you wanted to spend, you would have it. My father never cared about money, either. It was just sort of how he kept the score.' Bunker was, in all outward respects, a thoroughly capable businessman, the model of a Texas capitalist –

oil-based, ruthless, unconventional, and very successful. He was able to indulge a passion for breeding racehorses and cattle on a scale that was uncommon even in Texas, and he collected ranches as other men collect paintings. Many other sons of eccentric rich men had failed where Bunker had succeeded: he had survived an unhappy childhood, and a dominating father.

H.L. never alienated his children; on the contrary, Bunker always sought H.L.'s approbation. But, try as he did, Bunker was a dismal disappointment as a boy. He was awkward and shy, and quite hopeless at schoolwork. Unaccountably, H.L. sent him east to school, where Bunker was out of his depth, first at the Culver Military Academy, and then at the Hill School in Pennsylvania. His grades were only just good enough for him to become the first member of the family to attend a university back in Texas. He did not stay long.

There is a fine item of Hunt mythology about Bunker's exit from the University of Texas. It suggests that he quit in outrage after listening to a geology professor argue that natural resources should be controlled by the government. There is no doubt that he would have found the idea unpalatable, but it is probable that he left for the more prosaic reason that he could not pass his exams. The U.S. Navy was less discriminating, and Bunker finished his education at the end of World War II, in the Pacific. Bunker's youth demonstrated that whatever qualities he might have, they were not academic.

Unlike other undereducated sons of the rich, Bunker did not devote his early manhood to a flamboyant international social life. He started learning the oil business at home, and in 1951 he married a girl named Caroline Lewis, who was fresh out of Southern Methodist University in Dallas. They bought a comfortable if undistinguished house in the high-income, all-white Dallas enclave called Highland Park, and began a family. There were three daughters, Ellen, Mary, and Elizabeth, before their son, Houston Bunker, was born; and they left it at that.

Bunker travelled a great deal when the family was young, establishing habits that hardly changed when he became really rich. The family car is still an old Cadillac. When he flies, he will hire a private aircraft if necessary, but on scheduled flights it is always economy class. He does not drink much, and when he eats, he prefers bulk to quality. Bunker has always had an insatiable appetite for junk food, the results of which an occasional burst of jogging has never controlled. A real treat for Bunker is a plate of hamburgers or spareribs, and, if possible, a second course of the same thing, washed down with Coke or Dr Pepper and followed by ice cream. He is intimidated by European cuisine, and he does not like the prices. (Having eaten at the Ritz in Paris once, he said that when you got the bill, you thought you were buying the hotel.) And, wherever he goes, Bunker is always reluctant to leave a tip.

Bunker has acquaintances, rather than the kind of real friends known in Texas as 'asshole buddies'. Because he is so rich, those who call him their friend are often promoters; not that Bunker minds, because he loves to hear propositions for new ways of making more money. No matter how bizarre they sound, Bunker considers them carefully. There is, for instance, a former football player named Catfish Smith, who persuaded Bunker to invest in a new type of helicopter, whose main fault was a stubborn resistance to flight. A contemporary from his Navy days, Jack Graham of Abilene, interested Bunker in his eccentric schemes for raising the *Titanic* or finding Noah's Ark. Bunker likes most spectator sports; when we met, the subject that interested him most was soccer. He once toyed with the idea of buying a football team that would rival the Dallas Cowboys, particularly as this might offend the owners of the team, another oil-rich family, the Murchisons, who are old enemies of the Hunts.

Bunker, a passionate non-smoker, likes to escape Dallas and go to his nearby ranch, the Circle T, or farther afield to his farms in Oklahoma, West Virginia, and Kentucky, where he gulps in fresh air and indulges a childlike delight in throwing stones. And although he might have had the odd girl friend on the road (he was once greatly smitten with Ursula Andress), there is no second family to distract him.

But if Bunker has few friends, he takes his hobbies seriously. Conveniently, he inherited the phenomenal memory of H.L., who could remember the exact composition of poker hands he had played fifty years earlier. Bunker applies his memory to the bloodlines of racehorses, and he buys discriminatingly, almost as though he wants to have a representative from each good bloodline he has ever heard of. When he buys cattle, he chooses the biggest as well as the best, and populates his farms with Charolais; he likes there to be so many of them that when he flies over his herds they look like one large single object moving over the plain.

Bunker's politics are right-wing, like his father's, but although H.L. had been scornful of the John Birch Society, Bunker prefers its variety of political prejudice to H.L.'s *Lifeline*'s. In fact, Bunker's name first appeared in the newspapers because of his interest in right-wing politics. In the library files of the Dallas newspapers is a faded cutting dated May 19, 1963, reporting that a speech by Robert Welch, the founder of the John Birch Society, scheduled to take place at the home of Nelson Bunker Hunt at 4508 Lakeside Drive, Dallas, had to be moved to another location because the Hunt home was not big enough. In 1964 Bunker's name showed among the contributors to Strom Thurmond's racialist Senate campaign in South Carolina; a year later it was among the list of shareholders in the statement of ownership of the *Review of the News*, the monthly organ of the John Birch Society. He helped finance the society's bookshops, too. And, while no sums have to be declared, Bunker was not mean about his subsidies to the society; they were quite large enough to win him a place on its National Council. His wife, Caroline, organized a $1,000-a-plate dinner for George Wallace in 1968, and Bunker was enthusiastic about the nomination on a Wallace ticket for Curtis LeMay (he who wished to bomb the Communists back into the Stone Age). There was a common characteristic in all these donations: none was intended to buy real political power. Until the late 1970s, at least, Bunker's politics did not belong to Washington, D.C., or even to the state capital in Austin. He was a real right-wing eccentric; the difference between him and most of the others was that he had more money.

He spent it on religion, too. Bunker Hunt is an old-fashioned Southern Presbyterian, with a strong sense of mission and a blatant anti-Semitism; and he does not seem to believe that it is more difficult for a rich man to enter the kingdom of heaven than it is for a camel to pass through the eye of a needle. Bunker likes to think big about God, and promises to help raise One Billion Dollars for a campaign called the Campus Crusade for Christ, which intends to rid American colleges of the taint of Marxism and return them to the Lord, no matter what the cost.

His own contributions are generous, and one reward for them was immediate and glowing. A staff member of the Campus Crusade, a young man named Robert Pittinger, says: 'Bunker is a beautiful witness of our Lord. I have never seen him mad, impatient, or bitter. His heart is so good, so pure, I've met few people who are really real, but I've never met a man so down to earth as Bunker Hunt.'

His brothers, Herbert and Lamar, think highly of Bunker, too. He is the undisputed head of the family, and when they meet to discuss family business only his eldest sister, Margaret, regularly questions his judgments. Herbert does so rarely, and tentatively. An ex-employee of the brothers observes: 'Herbert holds Bunker in reverence; he follows him around just like a little puppy.' Herbert himself confirms his subordinate role. 'Bunker prefers to conceive something and then step back. I get more involved in the figures.' But Bunker can be a hard taskmaster; when he has been away and returns to

Dallas, Herbert is called upon to give an account of his stewardship, and it is sometimes found wanting. In such a case, Bunker snarls: 'You're unlucky, Herbert. I'm not doing any more deals with you.' Then he subsides and lets Herbert get on with the figures.

'Unlucky' is not the adjective most people would use to describe William Herbert Hunt. As a boy he was never brilliant, but he was notably more successful than Bunker, and graduated with a degree in geology from Washington and Lee University, in Virginia. H.L. was characteristically suspicious of Herbert's degree. 'It's going to cost us millions,' he told Herbert, 'because you'll end up drilling wells just to prove something rather than to find oil.' His fears were groundless. Herbert was an entrepreneur, not a wildcatter; he preferred clean hands, and concentrated on expanding Placid Oil and the Penrod Drilling Company.

Herbert is a plain man. He married a comfortable wife, Nancy, and lives in a comfortable house in the respectable Dallas suburb of University Park, where his three boys and two girls were brought up. Unlike Bunker, Herbert is not much of a collector, though he does buy coins, Greek statues, and the occasional picture, especially when he likes the frame. Perhaps the only singular thing about him is his fondness for health foods, which he inherited from H.L. On trips to New York (economy class, just like Bunker) he often takes his own wheat germ and orange for breakfast. It is healthful, and breakfast in New York is very expensive. His diet and the exercise he takes make him more presentable than Bunker. Herbert's suits are better cut, and they hang more elegantly on his slimmer figure.

Herbert arrives at the office on the twenty-fifth floor of the First National Bank Building on Elm Street in Dallas between seven and seven-thirty in the morning, while Bunker – if he is in town – is still fast asleep. He examines drilling reports from Penrod's rigs, and his employees' expenses, in an office that is cluttered with the impedimenta of the oil business – rock samples, drilling cores, and phials of thick black fluid. And Herbert has often done a good part of a day's work before Bunker comes on the phone in midmorning for a gossip about the business. Bunker rolls in just before lunch, which they often take together in the Petroleum Club; he prefers to work on into the early evening. He says it allows him to miss the worst of the traffic, but what it means is that the brothers get long days of work out of their employees. Herbert likes that.

Lamar is the exception to the family rule that the children and sons-in-law of H.L. work in the family business. He shares with them a determination to acquire even greater riches; he has, however, chosen a different area in which to do so: professional sports. 'None of my sports is a hobby, though,' says Lamar, like a true son of his father. 'Anything I put my money into has to be an intelligent investment.' Lamar invested in a new football league, the AFL, which turned out very intelligent indeed; he owns his own football team, the Kansas City Chiefs, as well as a soccer team, the Dallas Tornado; and he has a share in a basketball team in Chicago. But Lamar is best known – perhaps notorious is more apt – for World Championship Tennis, which cornered the market in top tennis players. Almost single-handedly, Lamar revolutionized a game with a strong amateur tradition and, for better or worse, made millionaires out of the best tennis players. But Lamar is also a vice-president of Placid Oil. So he is there, at the family business conferences, where the brothers and sisters listen to reports from their forty-one corporations, their seventeen partnerships, their two limited partnerships, their one joint venture, and the forty-one family trusts through which the profits of their enterprises are channelled into their innumerable bank accounts.

They are all exceedingly rich, and they conform to Scott Fitzgerald's dictum that the rich are different from us. Even so, for the most part they are no different from many other rich Texas families. But Bunker himself is different again, even from the rich. The scale on which he buys the objects of his desire is different, for a start.

There is something else as well. The story so far has been of remarkable good luck and great fortune. But Bunker has also been very unlucky, and there are enough examples of his ill-fortune to suggest that he is accident-prone. Moreover, Bunker is usually the architect of his own worst accidents.

There was, for example, the accident on November 22, 1963, that allowed conspiracy theorists to implicate Bunker circumstantially in the assassination of President John Kennedy. Bunker had contributed generously to the cost of an advertisement in the Dallas *Morning News*, which appeared on the morning of November 22, implying that the president was a traitor because he used taxpayers' money to subsidize international Communism. The advertisement contained its share of propaganda from the lunatic right, but it was the suggestion that the president was a 'traitor' on the day he was shot that provided the occasion for theorists to delve into Bunker's politics, especially as his father's *Lifeline* programme that same day was hinting at exactly the same thing: that the president was soft on Communism.

The timing of the advertisement in the Dallas *Morning News* was, to say the least, unfortunate, and inferences that Bunker was involved in the assassination plot dogged and upset him for years after the event. Finally tiring of the allegations in the late 1970s, he asked a feisty young civil-rights lawyer named Phillip Hirschkop to conduct his own private investigation into the insinuations. Hirschkop had the freedom of Bunker's own papers and gained access, under the Freedom of Information Act, to a thick pile of material from Bunker's FBI and CIA files. At the outset of the investigation Bunker told Hirschkop that if he found any suggestion of involvement in the assassination he must turn the evidence over to the Justice Department. It was the action of a man confident of his innocence. But some of the mud has stuck.

The second example of Bunker's bad luck takes us back to where we began, the Libyan oil field. Bunker has never been popular with the oil establishment. Because he had not drilled the Sarir Field himself, he was regarded as a freeloader. In return, Bunker convinced himself that none of the oil companies wanted him to make a dime. He thought British Petroleum was not developing the Sarir Field fast enough, and it was true that BP had been in no hurry, until the Six-Day War led to the closure of the Suez Canal in 1967, giving a strategic advantage to Libyan oil, which flowed directly to Mediterranean ports.

But Bunker felt basically secure, because of his belief in the Texas concept of 'good title'. He had shaken hands on the deal, and that meant half the oil was his and no one could take it away from him. Good title had been firmly established in arduous negotiations with the Libyans and BP; Bunker had had one of the shrewdest contracts negotiators on his side – another Texan, named Ed Guinn. (Guinn's negotiating skill was more elegant than his manners; he would arrive at a meeting with oil ministers wearing a replica of the *Manneken-Pis* as a tiepin, with a tube to a bulb of water in his pocket, which he would squeeze at an inappropriate moment.)

Bunker did understand that Libya was unstable because the regime of King Idris was crumbling fast. That was a reason for wanting to get the oil out quickly. He knew the Seven Sisters were making deals with Libyan officials that secured their own position at the expense of the independents. And he was not at all enthusiastic when a coup against the king on September 1, 1969, brought to power a Muslim Marxist, an unpredictable Army colonel named Muammar al-Qaddafi.

When Qaddafi took over, Libya had already become the largest single supplier of oil to Western Europe, and production in the Sarir Field was averaging 400,000 barrels of oil a day. Half of this was Bunker's, minus the 18,500 barrels a day taken by BP to pay for Bunker's share of the cost of developing the field. Even after Qaddafi began to squeeze the oil companies by raising prices, profits were still counted in tens of millions of dollars.

Then, in December 1971, Qaddafi nationalized BP on a slim pretext, and ordered Bunker to market BP's share. Bunker refused to do that, but he did send Texans into the field to produce his own share – a useful 217,000 barrels a day. Within a year Qaddafi was demanding that Bunker relinquish 51 per cent of his holding to the government. This outraged Bunker's belief in good title, and he refused. In retaliation Qaddafi ordered that production be cut back; next, in April 1973, Bunker was told he could lift no more oil. Finally, on June 11, Colonel Qaddafi, flanked by two men who were then his allies – Anwar el-Sadat, president of Egypt, and Idi Amin, president of Uganda – announced that Nelson Bunker Hunt was going to be nationalized. The reason, he said, was 'to give the United States a slap in the face'.

It hurt Bunker more than it hurt the United States. He was at a meeting in Dallas that day, when the phone rang. He listened for a while, and eventually said just one word: 'Fuck'. When the meeting was over, one curious participant asked Bunker why he had used such bad language. 'The Libyans just nationalized my oil,' he replied. He had more to say later. He was angry at the other oil companies, whose attitude was: why shouldn't Bunker go balls to the wall; it never cost him a penny. And he was furious with the State Department. Bunker would have sent the Marines into Libya, and Henry Kissinger's refusal to undertake the adventure merely confirmed Bunker's conviction that the secretary of state was just another Communist-loving Jew.

Another man who earned Bunker's lasting enmity was Dr Armand Hammer, the flamboyant chairman of Occidental Petroleum. Hammer had seen no matter of principle involved in a similar request that he should hand over a 51 per cent share to Qaddafi. The deal was done, and Occidental has been taking profits from its remaining 49 per cent share ever since – from vastly higher oil prices, at that. All Bunker got was $17 million in compensation. (The sum might have been higher if his original choice of lawyer to negotiate compensation had been able to do the job. Bunker hired the former governor of Texas, John B. Connally – once described as the only man who can sit and strut at the same time – on a contract worth $70,000 a year for ten years, to plead his case in Libya, but soon after he had signed up, Connally went to Washington as President Nixon's secretary of the treasury.)

By the time the Sarir Field was nationalized, 550 million barrels of oil had been recovered, 74 million of this by Bunker, after BP's enforced retirement from the concession. Bunker had done well by any standards but his own. How much he made is uncertain, but a profit of $100 million in six years is considered a fair estimate by oilmen. (This total was effectively boosted by a splendid method of U.S. tax avoidance, because all the taxes Bunker paid to the Libyan government could be offset against his very substantial personal income in the United States.) But Bunker could not forget the reserves, conservatively estimated at 8 billion barrels of oil, in a field that was expected to go on producing liberally until 1986. Had Bunker been able to retain his share, it would have been worth – using the most pessimistic assumptions – around $15 billion. Colonel Qaddafi had cut him off with only a few million, and Bunker was no longer the richest man in the world – not even notionally.

The Libyan nationalization continued to vex Bunker long after 1973. BP sued him in the English courts for the share of development costs they claimed Bunker still owed. Under a legal pretext that seemed fanciful to non-lawyers, BP was eventually (in March 1979) awarded damages amounting to $35 million. Bunker thought it was a hometown decision, and he showed his distaste for the judgment by refusing to pay the damages into court, as is British legal custom, before an appeal was heard. BP retaliated by asking the courts to freeze Bunker's assets. The requests were not confined to the United Kingdom, where Bunker had oil concessions in the North Sea. In a bonanza for the lawyers, applications for similar injunctions were also made in New Zealand, in four states of Australia, and in the Northwest Territories of Canada. By the summer of 1979, Bunker's refusal to pay the damages had resulted in his being officially declared a bankrupt in Britain. If he were to fly into Heathrow, he would be in danger of arrest. It was a great joke: Bunker, bankrupt! But there is no evidence that he shared the joke. For him, the evidence was that he had been screwed – twice: first by Qaddafi, and second by a shoddy alliance between Britain's oil 'sister' and her courts.

Another serious accident, which concluded with Bunker's having a criminal record, had taken place closer to home, and the cast included not only his brother Herbert but the president of the United States, the attorney general, the CIA, and the Palestinian terrorist group Al Fatah.

Late in the 1960s Bunker and his brothers decided that their father was being robbed by three of his senior employees; there was evidence of unexplained production runs at the health-food factory and curious land deals that would have been difficult to explain to anyone but a senile old man. Bunker hardly knew what to do until he met an old Texas buddy at a football game; the friend said he had dealt with a similar predicament by hiring private detectives to obtain evidence by tapping telephones. Bunker thought that an excellent solution. But the detectives he hired got caught; for tapping the telephones of H.L.'s senior men, they were sentenced to three years in September 1971. They had not named their employers, however, and Bunker tried to purchase their continued silence. But the cover-up was bungled, and the accused turned state's evidence, implicating both Bunker and Herbert. They claimed to have been tricked 'by men of vast fortunes who merely wanted to escalate their wealth and power'. After a protracted grand jury investigation the brothers were indicted in March 1973 on a charge of illegal wiretapping, a federal offence.

Bunker considered it 'a bum rap'; all he had tried to do was to protect his daddy, and he was determined to prove his essential innocence. But the methods he chose were not those of an ordinary citizen. Bunker regarded justice as a suitable subject for negotiation – not unlike an oil concession. Through his lawyers, he offered the federal government a deal. There is some uncertainty about what Bunker offered; one lurid version suggests that he said that if the charges were dropped, he would provide the FBI with a list of the American agents of Al Fatah, which was being financed by his old enemy Qaddafi and was making a dangerous nuisance of itself. (Quite how Bunker had obtained this list remains his secret.) And he made quite sure the message was put across: he buttonholed President Richard Nixon at a barbecue given by John Connally in April 1972, while the grand jury was investigating the case, and outlined his predicament again, before proceeding to rail against Henry Kissinger's Libyan policy. (It was an eventful night; in another part of the garden H.L. was loudly accusing the Nixon administration of dragging the Stars and Stripes in the dust.)

The president seems to have been interested enough to alert his deputy attorney general, Richard Kleindienst, because shortly afterward Kleindienst had a discreet meeting with Bunker at the ranch of Senator James Eastland, one of Bunker's few political friends who had any real power. When the meeting ended, Bunker assumed that the deal was on; and whether it involved cloak-and-dagger work or not, Bunker's friends in Dallas gave him the credit for the FBI's foiling an Al Fatah assassination attempt against the Israeli prime minister, Golda Meir, in New York in March 1973.

Then Bunker became an unlikely victim of Watergate. Implicated in the affair, Kleindienst slunk away from the Justice Department in April 1973, and the White House became more preoccupied with covering up its own illegal wiretapping operations. Nothing more was heard about any deal, and the case against Bunker and Herbert went ahead. Their lawyers told them that conviction could mean a jail sentence, and Bunker wondered who could possibly want him in jail. After some thought, he convinced himself that it must be the CIA, which had once wanted to place an agent in Bunker's Libyan operation. Bunker had said no; the wiretapping case, he felt, was the CIA's revenge.

Bunker sought help from an improbable quarter. He discovered that the most expert defender of wiretap cases was Phillip Hirschkop, a curly-haired, moustachioed Jewish lawyer who worked from a smart town house in Arlington, Virginia; Hirschkop's credentials were impeccably liberal and many of his clients were impecunious left-wing members of the peace movement. He was not Bunker's type at all, but Bunker was desperate. Hirschkop listened to the story and decided that Bunker was being persecuted by the Justice Department. Concluding that right-wing billionaires had civil rights, too, Hirschkop took the case. There was only one condition: if he won, Bunker would have to join the American Civil Liberties Union.

When the case was finally heard in Lubbock, Texas, in the fall of 1975, the basis of the defence was Bunker's naïveté; and his loyalty to his aged father. Hirschkop argued that Bunker had not known that wiretapping was illegal, and he had intended no evil. It was an ingenious defence, which worked so well that the brothers were acquitted. Bunker even joined the ACLU, though not for long. But there was still an obstruction-of-justice charge arising from the clumsy attempt to cover up their involvement in the original wiretap. Hirschkop told Bunker that he doubted whether a Texas jury would ever have convicted him on the wiretap charge, because they'd have understood that he was just protecting his daddy; but about the second charge he was less confident. Hirschkop persuaded the government to reduce the charges, and in April 1976 persuaded Bunker to plead *nolo contendere*, or no case, which is an admission of guilt. The fine was $1,000, and the consequence was a criminal record for Bunker.

Bunker was unusually grateful to Hirschkop. Considering the injury to his reputation – never mind his person – which a jail sentence would have inflicted, he had got off lightly. But he still felt that a great injustice had been committed. By the time the ordeal was finally over, in 1976, Bunker had decided that the federal courts were politically inspired and had punished him for his extreme views. The experience made him even more extremist.

His persecution complex is an essential element in Bunker's personality. The list of people and institutions he believes are conspiring against him is lengthy. Some were exposed by the wiretap case; the Libyan nationalization revealed others. But there were more – Exxon, for example. Bunker believes that the largest oil company in the world spends twenty-four hours a day thinking of ways to ruin him. The reason? Because Exxon is the Rockefellers; only Trotskyites are more suspicious than Bunker of the Rockefellers. He also suspects lawyers of professional conspiracy to lift as much of his money as possible. He has had to spend a great deal of his time in the company of lawyers, and a first impression of Bunker is that he uses them as other men use bodyguards, but he does not like them.

This persecution complex further influences Bunker's view of American politics, which is composed of unsubtle primary colours. When Bunker looks at Washington, D.C., he sees evidence of a conspiracy against the United States – and not only the one inspired by the KGB, which he takes for granted. He sees welfare as a conspiracy to stop people working; the civil service as a conspiracy to force up government spending and prevent a balanced budget. He believes government spending threatens free enterprise, which has made America great. He is quite depressed about the future of the Republic. In an interview in the John Birch Society's *Review of the News*, he said: 'I think our entire future as a free society is in the balance, and I'm not sure which way it will go.' (Bunker's personal protest against the creeping socialism is to pay as little money as possible to finance government spending. 'For him, tax avoidance is a religion,' observes an associate.)

Bunker's fondness for the conspiracy theory is perfectly illustrated by the following story. 'I was in Washington,' says one of his ex-employees, 'and Bunker called me late one night and told me to get down to Dallas first thing the following morning; there was someone he wanted me to meet. I did as I was told, and when I arrived he introduced me to a financial consultant with a strange accent, called Peter Beder, a man who believed the Rockefellers were using a research body known as the Trilateral Commission as their means of establishing dominion over the whole world. What I heard was the outline of a conspiracy to make David Rockefeller the richest man in the world. It was before Watergate became terminal, and the consultant's prediction began with the downfall of Nixon and the appointment of Gerald Ford, which did not seem so likely at the time. Next, he said, Ford would appoint Nelson Rockefeller vice-president, which seemed *very* unlikely. The punch line was that the first executive act of the new administration would be to legalize the sale of gold to American citizens. That was how David Rockefeller was to become the richest man in the world: he would know it was going to happen, and would buy up all the gold around. I returned to Washington thinking that Bunker's persecution complex was beyond a joke.' But as the months passed, Nixon went, Ford came in, chose Nelson Rockefeller, and very quickly made it legal for Americans to hold gold. That David Rockefeller did not subsequently become the richest man in the world is a quibble; the consultant had had the rest of the story right. While most of us would agree that Peter Beder had simply made a series of inspired predictions, for Bunker his story was proof that the conspiracy theory is right. I have noticed an intriguing and disturbing tendency among believers in the conspiracy theory: they assume that the threat posed by the conspirators with whom they disagree gives them the right to conspire themselves. It is a condition in which conspiracy can become a way of life.

But Bunker's own private world was formidably well financed. The Libyan adventure had ensured that it was, and as that money tree began to wither, Bunker's instinct told him to look for another way of multiplying his fortune. In 1972 he first suspected that he had found it, and it was territory free from Colonel Qaddafi, Exxon and the other thieving Sisters, the CIA, and Big Government. Bunker thought he had happened on something in which he could not possibly lose. It was the silver market.

Chapter 2
The Merchandise of Silver

Old H.L. always said that hundreds of oilmen insisted they had drilled his first oil well. Almost as many silver dealers claim to have first interested Bunker Hunt in silver. One story begins on a golf course in Chicago. A silver dealer named Don Dial is playing with a man named Ted Jansy, a roommate of Bunker's at the Culver Military Academy. Dial is an enthusiast for silver, one of the original members of an unorganized group known as 'silver bugs'. Jansy, believing that Bunker would also be fascinated, suggests that Dial try to convert him. Dial does so, and becomes one of Bunker's first brokers in the silver market.

Another story gives the credit to a New York commodities dealer named Alvin Brodsky, and it claims that Bunker's conversion was as dramatic as Saint Paul's on the road to Damascus. Brodsky visits Bunker at his Circle T ranch, outside Dallas, and as he ends his sales talk about silver, sees a pile of dry cleaning and asks, 'How much will those clothes cost next year?' 'They'll cost more; everything will cost more,' Bunker replies. 'So you've got to buy silver,' says Brodsky. Allegedly, Bunker is struck, as with the force of revelation, and buys silver.

Charles Matty, for whom Brodsky worked at the New York brokerage house of Bache Halsey Stuart Shields, has been in the market for fifty years and distrusts the tales of Bunker's sudden conversion. When Bunker entered the market, not even he remembers. 'I don't know, 1972 or '73,' he says. 'But it's a load of garbage that someone had to convince a Bunker Hunt,' says Matty. 'This was his idea all the time and I believe I can recite the reasoning verbatim. It's to do with the defence of wealth versus a deteriorating currency.'

Herbert Hunt lent credence to Matty's explanation when he gave evidence to a congressional committee in 1980. 'My analysis of the recent economic history of the United States,' he read from his script, 'has led me to believe that the wisest investment is one which is protected from inflation. In my opinion natural resources meet this criterion, and, to that end, I have invested in oil, gas, coal, and precious metals, including silver.'

Then Herbert named a source of the idea. 'I first became interested in silver as an investment, not as a speculation, in 1973 after reading about it in several publications including one entitled *Silver Profits in the Seventies* by Jerome A. Smith.' The attribution of the idea to a particular book was a great favour to the platoon of Hunt-watchers at the hearing, because the Hunts themselves rarely explain how they actually conceive an idea. *Silver Profits in the Seventies* became a sought-after volume, and it was uncommonly difficult to find. There is no copy in the Library of Congress, so on my first visit to Dallas late in May 1980 – when I telephoned their office and was told by one of their protective secretaries that Bunker and Herbert were not seeing any reporters, even if they had come all the way from London, England – I asked if I could borrow their copy of Smith's book.

After a lengthy silence, one of the Hunt lawyers, Bart Cozzens, came on the line and explained that the brothers had mislaid their copy, but he added that he had found one in the Dallas Public Library. When I took it out I discovered that Herbert (or Cozzens, as the case may be) had got the author's name wrong; it was Jerome F., not Jerome A., Smith. But reading it, I found it was the perfect expression of a phenomenon of the 1970s that deeply influenced the Hunts and thousands more who, if not so rich, were just as concerned about the erosion of their capital by the declining value of the dollar. Four months later, when I met Bunker in Paris, he said that he had never read *Silver Profits in the Seventies*, but many of his advisers and cronies had done so. Everything Bunker says about silver confirms that he absorbed the message, as if by osmosis. For that reason, it is worthwhile spelling out Smith's message.

Jerome Smith was a Corporate Man who dropped out in the late 1960s. Born in St Joseph, Missouri, he attended the University of Kansas before signing on as a middle manager, working for General Motors and then General Dynamics. Smith did well enough, but he did not like what he was doing, and his hobby began to absorb most of his time. He had started playing in commodity markets, and although he had no particular system, he had a theory: that modern economic management was all wrong. Under the influence of John Maynard Keynes, the great English economist, the United States government was printing too much paper money, and it would, Smith believed, end in tears. In response to Keynes's radicalism, Smith became a reactionary, believing passionately that a stable currency must be backed by a precious metal, such as gold or silver, which held its value. Moreover, he was willing to invest in his belief.

His confidence was so great that Smith quit the corporate life in 1967 and became a full-time investment analyst. To drum up business, Smith toured the nation, holding investment-advice sessions in hotel rooms for audiences drawn by small advertisements in the local papers. It was an arduous apprenticeship, but Smith's timing was impeccable. By the late 1960s the American economy was experiencing strains it had not suffered since the Great Depression, and for the first time since 1945 the dollar looked less than mighty. Any analyst who assumed that the worst was about to happen to the value of money was heard by a growing audience.

Smith was one of the most articulate pessimists among the newsletter writers. But to be successful it was also necessary to be able to preach some form of salvation. By the early 1970s salvation was silver, and the message was so popular that *Silver Profits in the Seventies* was reprinted three times in the two years following its publication in June 1972. That same year Smith started an investment newsletter that he called *World Market Perspective.*

Smith's preface to *Silver Profits* began confidently: 'If you have the patience to study this report and follow its logic – it could make you rich. If you are already rich, it can at least provide you with a means to keep what you have.' And the promise was alluring: 'Within our lifetime, and perhaps within this decade, silver could become more valuable than gold.'

Smith's exuberant recommendation was founded on a haphazard mixture of political and economic analyses. The economic was conventional enough; the political was bizarre. As Smith explained in an appendix to his book: 'This is devoted to what I believe to be the over-riding issue of all times – an issue which over-shadows all markets and affects all investments. It is the underlying, but seldom discussed, cause of all major crises: statism. Either there will be a fundamental change in our conception and action concerning government in this decade or we will have all our investments confiscated and become either employees or prisoners of the State before another decade passes.'

Smith believes that statism – the power of government – is a corruption of democracy. In his definition, democracy exists only when each man rules himself. Smith's anarchic principles are not divorced from his economic theory, however, because they provide him with a sweeping justification for free enterprise. The statement that explains the virtue of the marketplace is not quite Jeffersonian in its lucidity, but it does express the economic nonconformism that appealed to the alienated rich – men like Bunker and Herbert. 'Political democracy cannot exist,' Smith wrote. 'It is an illusion used to legitimise the rule of the few over the (easily manipulated) many. Democracy does not require elected or appointed mediaries; pure democracy in fact requires that there not be such likes. Democracy does exist, it does function (greatly hampered by the State). Its common name is the free market. The free market, to the extent that it is free, is an economic democracy. The unencumbered market, overall, operates like a societal guidance system that constantly makes multitudinous minute corrections through changing relative prices to direct and co-ordinate individual human actions towards the maximisation of total prosperity, the total well-being, the total happiness in a society.'

(Smith did not evade the tricky question about the way his stateless utopia might be financed and administered, and reached conclusions not dissimilar from those of H. L. Hunt in a novel the latter had once written, called *Alpaca* – cartons of which he would send to right-wing candidates for office who requested campaign donations. H.L. had decided that his political notions would be more acceptable if they were sweetened by a romance. His hero is a handsome young man, from a nation called Alpaca, who falls in love – in Paris, of course – with a beautiful opera singer; together they forge a state in which people who pay the most taxes get the most votes, a scheme which H.L. thought would lead to a drastic and rapid reduction in government spending. Smith's variant cuts out the intermediate stage entirely and effectively eradicates all taxation, replacing it with voluntary contributions to such services as national defence. 'As long as that danger of international attack exists,' he wrote, 'corporate boards of directors and wealthy individuals accustomed to being taxed 50 per cent or more, could be expected to voluntarily contribute some portion of their income, perhaps based more on the value of their physical property to be protected, as an insurance premium. Publication of lists of those who paid, and how much, would stimulate ultimate customers to favour the big contributors and avoid the shirkers.' Local services would be financed by charging an economic price for them, a price set by boards of elected managers; the ideal is voluntary government offering services competitively in the market – like any other business.)

Smith modestly described his ideas as an agenda for thought and discussion, and told his readers to buy silver while the debate was continuing. Incidentally, he suggested they keep their bullion in the vaults of Swiss banks, in case the discussion was overtaken by World War III. I could not find his explanation for this in later editions of

Silver Profits in the Seventies, but in the first edition he wrote: 'Suppose we lost World War III? I'd rather be a wealthy refugee than a resident pauper. Actually, as a reserve fund against the eventuality, the most patriotic thing to do is to have some funds in a safe place abroad, so you and other far-sighted Americans would have something with which to rebuild.'

When I first described these views in print, in articles in the *Sunday Times* in June 1980, Smith was upset. Later that summer he journeyed down from the mountaintop in Costa Rica to which he had removed himself in order to enjoy the delightful climate, the undoubted social stability which made it less likely that he would become a prisoner or an employee of the state, and the extremely advantageous tax rates. When we met, fortuitously, in London, he looked rather forbidding: he wore a fierce moustache and seemed to glare from behind his thick-rimmed spectacles. But the first impression was entirely misleading.

True, as a great guru of investment in precious metals, he was a little vain – his hair was fashionably curled and his cuffs showed gleaming white. He took himself immensely seriously, but that was not necessarily surprising, since *World Market Perspective*, which he had founded, now referred to him so reverentially. His publicity spoke of his economic insights, which have been 'translated into sound investment strategy for many thousands of people, resulting in profits and financial security for his adherents.' And the use of the word 'adherents', rather than 'readers', was significant, defining as it did the nature of Smith's appeal: he is an evangelist for the religion of old-time capitalism.

Far from being fierce, he was scrupulously polite, leaning over to light my cigarette while he explained that he was not right-wing at all. That, I inferred, was to locate him on a contemporary political spectrum on which he really felt he had no place. He explained that he is, instead, a Libertarian; a man who believes in the absolute virtue of free markets. But there was not a great deal to be gained from a dispute about the exact revolutionary implications of his philosophy, and we agreed that if it was not right-wing, it was certainly unconventional.

His is the kind of analysis that breeds on financial insecurity, which is one reason why it flourished. There were no secrets in the economic case Smith made for buying silver. It was the alliance of an eccentric set of political and economic convictions with an exhaustive analysis of an investment opportunity in silver that made the arguments so appealing to the rich and the super-rich. Men like the Hunts wholly shared Smith's scepticism about the stability of the American economy, and had enough money to feel the need to protect it – even better, to take the opportunity of making more.

What is so precious about silver? It no longer has the mesmeric qualities invested in it by the ancient Egyptians, who valued it more highly than gold; or by Ceylonese Buddhists, whose beliefs that silver brought luck was acted upon with remarkable extravagance by the builder of a pagoda in Kandy whose foundation is solid silver, 7 inches thick over an area of 500 square feet. The Bible, on the other hand, was always unremittingly stern about its properties. As in Proverbs (3:13–14): 'Happy is the man that findeth wisdom, and the man that getteth understanding. For the merchandise of it is better than the merchandise of silver, and the gain thereof than fine gold.' Or in Ecclesiastes (5:10): 'He that loveth silver shall not be satisfied with silver; nor he that loveth abundance with increase: this is also vanity.'

Yet it would be a strange person who did not have some love for silver. Because it is half the weight of gold, silver is the most practical precious metal for craftsmen to work into objects of great beauty. Great museums contain pieces of stunning sophistication from ancient Persia, crafted many centuries before the birth of Christ, and silver spoons are Biblical objects. Christian churches became the great patrons of the silversmith's art, ordering cups and candlesticks (though the latter were introduced only after the fifth century), and effectively cornering the market in fine silver objects for ten centuries until the English kings and the aristocracy in the fourteenth century decided that functional secular objects such as plates and tankards could be expensive and beautiful, too. The standard for sterling silver was set as early as 1335 (according to some historians, the name comes from Easterlings, because the smiths came to London from Germany, in the east). Sterling silver must contain 92.5 per cent pure silver, and for hundreds of years the penalty for including any less in an object allegedly made of sterling silver was death.

The high quality of the silver, allied to fine workmanship, made England the source of more fine silver than any other nation. Much of it was melted down during the Wars of the Roses, and then by Charles I to pay for his armies in the Civil War, but the permissive age of Charles II and the simultaneous introduction of tea to England led to a spate of teapots, trays, sugar bowls, and creamers as well as the more common plates, knives, forks, and spoons. In the eighteenth century the work of the silversmith reached its apogee, occasionally becoming an art in itself, and by then the English tradition had spread to America. (Although Paul Revere, whose Midnight Ride from Boston to Concord meant that he was the most famous as well as one of the very finest silversmiths in the United States, was actually the son of a French Huguenot.) By the nineteenth century every family of substance on both sides of the Atlantic had its silver, and the collections were added to by successive generations. They form part of the cultural heritage of a nation.

Silver was money, too. Its scarcity allowed the ancient Greeks to use it as a medium of exchange; the Romans continued the tradition, which lasted through the Dark Ages into modern Europe and America, when the relationship of gold and silver as to their relative scarcity was reflected in a sum known as the gold/silver ratio. For centuries the value of gold relative to that of silver was stable at 1 ounce of gold to 15 or 16 ounces of silver, and until the nineteenth century, silver was used as the backing for the currencies of great and small Western nations. America had a dual gold-and-silver standard, known as bimetallism, until 1873; and the ending of this principle inspired such controversy that it was known as 'the Crime of '73'. Into the mid-1890s the bimetallists were demanding free and unlimited coinage of silver. At the Democratic National Convention of 1896, William Jennings Bryan declaimed: 'You shall not press down upon the brow of labour this crown of thorns, you shall not crucify mankind upon a cross of gold,' and became the party's presidential nominee.

But the discovery of the Comstock Lode, and of many other silver veins in the Western states, meant that silver was freely available, and, like paper money in the 1970s, too much of it was in circulation. The result was inflation. Gold, on the other hand, remained scarce, so that became the medium through which international trade was conducted, and silver was relegated to the small change of the currency – dimes and quarters. It was still handsome enough to be used for decoration, and cheap enough for millions of buyers to acquire some family silver. By the mid-twentieth century, silver had become associated in the public's mind mainly with christenings and wedding anniversaries.

But it did have other uses, to which there is a clue in the dry definition of 'silver' in Webster's New Collegiate Dictionary: 'A white metallic element that is sonorous, ductile, very malleable, capable of a high degree of polish; and chiefly univalent in compounds, and that has the highest thermal and electric conductivity of any substance.' Conductivity makes silver important in the late twentieth century because it has become an essential raw material for the engineering and photographic industries.

After World War II, demand for the metal rose, but the price remained the same. Silver seemed to contradict the most basic law of economics, the law of supply and demand, which states that when the demand for a commodity whose supply is limited rises, the price will rise also. But the silver market was not a free one; the supply was then controlled by the United States government in Washington, D.C.

The first two decades of the twentieth century had been disastrous for silver producers. In the days of bimetallism an ounce of silver was worth $1.29; by the late 1920s it cost 50 cents an ounce, and demand for silver products slumped so badly that in London a spokesman for silversmiths was talking anxiously of the need for an invention that would prevent silver from tarnishing, so that it would be bought by the mass of people who did not have servants to polish it. By 1933 the price had fallen to 25 cents an ounce.

In 1934 the Roosevelt administration intervened in the silver market on two pretexts: first, in the belief that if the price of silver rose, more money would be available for world trade, especially in Asia; and second (more familiarly), because a block of fourteen senators from the seven Western states in which silver was mined – Idaho, Utah, Arizona, Montana, Nevada, Colorado, and New Mexico – had used their political muscle to help miners, owners and smelters.

The Silver Purchase Act of 1934 was one of the finest achievements of any political lobby in Washington in this century. It directed the United States Treasury to buy silver, wherever it was sold, until the world price rose back to $1.29. To ensure that the market could not be confused by private buyers, the administration sequestered all privately held bullion, paying 50 cents an ounce for it, and closed the New York silver market.

Government intervention raised the price briefly. By 1939 the Treasury was buying silver on the world market for 35 cents an ounce, while paying the Western mines a subsidized price exactly twice as high. But the silver bloc in the Senate successfully resisted any change in the law. So by the time war was declared, the United States government owned 3 billion ounces of silver, an amount equal to one seventh of the world's output of silver since the discovery of the Americas. The purchases were paid for by printing silver certificates – which were dollar bills, with an inscription at the top reading 'Silver Certificate' instead of 'Federal Reserve Note'. The Roosevelt administration had cornered the market in a commodity that no other nation wanted, though in wartime silver was used for paying bills again, and when thousands of tons of it were required for miles of electric wiring used in the Manhattan Project, which produced the first atomic bomb, the Treasury provided them without feeling any disquiet at all. ('In the Treasury we do not speak of tons of silver. Our unit is the troy ounce,' the bomb builders were told; they then asked for millions of ounces instead.)

U.S. Treasury silver purchases did not end until 1963, when the silver price reached $1.29 an ounce at last. The silver market of New York's Commodity Exchange (known by the acronym Comex) reopened for the first time in thirty years. But sales from the immense stockpile then met all the needs of industrial users of silver, and the price stayed steady until 1967. After that the price began to rise again, and a delightfully profitable little market arose in converting silver certificates – alias dollar bills – into silver that was worth a few cents more than one dollar. This method of making money attracted Dr Henry Jarecki, a psychiatrist teaching at Yale, into the bullion market, and he supplemented his professional salary by converting silver certificates into the genuine article until the Treasury spotted the loophole and stopped redeeming dollar bills for silver in 1968.

In the same year the Treasury also decided not to use any more silver in the coins it minted; dimes and quarters were to be made of cupronickel, just as nickels were. The silver price rose, but never sharply, because the government was still selling off its stockpile; and the price remained stable until November 10, 1970, when the greatest hoard of a precious metal the world has ever known was finally reduced to a level at which the administration decided it should remain, for strategic purposes. In the previous five years the administration had sold 693 million ounces of bullion, and Jerome Smith needed no genius to work out that the end of the government silver sales meant the end of a useful subsidy to industry, which ought to have some effect on the price.

The next question to engage Smith was: Where does silver come from, and how is it mined? Unlike most precious metals, which are found mainly in southern Africa and in Russia, there are no serious political inhibitions on the supply. The major producers are in the Americas – in the United States and Canada, in Mexico, and in Peru. In 1970 two-thirds of the silver mined in the non-Communist world came from these four nations. But silver mining was now quite different from the process of a century earlier, when the Comstock Lode was discovered in Nevada. The purest seams of silver are found near the surface, so the nineteenth-century miners could dig silver out with a shovel or even with their bare hands. A hundred years later it is harder work, because the amount of metal in each ton of ore generally diminishes as the mines are dug deeper. By the 1970s only a quarter of the silver produced actually came from silver mines.

Most silver now comes as a bonus from mines whose real function is to retrieve base metals – copper, lead and zinc. When these are smelted, the ore leaves a residue of silver. So even when the demand for silver is rising, the mine owners cannot meet it unless demand for their base metals is going up, too. Smith, and other investment analysts, reasoned that the demand for silver would certainly rise faster than that for copper, lead, and zinc – and they were right.

The silver bugs became obsessed by what they called The Gap. In 1971, when Smith was preparing *Silver Profits in the Seventies*, industry in non-Communist nations used 351 million ounces of silver, and the mines produced only 247 million ounces. The gap was plugged partly by scrap: by the accumulation of silver from melted-down coins or unwanted family silver, and by what could be retrieved from such articles as used X-ray film.

The other important source was India, from which silver, whose export is illegal, is smuggled to Dubai on the Arabian coast. Over the centuries silver has become an integral part of the Indian social fabric, and hundreds of millions of ounces had been imported. Indian inheritance customs make it possible for a woman to keep only what she is actually wearing on her body when her husband dies, so fond parents often give their daughters dowries of silver and gold jewellery as an insurance policy against their husbands turning ungenerous later in life. This practice intrigued Dr Jarecki, who observed: 'The result is that a bad monsoon causes some of the good marriages' silver, but little of the bad marriages' silver, to come onto the market. In the bad marriages, the women hold on to it.' The combined impact of the weather and marital harmony means that India fills an unpredictable quota of the difference between industrial consumption and mined supply.

The next factor to interest Jerome Smith was the growing industrial use for silver, which had consistently outstripped mine production since the mid-1950s. He listed the variety of uses to which silver was being put, and it was impressive: not just in photography, but in electronic components, aircraft spark plugs and engine parts, silver-plating, submarine and torpedo batteries, dental fillings, medical compounds, mirrors, photochromatic glass, and optical and heat-reflecting surfaces. Without even pausing for breath, Smith went on to report twenty-two recent developments that would increase the demand for silver. But the greatest demand of all did not require any new developments. Try though they might, Eastman Kodak, the world's largest producer of photographic materials, could not discover any substitute for the chemical salts, made from silver, that react with light in such a way as to give the clearest picture.

In 1971 American manufacturers bought 130 million of the 351 million ounces consumed industrially outside the Communist bloc. Three of every 10 of these ounces were bought by photofilm makers; the same proportion went to silver-plating; a further 2 ounces went to the engineering industry. And the most delightful thing, Smith noted, was that because silver comprised only a small part of the cost of the manufacturing process, industry would not reduce its consumption even if its price doubled. He concluded: 'In this decade the shortfall cannot be met. It cannot be met for even half this decade! It can be met for two years, through 1973, only on the assumption that the users bid high enough prices to draw out ¾ of the speculatively held silver in the world. By 1974, no matter what the users are willing to pay there will have to be a sharp curtailment in consumption because *enough silver will not be available at any price*! [Smith's italics].'

Smith's case might have rested there, but he continued to develop it relentlessly. His next argument involved some complex economic analysis, but complexity does not deter investment analysts. Like astrologers, they tend to use a crystal ball and see what they believe ought to be there; like astrologers, too, they tend to forget those predictions which turn out to be inaccurate. But Smith was right again.

Since 1945 the international monetary system had been based on fixed relationships between currencies; a traveller could move from one country to another and know exactly what he would receive for his dollars in the bank. All international trade was conducted in dollars, and world bankers and businessmen trusted America because of the government's promise that all dollars could be converted into gold from the American reserves. This system had originated with an inventive scheme, produced by the Allies to organize postwar international trade and agreed in the hills of New Hampshire at Bretton Woods, in 1944; it made the dollar pre-eminent currency of the non-Communist world.

By the late 1960s the system had begun to creak. The trouble was that the strength of the dollar depended on the superiority of the American economy, and that had been weakened, not only by the cost of the Vietnam War, which had led to inflationary deficits in government spending, but also by competition from some very able businessmen in West Germany and Japan, who produced cars and cameras, tape recorders and televisions that many consumers preferred to those made in America. The country was spending more abroad than it was receiving; there was a balance-of-payments deficit, and when that occurs, the currency always suffers.

In July 1971 Smith predicted that the dollar would be devalued within two months – 'mid-August being the most probable time'. And so it was, on August 15, when the dollar also ceased to be convertible into gold. In September, Smith forecast another devaluation for mid-December, and once more he was entirely correct.

These two accurate predictions gave him the confidence to extrapolate extravagantly. The meaning of the decline of the dollar, he announced, was 'the first world-wide runaway inflation and depression in the history of the world.'

'The world monetary system is on a collision course to chaos,' he wrote. 'What can the individual do about it, to protect his own resources? The individual can do something about it, in fact only the individual can protect himself from the forces of destruction. The solution is contained in the problem: one can protect oneself from the forces of destruction by converting those resources that are dominated by paper "money" into hard assets, into real values, preferably into assets whose values are not subject to the arbitrary mismanagement of anyone, ideally into assets that are both hard and highly liquid, into real money . . . gold and silver.'

When Smith wrote his tract it was illegal for Americans to buy gold; this invested silver with one more virtue. And the final inducement, if one were still needed, was his prediction for the course of the silver price. Smith assumed that the ratio of silver's value to gold's – 32:1 – would fall to at least the traditional level of the old bimetallism, or 16:1; and he calculated that this would raise the silver price to $4.37 an ounce. That sum did not take account of the effect of increased industrial consumption, so he added: 'Silver will trend upward thereafter because of the underlying shortage, and the silver price will reach $8 or $9 within two or three years.' At the time Smith made this prediction, the price of silver was a mere $1.60 an ounce. His conclusion was: 'There is literally no historical market precedent for the conjunction of so many strongly bullish factors on the price of silver in the 1973–75 period!'

Smith's study of silver was heady stuff. Other investment newsletters were circulating conclusions based on the same statistics, but none gave advice so firmly as Smith on how to go about silver buying. He believed that the most direct way to profit lay in owning bullion and storing it in Swiss banks – despite the opprobrium which might attach to that. (Smith, ever thoughtful, wrote: 'If your account is over $1,000,000 and you fear blackmail by someone who is in a position to intercept your mail, please contact me by phone and I will assist you to work out appropriate and effective safeguards.') He was, however, less impressed by the silver futures markets in New York and Chicago: 'Silver futures are a way of speculating in silver, not investing in silver.'

By 1973 Bunker had caught the silver bug, so much so that he made his own forecast, which was more optimistic even than Smith's. Bunker foresaw the ratio falling to 5:1, so that when gold cost $100 an ounce, silver would cost $20 an ounce. He had swallowed Smith's analysis whole, though whether he would also follow Smith's advice about investment methods was less certain.

Jerome Smith did not meet Bunker Hunt until the spring of 1979, when a mutual acquaintance – another Texas multimillionaire, Gordon McLendon – brought them together. Both were, at the time, in Zurich, where Bunker was buying an astonishing quantity of rare coins at an auction. Smith wandered in and out, finding the proceedings less absorbing than Bunker evidently did. When the sale was finally over, the two went for a cup of coffee. Smith recalls repeating his conviction that silver was a long-term investment, not a short-term speculation, and that Bunker rose to leave after only five minutes or so. 'He did not appear to want to hear what I was saying.'

Chapter 3

The Futures Market: A Game of Chance

When Bunker started buying silver seriously, in 1973, he acquired plenty of bullion; more even than Jerome Smith dreamed of. But Bunker takes advice selectively, discarding the bits he does not like. He accepted the advice about bullion and neglected the advice about the commodities futures market. Smith thought the futures market was too speculative for the amateur investor. But Bunker behaved as though his wealth endowed him with professional status; and he was fascinated by speculation – the one obvious similarity between oil and the silver market. When he was in Dallas and made his first telephone call to Herbert around ten a.m., the silver market was, observes one employee, 'always the first order of the day'. No matter where he was – New York, California, Australia, or Europe – Bunker always telephoned to find out what was happening on the market.

For most people, commodity futures markets are MEGO affairs. (MEGO is an acronym that describes particularly obscure happenings; it stands for My Eyes Glaze Over.) The markets are difficult to understand, partly because they have their own language, and partly because their economic function is less easy to grasp than that of a bank. In fact, they are not unlike banks, except that they are imprudent, less pompous, and more fun. Therefore, they attract gamblers, who often have more money than expertise. The secret is that the markets cannot operate without the gamblers.

My own eyes glazed over regularly when kindly men first tried to explain how the futures markets work, and my vision began to clear only when one of them, taking pity on me, started at the beginning, with a story about the California grain trade. He explained that in the 1840s the land and the climate in the Sacramento Valley was so ideal that the early settlers grew much more wheat than the population of California could consume. Since there was no need for wheat in the Eastern cities, the only possible market was in Europe, and before the Panama Canal was dug, the sea route around Cape Horn was dangerous and time-consuming. The shipowners could insure their vessels at Lloyd's, but there was at first no way the farmers could insure against a ruinous fall in the European grain price; nor, if the price rose quickly, was there any certainty that the flour millers would be able to buy the grain when it arrived.

The farmers and the millers needed some way of transferring the risk, and to facilitate the trade, some enterprising merchants in Liverpool drew up a contract that guaranteed the price a cargo of grain of specified quality, loaded in San Francisco, would fetch when it arrived in Liverpool three months later. This was called a futures contract. The idea was not new (the Japanese had had similar contracts in the seventeenth century), but with its application to international trade in commodities such as grain, its time had come.

The farmers who sold grain, and the flour millers who agreed to buy it, were hedging – that is, eradicating the risk of sudden changes in price that would throw their business into turmoil. The Liverpool merchants were gambling on the movements in prices in the future. If they thought the grain price was likely to rise, they would buy futures contracts, and they would sell them if they thought it was likely to fall. The peculiarity of their role was that they were not interested in actually possessing the grain; normally they took their profits or their losses before the contract expired. They did not create the demand for wheat, but by buying and selling futures contracts they financed the trade. If they had not been willing to take the risk of price changes, California wheat would have stayed in California. The futures contract made speculation respectable; it also made some Liverpool merchants wealthy and bankrupted others.

Traders in Chicago had a similar idea at much the same time. (The Chicago Board of Trade boldly claims to have initiated futures contracts – on March 13, 1851, to be exact.) By the end of the nineteenth century there were active markets in New York and London, and the concept had spread from grain to cotton, then to metals like copper, tin, and silver, as well as foodstuffs such as tea, coffee, sugar, and cocoa.

The speculator quickly became a fixture, regarding commodities no differently from stocks and shares, and the peculiar state of mind that speculation induced was described in magnificently florid prose by a dealer named William Worthington Fowler in a book published in 1880 called *20 Years of Inside Life in Wall Street.* The speculator, he wrote, 'produces nothing, he drives no plough, plies no hammer. And yet what life is more trying than his? Amid the convolutions of his brain a silent invisible struggle is going on which, if put into bodily shape, would startle the beholder. There the vulture passions are at work, led on by their generals, ambition and avarice. Pining envy, fear of an evil which always impends, rage over injuries inflicted by others, jealousy and hatred of successful rivals, all hold carnival in the space of an hour. He climbs on the edge of a sword to a fool's paradise, where he tastes brief joys as in a dream, and in an hour is abased to the earth where he drinks the cup full of humiliation and want.'

It is doubtful whether Bunker would put it quite that way, but what Fowler meant is that most amateur speculators are losers. Not that this prevents them from playing, especially in the markets in New York and Chicago, where the number of speculators increased so quickly in the 1970s that they now vastly outnumber the industrial consumers and producers of commodities. In theory, the futures market is a delicate financial instrument; in practice it is more like a casino. Futures contracts still state that a purchaser may take delivery of a commodity, but the main purpose of that clause is to draw a legal distinction between the commodities market and a gaming house. It would be unfair to attribute no economic function to the markets, because they are still used by hedgers and they do establish commonly agreed world prices for commodities, but essentially they are a game of chance played between sellers who do not own a commodity and buyers who do not want it.

The game is played according to strict rules. Trades have to be settled each day, through an institution known as the clearinghouse, where the winners and losers are sorted out – because the odds are even: for each winner there is a loser. And anyone who does not pay cannot play. Because the members of the clearinghouse are responsible for the debts of a defaulter, the old market adage states: 'He who sells what isn't his'n,/pays it up or goes to prison.'

Business is conducted in a vernacular language. The people who own a commodity, or a futures contract to buy it, are the longs. Those who have contracted to sell (and to deliver what they usually do not possess) are the shorts. The buyers of futures contracts, who believe the price will rise, are known as bulls; the sellers, who expect the price to fall, are bears – apparently because eighteenth-century speculators who wanted prices to fall 'were acting the part of a man who would kill a bear for the sake of his skin,' reports Fowler.

The game is cheap to play. A single silver contract on the Comex exchange in New York and the Board of Trade in Chicago is 5,000 ounces of silver, so if the market price stands at $10 an ounce, the value of a contract is $50,000. But since delivery is not normally part of the game, no one is asked to put up a stake of $50,000. Instead, a speculator pays his dealer a down payments as an insurance against his losses if his forecast of the movement in price turns out to be wrong. The payment is called margin, and it is an earnest of good intentions. In August 1979, when the price actually was $10 an ounce, the margin payment on Comex was $2,000 for each contract, a mere 4 per cent of its total value – much lower than margins on the stock market, where they will vary from 50 to 90 per cent of a share's market value.

The catch is that, unlike on the stock exchange, commodity deals have to be settled daily in the clearinghouse; if the price has moved, the value of every player's position will be different at the close of the market. If the price has gone down, a speculator who is long in the market (a buyer) will be asked for more margin. So, let us say the price has fallen from $10 to $9: the contract's value has declined from $50,000 to $45,000, and the dealer would then ask the speculator to cover the whole of the loss; the sum is often greater than the original margin payment, and the speculator can lose the whole of his stake in a single day, and then some more. But few speculators gamble on a single contract. So let us say, for example, that a player has 300 contracts; his additional margin on the day the price fell by $1 an ounce would be $1.5 million. And since each side of the market mirrors the other, a speculator who was short would pay similar sums if the price *rose* by $1 – from $10 to $11 – instead of falling.

The additional margin money, known as variation margin, does not go into the broker's account. It is transferred to the account of a speculator who has anticipated the price movement correctly. If the price rises from $10 to $11, a speculator who is long and has 300 contracts would be $1.5 million better off. And by a process of increasing his position, known as pyramiding, he can use that gain to purchase a further 750 contracts without putting up another penny to his broker. For a speculator who is long when the price is rising, or short when the price is falling, the commodity market is a most delightful institution.

By the late 1970s, however, a growing number of speculators did not bother to gamble at all. They simultaneously bought and sold contracts, in a transaction known as a straddle; most of the contracts showed a loss in the first leg of the straddle, which would be balanced by a profit later on. Stated thus baldly, a straddle seems to be a purposeless transaction; but it actually had nothing to do with hedging or price fixing, or even speculation. Most straddles were for the sole purpose of avoiding taxes, because short-term losses could be offset against profits made elsewhere – in real estate or the stock market – without risking the long-term gain on the second leg of the transaction. Until President Ronald Reagan's 1981 tax law, which ended the use of straddles for tax avoidance, the futures market was becoming a fairly blunt economic instrument, allowing wealthy speculators to convert short-term capital gains, taxed at 70 per cent, into long-term gains, taxed at 28 per cent. It was good for business, because the brokers got the commissions from the straddles, but bad for the U.S. Treasury, since the Internal Revenue Service calculated that lost revenue amounted to $1.7 billion a year.

This form of market activity never appeared in the economic textbooks. Its origin was in the native intelligence of dealers and speculators looking for ways of maximizing their income. And even if it had been written down, not many dealers would have bothered to read it, because they willingly concede that they are not, on the whole, given to literary reflection. But a remarkable number of them name a single book that illuminates the compulsion to speculate. It was published in 1841 in London under the title *Extraordinary Popular Delusions and the Madness of Crowds.* Written by one Charles MacKay, LL.D., it owes its presence on the shelves of so many market men to Bernard Baruch, the Wall Street financier, who knew a thing or two about the madness of crowds. He paid for the republication of MacKay's book in 1932, a year in which Baruch thought its lessons about human folly would benefit from repetition. One reason why dealers read the book with such fascination is that it confirms their own experiences, which show that speculators never learn.

There are entertaining chapters about the Mississippi Scheme and 'tulipomania', the frenzy to possess tulip bulbs in Holland in the 1630s, when they were imported from Constantinople and were very rare. The desire for the finest bulbs grew so intense that a single root was exchanged for the following collection of household objects: 2 lasts of wheat, 4 lasts of rye, 4 fat oxen, 8 fat swine, 12 fat sheep, 2 hogsheads of wine, 4 tuns of beer, 2 tuns of butter, 1,000 pounds of cheese, a complete bed, a suit of clothes – and a silver drinking cup. One particularly valuable bulb was consumed along with some herring by a sailor who thought the bulb he saw lying on a merchant's counter was an onion. The cost of that breakfast, commented the distraught merchant, could 'have sumptuously feasted the Prince of Orange and the whole court of the Stadtholder.' By 1636 tulips had become a commodity whose price bore no relationship to its real value. When that finally became evident, the bubble burst, the price collapsed, and speculators were ruined. 'The commerce of the country', MacKay reported, 'suffered a severe shock, from which it was many years ere it recovered.'

But the most relevant of all MacKay's tales is about the South Sea

Bubble in 1720, when the English learned, says our author, that 'nations, like individuals, cannot become desperate gamblers with impunity. Punishment is sure to overtake them sooner or later.' The story begins with the formation in 1711 of the South Sea Company, which had the remarkable objective of taking over the national debt in return for a monopoly of trade in South and Central America. The prospect was exciting because, as MacKay observes, 'everybody had heard of the gold and silver mines of Peru and Mexico; every one believed them to be inexhaustible, and it was only necessary to send the manufactures of England to the coast to be repaid one hundred fold in gold and silver ingots by the natives.'

The only problem was that the monopoly was not in the gift of the English Parliament; it belonged to Philip V of Spain, who had no intention of sharing it. But that little difficulty did not deter speculators from feverishly buying the company's shares. In 1720 the price rose from £290 to £890, and other bubbles formed to satisfy the public passion for speculation, including 'a company for carrying on an undertaking of great advantage, but nobody to know what it is.' The ingenious promoter of that scheme raised £2,000 in twenty-four hours before fleeing to the Continent, never to be seen again. As Jonathan Swift observed:

> Subscribers here by thousands float.
> And jostle one another down.
> Each paddling in his leaky boat,
> And here they fish for gold and drown.

The directors of the South Sea Company deliberately manipulated the share price to keep it high, by buying their own shares when necessary, but by the summer of 1720 'the bubble was then full blown, and began to quiver and shake, preparatory to its bursting.' The dream – that metal from the mines of Postosí-la-Paz was to be brought to England until silver became almost as plentiful as iron – was finally scrutinized and found to be an illusion, and the bubble burst. Intervention by the Bank of England – the first attempted bailout by a central bank – failed to halt the collapse of the share price. Thousands of speculators were ruined, and the directors were eventually exposed as frauds and market manipulators.

It is diverting to discover that this recital of human folly should still be regarded as a reliable guide to the nature of modern commodity markets, but in fact four out of five amateur speculators in the markets do lose money. The inflexible rule of the market is that there is a winner for every loser, but most of the winners are the market professionals, and the hedgers who are protected against price fluctuations. So it is not difficult to understand why the professionals are a cliquish crowd who prefer to keep their secrets to themselves.

The public is kept at a distance; they can see, but not really hear, the markets from the glassed-in observation galleries in New York, Chicago, and London. Comex is one of four separate exchanges on the floor of the Commodity Exchange Center in New York, a single vast room – the size of four basketball courts – in one of the new, low buildings that flank the towers of the World Trade Center. Comex specializes in metals – gold, silver, copper, and zinc. In Chicago, silver is traded at the Board of Trade, which occupies a floor almost as large, in a great, stone-faced monument to capitalism on La Salle Street. In London the Metal Exchange occupied a crowded room just off Leadenhall Market in the City for a hundred years; there, metals would be traded separately at five-minute intervals, and, in the case of silver, trading usually reflected the price fixed by the bullion dealers – Mocatta and Goldsmid, Samuel Montagu, and Sharps Pixley – whose representatives meet in Montagu's offices in Old Broad Street each day with files of orders to buy and sell, which, when completed, produce a fixed price for that day's trading. In 1980, when the room by Leadenhall Market became too cramped, the London Metal Exchange moved just a few blocks away to larger quarters on Fenchurch Street, which were not unlike the exchange in New York – though smaller, because there are many fewer dealers with seats on the London Exchange – right down to the glassed-in gallery.

The glass does not entirely drown the noise of the traders, whose hoarse voices are the sound of what is known in the market as public outcry. The floor traders in New York and Chicago mill about in pits built into the floor, one for each metal, and the members wear coloured cotton jackets to identify the exchange on which they own a seat. Since a dealer must have a seat on the exchange before he can trade, the seats have become a commodity, too. In 1979 they changed hands (because nobody actually sits in them in the United States; although they still do in London) for $200,000 on Comex; a year later the value of a seat had risen to $350,000.

When the market price of a commodity is moving fast, the pit becomes a frenzy of waving arms and yelling voices, apparently incoherent, but translated with remarkable speed into price movements that are recorded on large scoreboards on the walls. The sellers wave their arms outward; the buyers wave them inward; and the most highly skilled operators are known as two-handed dealers – for by making opposite motions with their hands they can buy and sell almost simultaneously. Some of the dealers trade for themselves, and they are known as scalpers, or locals; but most of the men and women on the floor (women are there in growing numbers) take their orders from brokers, agents for bullion merchants or for larger brokerage houses such as Merrill Lynch. The pit is, as it were, only the tip of the iceberg.

The real action takes place in the trading rooms of brokerage houses and bullion merchants scattered around the financial districts of New York and Chicago. Although modern communications make it possible to run an operation from the leafy lanes of Connecticut – or from the middle of the desert, for that matter – habit so far ensures that most traders still cluster around the exchanges. Because trading is not easy to understand, I sought a tutor. I shall call him Theo Hook, because he was willing to exchange a frank, beginner's course in the market for anonymity. Since frankness is uncommon in the market, it was a bargain.

Theo Hook is in his late thirties, slim, about five feet eight, pale, with sharp brown eyes, a quick nervous smile, and a preoccupied expression. He was born in Providence, Rhode Island, and left school at sixteen, wiser about the ways of the streets than about his schoolbooks. The evidence of a misspent youth was his skill at the pool table. He had already learned something of the human capacity for self-delusion from a saloonkeeper, who was so sure he could beat the adolescent Hook that he bet his saloon on a game of pool, and lost it. Hook told his opponent to forget the bet, and learned that charity earns no gratitude. He was barred from the saloon forthwith. In an Army signals unit, he discovered another skill: his power of concentration was so intense that he could isolate a single faint transmission on a band where two or three others were competing and confusing the sound.

When he left the Army, Hook decided it was time to get an education, and went down to Wall Street, where he thought his peculiar skills might compensate for an absence of book learning. He started as a runner, carrying messages and orders to the traders on the floor, and played the market on the side. Within a decade he had become a partner in a firm of bullion dealers. His special reputation is for his memory for price movements, and his ability to do sums in a few seconds faster than a computer. He smokes incessantly, and drinks hardly at all.

Theo Hook wakes early in his house in suburban Westchester County, and phones London at six a.m. to find out how the gold and silver markets are behaving. (Before he goes to bed he makes a quick call to Hong Kong to see what is happening as trading opens there.) Hook arrives in his office on Water Street in Manhattan's financial district at about nine-fifteen, twenty-five minutes before the silver market opens, holding the first of many cups of coffee from a carryout on the corner, and sits at the head of the trading table. He glances at the computer printout, which has been sent from the clearinghouse, listing any margin calls his firm might have to pay, and looks down the list of bank loans the firm has taken out to finance its operations. His desk is then uncluttered, but within half an hour it is piled with papers, particularly with sheets printed either black for an order to buy or red to sell.

Down the table are more traders, whose view of each other is obscured by the bulk of the monitors on which they can call up anything from the Chicago soybean price to the latest world news on the Reuters wire. In case they miss anything there, a secretary looks down the tape from the Associated Press machine every ten minutes and calls out any news that might affect gold or silver prices. In front of each dealer is a telephone bank, with direct lines to the exchange floor and to all the major bullion dealers; along the wall are telex machines linked directly to London and Zurich. The company's telephone and telex bill is $192,000 a year. 'It's not that big,' says Hook. 'Most people call us.'

Business is conducted in a code.

'Buy a half,' Hook shouts.

'Half of what?' I wonder.

'Half a lakh.'

'A lakh?'

'A lakh is the Indian measurement of one hundred thousand, and it's still used in the silver market. Half a lakh is fifty thousand ounces of silver.'

When Hook gives a price, he shouts two figures. 'Seventy-five–eighty-two,' he calls to a dealer. The figures mean that, at that moment, Hook is offering to buy silver at $17.75 an ounce or sell at $17.82. It is known as the bid-and-offer price, and there are two figures because when an inquirer comes on the phone or the telex, Hook does not know whether he intends to buy or sell. The trader must give him the option to do either.

That momentary uncertainty about the caller's intention is the key to the puzzle about commodity markets. Dealers like Hook do not make money only when the price is going up. The beauty of the business for professional traders is that, unlike amateur speculators, they take money whichever direction the market is moving. The only time they make no money is when the market is not moving at all.

Simple silver-trading was illustrated by one of the transactions I overheard at the table.

A telex machine chatters; one of the traders down the table calls to

Hook that a Swiss bank is asking about silver. 'Seventy-five–eighty-two,' replies Hook.

The price is tapped out on the telex, which replies immediately: Swiss bank buys 50,000 ounces of silver at $17.82. 'Okay, done,' the trader replies, confirming the sale of half a lakh.

Hook simultaneously calls a huge bullion dealer, Engelhard's subsidiary Philipp Brothers, on a direct line and asks their price for silver. They are selling at $17.79; Hook buys as much as he has sold the Swiss bank. Meanwhile, the telex machine is chattering again: *How is your market now?*

'Seventy-eight–eighty-five,' goes the reply, and within seconds the Swiss bank has bought another 100,000 ounces of silver at $17.85. Hook gets back to Philipp Brothers again and buys 50,000 ounces at $17.82, and at the same time his assistant phones Mocatta Metals, which, unaware of the previous transaction, sells Hook the other 50,000 ounces at $17.81.

The slips are written out – sales on the red forms, purchases on the black ones – and the trade is over, completed within two minutes. The Swiss have bought 150,000 ounces of silver for a total of $2,676,000. Hook has bought the same amount from two bullion dealers for $2,671,000. The profit on the deal was $5,000. Hook told me that, with a quick grin, seconds after it was done; it took me fifteen minutes to check it. 'You win by knowing where to go,' he explains. 'I bought a bit of silver earlier in the morning to find out who was selling. I knew Philipp's was a seller.' There is nothing unusual about such a transaction, either. The daily turnover in Hook's trading room varies between $75 million and $200 million.

This kind of silver deal is called back-to-back trading, and it is bread and butter to Hook. The jam is arbitrage. This is a more demanding test of Hook's skill, since it involves buying and selling silver contracts at future dates in different markets. Even Hook reaches for a pencil and paper to explain the complexities of futures trading. He draws a graph, and in the bottom left corner he marks the spot price of silver – the price, in ounces, of silver bought that day. Then he marks points on the graph showing the price rising through the successive months of Comex futures contracts: January, March, May, June, September, and December. (The last is always known as 'the Deece'.) Each point on this ideal graph is higher than the previous one because of the cost of borrowing money to finance the purchase of the contract, and the graph assumes no variation in demand.

Next, Hook draws a line that represents the actual futures prices in the markets in New York, Chicago, and London, and the points of the graph diverge from the straight line to reflect differences in supply and demand for silver contracts in future months. If demand for March silver is heavy, the price will rise above the straight line; if demand is light in June, the price will fall below the straight line. Arbitrage is spotting where the lines on the graph differ between two markets – between New York and Chicago or between the United States and Europe. Whenever the differential between the two markets is great enough for Hook to make a profit by buying in one market and selling in another, he will trade.

In the dealing room, arbitrage is a discordant duet between Hook on the phone to the pit in Chicago and a trader down the table talking to Hook's man in the New York Comex pit. The duet ends with one or the other shouting: 'We're out!' Hook's skill is in spotting the divergences between prices more quickly than the other market professionals. In a normal market these divergences created by speculative demand last only minutes before the prices come back into line. When they do so, Hook sells up and takes his profit. The game has to be completed by the end of a day's trading. Hook's profits from arbitrage on a good day are counted in tens of thousands of dollars. For the big bullion merchants like Mocatta and Philipp Brothers, the daily profit often amounts to hundreds of thousands.

Hook shows me the sheet of the day's silver trading. He has bought (or is long) 963 contracts, and has sold (or is short) 958 contracts. He says he prefers his purchases and sales to balance exactly so that they will cancel each other out, leaving him simply with the profit from arbitrage and back-to-back trading. 'I let some other genius figure out tomorrow's prices. I want to go home and sleep at night.'

'In this business,' Hook continues, 'you can never predict what is going to happen at the end of the day. You're always at school, and the hardest lesson is learning to take a loss. To make five thousand dollars is easy; but a five-thousand-dollar loss will become a fifty-thousand-dollar loss nine times out of ten.' The theory is that speculators should run their profits, which means not selling too soon, and take their losses, but it is remarkable how few learn the lesson. Their failure to do so is a reason why so many of them lose, and why professionals usually win.

Driving in Hook's long maroon Cadillac (his only ostentation), I ask Hook why he trades. 'It's sitting down with the best cardplayers in the world and making more money than they are. Not that I worry much about money. Like Bunker says, it's a way of keeping the score. Anyway, it beats walking to work.' I ask if he ever traded on his own, rather than his firm's, account, and he replies: 'I did once, until I lost four hundred thousand dollars in the silver market in August 1979. I managed to make three hundred fifty thousand back on a dangerous speculation, but it made me sweat, and I've never done it since.' I wondered what he would say if I were to ask him to trade with $5,000 of my own money. 'If I wasn't absolutely convinced that you could afford to lose it all, I'd tell you to put it in Treasury bills.'

The market is a big numbers game, Hook says, adding that since the market is a game, he finds it more fun when it is honest. And is it? Hook looks baleful. 'On the floor, eighty per cent of the traders steal in one way or another. The temptation is so great; it's just like taking an apple from the barrel. A straight guy, making maybe a hundred thousand a year, knows that the slob next to him doesn't know a thing, but there he is in the pit tweaking an ear or stroking his chin, signalling to a friend that he has just received a large order to buy or sell, so his pal can rip off ten cents an ounce on fifty contracts. That's twenty-five thousand dollars; he's made in a few minutes what it takes the straight man three months' hard labour to make. That's why the temptation is difficult to resist.'

The fiddles may be entirely invisible to any speculator watching through the glass windows of the exchanges, but they exist, nevertheless. The best known, and simplest, is when a trader, knowing a large order to buy will be placed at a certain time of the day, buys for himself beforehand, confident that the price will be forced up by the later large order. He sells again before the market closes, and takes his profit.

Off the floor, in the brokerage house, there is another version of this deception. The customer will call in an order, when the price is at $10.00, to 'buy at best' – the best price the floor trader can get. If the market falls to $9.50, the dealer buys then, but he tells the customer that he bought at $10.00 and pockets the difference. (This is another reason why the speculator so often seems to lose.)

The speculators, men like Bunker, tend to be bulls, relying on a conviction that prices are more likely to go up than down. To many it seems like a contradiction of common sense to make money out of falling prices. If the speculators, trading through their brokerage houses, make up a majority of the bulls, it follows that the bears – the sellers – are mostly professionals. Scalpers on the floor of the exchange are in a better position to be sellers than a hardworking dentist in Kansas City. The most substantial group of shorts in the market, however, are the hedgers – known as the commercials.

Commercials are not only producers and industrial users of silver. They include major bullion dealers, such as Mocatta Metals, Philipp Brothers, and Sharps Pixley, who act as middlemen between producers and users. All of these commercials want to insure themselves from the uncertainties of a cash market. They all hedge, though each does so for a different reason. Bullion dealers usually have large supplies of silver in their warehouses, so they hedge against a fall in the market price, which would reduce the value of their stocks, by going short in the silver market. (Remember, these shorts do not lose money when the price falls.) A silver producer does the same thing. A manufacturer using silver, on the other hand, wants protection against *increases* in price, so he goes long on the futures market. If the price goes up, his profit in the market offsets the increased price he must pay for silver when he wants to use it. The biggest users, companies like Kodak, hedge only when the market is volatile and appears more likely to go up than down; the bullion dealers and the silver producers are thus left as the largest holders of short positions.

In theory, especially, the futures market is a remarkable financial mechanism, and the exchanges are immodest about it. Theo Hook's scepticism does not feature in their promotional literature. In Chicago, particularly, the members who hold seats on the Board of Trade exchange boast that it is 'the last, best, free market in the world.' Unfortunately, the history of commodity markets is littered with cases of speculators who tried to manipulate the market to improve their chances of winning. Among the professionals the motive for manipulation is often the challenge: they want to see if it can be done. Among the speculators, the motive is more usually greed in its classic dictionary definition: 'inordinate or all-consuming and usually reprehensible acquisitiveness, especially for wealth or gain.'

As we have seen, the convention of the market is that speculators do not need the commodity they are dealing in. If they are bulls, and their long contracts expire, they either take their profits or roll them over – which means they sell contracts that are about to expire and buy the same number of contracts for a month in the future. That is the convention; it is not the rule. A bull can in fact demand delivery of silver from the bear. When there is not enough silver in the warehouse, the spot price (or 'today's' price) is forced higher than the futures price. This is known as a squeeze. When the bull demands a delivery, knowing that there is not enough silver available because he already owns so much of it, the bear has been cornered; he has to settle his contracts with the bull by buying from the bull's store, and the bull is virtually free to name his price. The corner is the most ambitious form of all manipulation, and is perhaps best described by an actual case.

The time was 1907; the market, silver, the place, India, then the world's largest silver buyer because its currency, the rupee, was still minted in silver. In the first five years of the century, the Indian government, through the India Office in London, had bought an astonishing quantity – 205 million ounces of silver – for a new rupee issue. Shrewd speculators were quite sure that before long the India Office would have to come back for more. The story is taken up by a journalist in the *Morning Post* with the impressive, if vague, by-line, 'An Expert Correspondent':

> In these circumstances the brain which could conceive a plan for cornering silver needed to be daring and reckless to an extreme degree, for the opposing forces were not the public, to whom silver is an article of luxury and not of necessity, but Governments, whose use of silver forms but an adjunct – in many cases certainly a most important adjunct – to their currency systems.
>
> In the last few years a powerful movement described in the vernacular as 'swadeshi' has been initiated by the native-born inhabitants of India, with a view to conserving with their own hands the management and affairs of India, both Governmental and industrial.
>
> The movement comprised the formation of banks, whose officers and capital were to be native. One of the most important of these institutions was the Indian Specie Bank, the capital of which had been enthusiastically subscribed and whose directors included Maharajahs and other prominent native personages. Under these circumstances the concern found no difficulty in obtaining an important share of native business, and enjoyed the advantage of a substantial amount of deposited funds.
>
> The management devolved into the hands of Mr Chunilal Saraya, whose experience and abilities appear to have compelled the bank in the long run to entrust him with unchecked control over the operations and funds of the institution. This gentleman set himself to dominate the silver market in Bombay. Flattered by success and imbued with the idea, so fascinating to the Indian mind, of Napoleonic ventures in finance, he conceived the idea of cornering the world's supplies of silver.

It is not only the Indian mind that is fascinated by Napoleonic ventures in finance, but never mind that for a moment. Saraya invaded the London market and persuaded a highly respectable London firm called Sharps and Wilkins to let him buy massively on generously low margins. They might have been more circumspect if they had grasped the scale of Saraya's ambitions. He proposed buying so much silver that he would control the world market price in London. The objective was simple, although admittedly expensive, but if he pulled it off it would be a great coup. He wanted to force the British officials of the government of India to come to him – an Indian banker – when they needed the silver for another issue of rupees; he wanted them to grovel, and to pay his price for his bullion and his futures contracts.

By the end of 1912, five years' vigorous buying in the market had created a great hoard of 50 million ounces of silver, half of it in bullion, half in forward delivery contracts. The hoard was large enough for Saraya, on his way to a corner, to squeeze the London market. Twice in 1910, when the supply of ready silver was desperately scarce, Saraya was able to unload a part of his hoard to satisfy demand, and each time the squeeze brought him a nice profit.

That was on the credit side of Saraya's ledger; the debit side – which was made up of lost interest on money that was tied up in bullion and forward contracts, plus warehousing and transport costs – was substantial enough to wipe out profits from the squeezes. But Saraya remained confident of the wisdom of his investment; it could only be a matter of time before silver was needed for a new rupee issue.

A common characteristic shared by the architects of market corners is the conviction that they have thought of everything. This leads to a dangerous assumption that their victim will be powerless in the face of market forces. But the victims are rarely so meek. In this case the India Office, in London, at last aware of the danger of a corner, began to buy silver secretly through a broker it had never used before. By 1913 enough silver had been acquired by this method for the Indian government to be able to announce a new currency issue, and although they did go to Saraya, the government wanted only half his hoard; consequently they were able to buy on their terms at market prices, not Saraya's artificially inflated price. The cost of financing the other half of the silver hoard broke the Indian Specie Bank. In November 1913 Chunilal Saraya shot himself.

Saraya had lost fatally, but the game was not over. His London bullion dealers, Sharps and Wilkins, were left with forward contracts for 26 million ounces of silver, which had been bought for Saraya without their ever asking for prudent margin payments. If they had to dispose of those contracts suddenly on the market, the price would collapse, and Sharps and Wilkins would collapse with it, undermining confidence in the market itself. To prevent all London's bullion firms falling like dominoes, the leading bullion dealers, Mocatta and Goldsmid, put together a syndicate from the trade, backed by banks, including the most famous of the British banks in India, the Chartered, to buy all Saraya's silver and organize its orderly disposal. Within four months all 26 million ounces had been sold, and the price had remained so stable that the syndicate made a small profit.

But speculators learn nothing from history; they believe that they can avoid the errors of their predecessors. Memoirs of the markets are full of stories about attempted corners, and they usually have two things in common: greed and failure. William Worthington Fowler, who had seen many corners attempted on Wall Street in the nineteenth century, noted: 'These combinations are traps in more senses than one, for they not only serve to ensnare the bears by cornering them, but they generally result in losses to members of the combination themselves.' Fowler observed the attempt to corner the New York gold market in 1869 by 'the oiled and curled Assyrian bull of Wall Street', James Fisk, and his partner, Jay Gould, who lost $20 million in an hour when their corner collapsed. In 1888 a Parisian banker named Denfert Rochereau tried to corner the world copper market. The nineteenth-century grain market in Chicago was littered with examples of attempted squeezes and corners; to a lesser extent it still is. Rings and corners in the stock market ended with the Great Crash and the establishment of the Securities and Exchange Commission in 1934. But commodities remained a temptation to the corner men. In the last generation corners were attempted in eggs, onions, vegetable oil, soybeans, and potatoes. The fact that market manipulation is now illegal does not stop people trying.

Not all manipulations fail, however. I asked a London dealer about corners one day, and he said the easiest way to explain how they worked was to describe how he had cornered the bismuth market. He showed me a graph of the bismuth price in the 1970s; it curved up gently except for a sudden sharp jump in 1974: his corner. My companion was only in his early twenties then, but he believed no one in the world knew more about bismuth than he did. He knew the suppliers in Peru, Bolivia, Japan, and South Korea; he knew the users, who are found mainly in France, where bismuth is an essential compound in the manufacture of suppositories. Moreover, he knew that demand was likely to rise because Sohio, in America, had invented a new catalyst that required bismuth. So he bought; soon he had contracts for forward delivery for 10 per cent of the world's supply of bismuth, all bought on credit. Eventually the dealers who had long-term contracts to supply bismuth to the users in France had to come to my companion: his 10 per cent share was all that was available on the market. They bought his forward contracts, and he charged twice the price the bismuth dealers had paid a year earlier. The corner netted £1 million for his company, and it was all over before anyone except a few manufacturers of suppositories knew anything about it. My companion had satisfied himself that it could be done, and only after the corner had been successfully made did he suffer mild pangs of conscience.

Episodes like this are well known to the market professionals. For public consumption they are dismissed as isolated aberrations, exceptions to the general rule that no man, or group, is bigger than the market. The rule insists that when a price rises or falls too steeply, the market will adjust; for example, when a commodity is in short supply, new sources will be found and the price will fall. Nelson Bunker Hunt must have been told that, but if so, it was another piece of advice he chose to ignore. He behaved as though the rule about no one's being bigger than the market did not apply to him.

Chapter 4

Insane About Silver

When Bunker Hunt discovered the futures market in silver in 1973 (or 1972, as the case may be), it was still dominated by industrial users and bullion dealers hedging the value of silver they actually used. A few of the followers of Jerome Smith were beginning to buy, but the price rarely moved by more than a few cents a day – until Bunker became involved, that is. He began to buy silver with the proceeds from his Libyan oil fields, for, although outraged by Qaddafi's expropriation of his assets in mid-1973, Hunt had still extracted more profit from the Sarir Field than an efficient, medium-sized corporation would expect to earn in a decade or so. By applying a great deal of that cash to silver futures, Bunker immediately became one of the major participants in the market. (Any other role would have bored him; small was never beautiful to Bunker Hunt.) And once Bunker was persuaded that silver was to be his newest passion, Herbert embraced it, too. Herbert was not much interested in racehorses or cattle, but silver was something he could understand.

Both applied their native cunning to the futures market and learned quickly: about margins, which enabled them to buy futures contracts with a value of $20 million for an initial outlay of $1 million; and about pyramiding, by which they could increase their position in the market without putting up an extra penny. Bunker quickly understood that the way to reduce the odds was to be long – a buyer – when the price was going up. He never was much interested in selling short, and soon he became the biggest bull in the business.

From the first, Bunker and Herbert were different from most other speculators, and it was not just their money that made them so. The other difference was that they wanted to possess silver, and so they took delivery of many of the silver contracts they bought. That cost real money but did not deter the Hunts. They had been told, no doubt, that the custom of the market was to roll their contracts over into more distant months before they become due for delivery, but the brothers never had much time for custom. And Bunker had grasped that taking delivery of silver and then removing it from the warehouse reduced the stocks in the Comex and Board of Trade warehouses and, therefore, the amount of silver available for delivery; the lower the visible stocks, the higher the price tends to go.

Bunker had also learned where the big bullion dealers purchased the silver that became part of the warehouse stocks in New York, Chicago, London, and Zurich. One source, for example, was a tiny emirate on the Persian Gulf, Dubai – the port at which the daring skippers of souped-up dhows plying the Indian Ocean trade land the silver they have smuggled out of India. The biggest bullion dealer in Dubai was, and is, a Pakistani named Haji Ashraf, and by the autumn of 1973 Bunker had already made his acquaintance. He bought $20 million of the silver that Ashraf had himself bought from the seamen who carried the smuggled silver from their moorings on Dubai's Creek to his small office on the edge of the Souk – the marketplace. Purchases like this put pressure on the warehouse stocks by cutting the supply lines, and by the end of 1973 the Hunts not only had bought bullion but had substantial holdings – for beginners, especially – in long futures contracts on the New York and Chicago markets. Bunker Hunt felt strong enough to apply a sudden squeeze to the silver market.

In December of 1973 the classic preconditions of a squeeze existed. The price was $2.90 an ounce and the Hunts had contracts for some 35 million ounces of silver; moreover, it was unlikely that there was enough silver in the warehouse to satisfy normal industrial demand *and* those contracts if the Hunts were to demand delivery of them all; worse still, none of the market professionals felt able to predict exactly what the newcomers would do. The fear of a squeeze, together with loud, orchestrated bidding by Bache's dealer, Alvin Brodsky, which made other dealers feel nervous, sent the price up through $4.00 in January 1974 and then on up to an unprecedented $6.70 on February 26. It seemed a good bet that the Hunts would find an unhappy figure known in the commodity markets as 'the naked short' – a broker or bullion dealer who would be incapable of delivering enough silver to settle the Hunts' long position, and who would have to cover his own short position by buying long contracts himself. The market even had a single candidate for this embarrassing role (although there were probably others): Dr Henry Jarecki, of Mocatta Metals. If Jarecki, unable to deliver the silver, were forced into the market as a buyer, the impact would, of course, send the price even higher – up toward the $8 Jerome Smith had forecast so confidently for 1974.

That was the theory: demand was greater than supply, so the price must go up. But there was one lesson that apparently had not been included in Bunker's rapid education. If someone could find a hoard of silver and persuade its owner to sell, the balance between supply and demand would be restored, and the price would come down. There was such a hoard; and Henry Jarecki knew where it was located. In the vaults of the Bank of Mexico there were 50 million ounces of silver that had been accumulated at less than $2 an ounce. Just in case the Mexicans had not noticed, Dr Jarecki pointed out to them that he believed the price in New York was artificial; they had only to sell now, and they would make windfall profits. The Mexicans needed little persuasion, and quickly sold all 50 million ounces – much of it to the Hunts, who had to keep on buying if their squeeze was to maintain its momentum. Afterward, the explanation of the Bank of Mexico's sudden intervention in the market was that it badly needed foreign exchange, but that was only a half-truth; a more plausible interpretation is that the bank saw an opportunity to make a great deal of money, and sensibly took it.

Although the flood of Mexican silver brought the price tumbling back to $4, it never fell to the bargain price at which it had stood when Bunker began his silver caper. Bunker's squeeze had miscarried, but, as a gambling man, he took it philosophically. He understood that you have to pay to learn. Being singed did not make Bunker frightened of the fire. He announced his belief that silver remained a first-class investment, claimed that he and Herbert had still made a lot of money in the flurry during that winter, and added that the Hunts were not sellers. They would keep what they had.

It emerged later that they did not intend to keep it in America. The brothers took Jerome Smith's advice about storing bullion abroad quite literally, and flew 6 million ounces of silver to London in 1975. Since the Hunts had little faith in conventional methods of security, hands at the family's ranches in Texas were given pistol target practice, and selected hands formed a guard that rode shotgun on the aircraft flying the silver across the Atlantic.

(There is an even more extravagant story about the Hunts' trans-Atlantic silver traffic. It is so improbable that most people who hear it dismiss it as pure fantasy; its very improbability persuades me that it might be true, though my attempts to check it with one of the participants, Randy Kreiling, brother-in-law of Ray Hunt – of the second family – proved unsuccessful. The story goes like this. On one of the freight aircraft carrying the bullion to Europe, the silver was carefully arranged around the sides of the hold to distribute the weight, leaving a large gap in the middle, which was filled by a cage containing a circus elephant. Over the Atlantic the aircraft suddenly began to yaw wildly, and Kreiling, who was accompanied by Lamar Hunt – so the tale has it – rushed back to discover that the elephant had pushed its trunk through the bars and was playing with the wires that controlled the aircraft's flaps. Acting with the inspiration that is prompted only by impending death, our heroes opened the cage and threw a rubber tire at the elephant – which transferred its attention to its new toy – and thus saved their own lives and the family silver.)

The account of the co-option of cowboys to guard the silver is contained in testimony given by an ex-employee of Bunker and Herbert Hunt's, a lanky and engaging Texas oilman named Bill L. Bledsoe. He had first worked for H.L. Hunt and Bunker inherited him after H.L.'s death. Bill Bledsoe was Bunker's loyal lieutenant, running errands and making acquisitions, until he resigned in March 1979 to become an independent in the oil business. ('You've got to be a monkey not to make money out of oil these days,' he claimed, having decided that he would rather make it for himself than for the Hunts.) Bunker's automatic response to Bledsoe's resignation was to sue him, claiming conflict of interest, diversion of company funds for his, Bledsoe's, personal use, and breach of fiduciary relationships with Bunker and the Hunt Energy Corporation. Bledsoe vehemently protests his innocence, and there is little doubt that another reason Bunker wanted Bill Bledsoe driven out of town was the evidence Bledsoe gave of the business activities of his former bosses to congressional investigators in May 1980. The brothers hated him for it; they stepped up the inquiries on which they based their lawsuit, and Bledsoe was eventually indicted in May 1981. But Bledsoe is a difficult man to silence, and he became a sought-after figure for any reporter arriving in Dallas to inquire about the Hunts – myself included. He may be a prejudiced witness, but he is not one who can be ignored, and, in a curious way, his loyalty to the brothers remains real enough. 'I love Bunker', he announced one evening to his wife and myself, though each of us was rather at a loss to understand exactly why.

Bledsoe gave a vivid account of Bunker and Herbert's activities in the silver market to Barbara Timmer, a lawyer for one of the many congressional committees that in 1980 investigated the brothers' activities in the silver market.

'Silver transactions are made by William Herbert Hunt and Nelson Bunker Hunt in concert,' Bledsoe told Timmer. 'They buy and sell silver together. It is more than having lunch together or working in the same building. Silver is looked on as the first order of business in the morning. It is reviewed all day long, and strategy is determined daily on whether Bunker or Herbert will buy or sell in their own names, or in family names, or in corporate names.

'The brothers are very brilliant individuals. They have phenomenal memories. They can tell you what they paid for an acre of land twelve years ago. They do not do business haphazardly. They do it on a planned attack, whether it is to buy or sell. They know precisely the amount of silver they have at any given moment. They could tell you precisely what they paid in 1974. Not only do they have phenomenal memories, they have documents fed to them daily by their personal accountants.'

Bledsoe went to work for Bunker shortly after the silver squeeze had failed in its ultimate objective, and he was one of the few people allowed to observe a most uncommon circumstance: Bunker and Herbert were strapped for cash. A slab of their capital was tied up in 50 million ounces of silver, now at roughly $4.50 an ounce, worth some $225 million, on which the brothers were earning no interest, and which cost them money to ship and store. They were even short of half a million dollars in 1975 to buy some promising oil leases. (Their sisters bought them instead and, to the chagrin of Bunker and Herbert, found oil and gas properties near Baton Rouge whose value Bledsoe estimates at $1 billion.) After the attempted squeeze, the silver price was immobile, the brothers were in the doldrums, and Bunker knew only one way to combat that. Always the captain of his fate, he decided it was time to apply some pressure on the market again.

By this time, in the winter of 1974–75, Bunker had met the shrewd Dubai bullion dealer Haji Ashraf in London, and Ashraf reports that Bunker asked him how the silver price might be heaved in an upward direction. Ashraf, who daily saw visual evidence of the explosive economic effect the vast accumulation of newly acquired oil wealth had in Arabia, told Bunker that the problem was easily solved. He simply needed to interest some very rich Arabs; if he could persuade them to buy, they would, by nature, do so on such a scale that the price would float up and up. Bunker thought it was a fine idea from the very beginning. Even a reflective man could hardly have known that this idea contained the seeds of his undoing.

The Arab ploy began early in March 1975 when Bunker Hunt asked Bill Bledsoe to accompany him on a trip. 'He wanted me as a bodyguard, though I didn't have a gun or anything. I wasn't much more than a lackey, really.'

Bledsoe discovered the destination only when he was sent to the Iranian consulate to get the visas, and not until they were airborne did Bunker reveal the purpose of the mission. He then showed Bledsoe some articles about silver that had been carefully underlined and that concentrated on the gap between production and consumption, as well as the value of silver as a hedge against inflation.

They were in the economy class of the aircraft – naturally – and Bledsoe interrupted his reading when the hostess came down the aisle selling headsets for the movie. 'We were going from Miami to London, long flight, so I spent two and a half bucks on a headset,' says Bledsoe.

'What you doing that for?' Bunker asked.

'I'm going to watch the movie; I want to kill some time.'

'I never buy those things. I can tell what's happening just by looking.'

When the movie began, Bledsoe settled down to watch. The plot involved some men blowing up a ship, and after a few minutes Bunker leaned over to Bledsoe and asked:

'What did he say?'

'He said they were going to plant a charge.'

'Why are they doing that?'

So Bledsoe extracted one of the earplugs and gave Bunker a running commentary on the dialogue. 'Bunker kept saying, "I can't figure out why they did that." Still, he saved his two and a half bucks.'

Bunker started ambitiously, right at the top. His plan was to persuade the Shah of Iran to invest in the silver market the amount of revenue he personally received in one month from oil, to take delivery, and to hoard the bullion in Switzerland. The effect of this would have been not to massage the market but to pummel it; a man who worried about two and a half dollars for a movie was talking about an injection of hundreds of millions of dollars in the silver market – though the irony would have been lost on Bunker.

The meeting had been arranged by the Shah's half-brother Prince Mahmoud, who had been a houseguest of Bunker's some ten years earlier when he was a student in Michigan. The prince was at Tehran airport to meet Bunker, and he was a bearer of bad tidings. The Shah was too busy with Henry Kissinger to see Bunker (another strike against the Jewish professor), but the finance minister, Hushang Ansari, had been told to see Bunker instead. When they met, Ansari said politely that he was not acquainted with Bunker's business, and asked how much he was worth.

'I don't know,' Bunker replied, his phenomenal memory unaccountably failing him. 'How much did we make last year, Bill?'

Bledsoe remembered the score; Ansari learned that profits had been around $50 million, and, satisfied with Hunt's credentials, listened to the well-rehearsed story.

'Well, Bill, how'd I do?' Hunt asked when they left Ansari.

'It was a good presentation, Bunker.'

'Think they're going to do it?'

'Well, I believe they're going to think a lot before they do. You hit them pretty cold in there,' replied Bledsoe diplomatically.

Bunker, who found that he was quite literally allergic to the atmosphere in Tehran, fled. Bledsoe took him to the airport and booked two seats on the first flight to Europe. This landed them in Zurich, where Bunker's head had cleared sufficiently to allow him to see that he would have to activate his second option: the Saudi Arabians. The man to whom he wished to tell the story was King Faisal Ibn Abdul-Aziz himself. Bunker had an obliging friend in New York named Benjamin Freedman, who, despite being Jewish, had remarkably good contacts in Riyadh, and he thought Freedman could fix the meeting. Optimistically – because King Faisal had no taste for commerce – Freedman thought so, too, but counselled Bunker against going to Riyadh right away. Since Bunker's trip to Tehran had become the subject of much gossip in the Arab world, Freedman felt Bunker should wait a couple of weeks, so that the proud King Faisal would not think he was Bunker's second choice.

Bunker agreed and went off to inspect his horses in Chantilly, outside Paris, before returning to Dallas. But he instructed Bledsoe to stay behind in Switzerland for a few days and see some bankers. 'He said to mention that we're seeing the Shah and Faisal about silver – just casually, to get them thinking.' Bledsoe found that a visiting card describing him as the personal representative of Nelson Bunker Hunt had a wonderful way of opening doors, and the message was duly passed on to the Union Bank of Switzerland, Crédit Suisse, the Swiss Bank Corporation, and the Banque Populaire Suisse. Herbert Hunt had also told Bledsoe to ask how the banks would react to a request for loans of some $100 million to buy a further 25 to 30 million ounces of silver – a signal that the Hunts were not dismayed by the stagnant market.

Bunker Hunt's second option collapsed dramatically on March 25, 1975, when King Faisal was murdered in his palace by a disenchanted young scion of the royal family. That terminated at a stroke Bunker's first flirtation with Middle Eastern potentates. But the idea did not die with Faisal; it merely lay dormant. And the traffic between Texas and Arabia had given Bledsoe an insight into the ultimate intention of Bunker and Herbert Hunt. 'As I saw it at the time, the Hunts were making a concentrated effort to manipulate or control the world's supply of silver.'

Bunker Hunt's preoccupation was not, of course, entirely with overseas business. In the United States the brothers had found a new vehicle for speculation in commodity markets. This was a company called Great Western United, a conglomerate with its roots in the sugar industry. It was the largest refiner of beet sugar in the nation, and owned a range of subsidiaries, the best known of which was Shakey's Pizza Parlors. The brothers originally bought a small stake in Great Western but, dissatisfied with the management, decided to buy a majority shareholding. With 65.7 per cent of the stock they were able to run it their way, eventually renaming it Hunt International Resources Corporation, with Bunker as chairman of the board and Herbert as president.

Great Western had, perhaps properly, been a commercial hedger in the sugar futures market. Then, in 1975 and 1976, through a subsidiary called Western Investments, the company became a big player in all futures markets, mostly metals, and especially silver. The change was so sudden that it provided Wall Street with an illuminating case study in the business methods of the Hunts. Western Investments' broker was Shearson Hayden Stone, a respected firm, and the account soon became substantial enough to come under the scrutiny of the senior managing director, George Lamborn, an upright man with an uncommon sense of what is right and wrong in the markets. Lamborn did not like what he saw; Western Investments had a modest capital of $6 million, which bore no relation to the outcome of the speculative orgy the company undertook in 1975 and 1976. From Western Investments' financial statement Lamborn counted between 43,000 contracts in sugar, silver, gold, and copper. The book value of these was $67 million, and it was secured by margin payments of a mere $4 million. Lamborn's first action was to demand an additional margin payment of $1 million. When the Hunts discovered that an underling had obliged with the money, they were angry and demanded that Lamborn return it.

But margin was not Lamborn's only concern. 'My feeling,' he remembers, 'was that Western Investments was a non-guaranteed subsidiary of a publicly owned sugar company, and I feared that some shareholders might do the same calculations as I had, and sue the Hunts for speculating in commodity markets with the sugar company's money.'

A chance meeting in 1976 finally persuaded him that radical action was needed. Lamborn had visited a friend who had, until recently, been involved in one of Great Western's subsidiaries. The company was doing well; sales, earnings, and profits were all up. Nonetheless, Lamborn's friend had been fired, and when he had made a routine request to cash in some stock options, he was told to forget them.

Lamborn's friend complained bitterly and said he would fight for his money. What happened next is not necessarily a consequence of this wrangle, but it is a fact that Lamborn's friend received through the mail glossy photographs taken with an infra-red lens of him *in flagrante delicto* in a motel room with a woman who was definitely not his wife. There was no message enclosed; the source could only be inferred. A man of some character, he showed the pictures to his wife, telling her that he believed he had been set up to silence him. He let that message circulate. Shortly afterward he received all the money owed from the stock options, plus interest.

The incident, whether it actually was inspired by the management of Great Western or not, convinced Lamborn that Shearson should stop doing business with the Hunts. Lamborn deliberately provoked the brothers by insisting that he would not return their additional million-dollar margin payment, as they had demanded; nor would he automatically remit to Western Investments daily profits when commodity prices were going up. Moreover, he said he would not be told by the Hunts how to run his business. Bunker and Herbert took these broad hints and withdrew the Western Investments account. Despite the size of the transaction, it took them only two weeks; there were plenty of brokers who were eager for the Hunts' business.

This incident did not deter the Hunts for a moment from plunging even more deeply into the silver market. In one month, June 1976, Western Investments took delivery of 21 million ounces of silver; the professional dealers defined this as a mini-squeeze, a dry run to see if the market were vulnerable. It was not; by the beginning of November that year, Bunker, Herbert, and Western Investments had registered vault receipts from the Comex and Board of Trade warehouses for 53 million ounces of silver, and still the price would not move as Bunker thought it should. The price had risen briefly to $5.20 in August, but by December it was down at $4.30, where it had languished exactly one year earlier. Jerome Smith's confident predictions were going sadly awry, despite Bunker's attempts to see that they were fulfilled, with some help from himself to overcome any resistance from the market.

Equally provoking was the Commodity Futures Trading Commission. For the first time, in 1976, the Hunts attracted the attention of the CFTC, which was concerned at the concentration of so much silver in so few hands. The brothers had an ingenious explanation; they said they were buying heavily because they had arranged to pay in silver for sugar from the Philippines, to be refined by Great Western. Further, the Hunts explained, the Philippines would use the same silver to buy oil from Arabia. The object of this complex barter deal, Bunker apparently calculated, was that the Arabs should hold on to the silver, and as a result of their extracting millions of ounces from the market, the price would be forced up. The greatest fault with the explanation was that the barter arrangement was never consummated by any of the parties involved.

The failure of this extravagant scheme was no doubt irritating, and so increasingly was the presence of federal regulatory agencies in Washington. To escape the scrutiny of the Securities and Exchange Commission, and the possibility of the kind of shareholder suit that had concerned Lamborn when he looked at Western Investments' portfolio, Bunker and Herbert Hunt went into the stock market and bought the remaining publicly held shares in Great Western. Since the company was no longer responsible to anyone other than its chairman and president, it was exempt from the SEC's stringent reporting requirements. A veil of silence was drawn over its affairs.

The problem of the CFTC remained. Until April 21, 1975, when the CFTC first opened for business, there had been no federal regulation of the silver futures market. The very principle of federal regulation was abhorrent to Bunker and Herbert Hunt – a view they shared with the market traders – but since it existed, the brothers decided they must define their legal position as exactly as possible. Consequently, in February 1976, they asked for a legal opinion about the relationship among the futures market, Great Western, and themselves. Xeroxed copies of this opinion turned up in New York City four years later, though the name of the law firm that had written the document had been blacked out, as if the author had been mildly ashamed of its provenance. It addressed itself not just to the law as it stood but to the particular concerns of Bunker and Herbert. The inferences that can be drawn from these concerns make the opinion material evidence.

One purpose in the Hunts' commissioning the document soon became clear. It noted that Great Western Sugar (one of the conglomerate's subsidiaries) had paid $74 million in taxes in 1975 and that the company 'proposes to engage in transactions in the commodity futures markets, looking towards the recoupment of a substantial proportion of such taxes.' The problem, as stated by the lawyer author, was that since Bunker and Herbert were personally active in the market, federal regulators might suspect that Great Western Sugar was being used in association with their personal holdings to manipulate the market. (It is possible that such a suspicion might not have been far wrong.) 'I also understand,' the document continued, 'that Nelson Bunker and William Herbert Hunt have been active in the silver market for some years; that they presently own substantial amounts of silver bullion; and that they may engage in activities of some considerable magnitude in the same period when Great Western Sugar will be engaged in silver transactions. Consequently the provisions of the Commodity Exchange Act must be reviewed and considered . . . because it is not necessary for the courts to show that the market activities of the accused are the sole cause of price distortion, only that they were the principal cause.'

The memorandum outlined the difficulties involved in Bunker's, Herbert's, and Great Western's separately taking large positions. 'In view of the individual activities and well known participation by the two principal officers of the company in the commodity markets, particularly silver, in the event that reprehensible conduct under the act were alleged against Great Western Sugar, Nelson Bunker and William Herbert Hunt would undoubtedly be brought into the matter in one of two ways: (*a*) They would be treated as a single entity under the Act. (*b*) In the event that the company and its controlling persons were not "thrown into the same pot" it would be surprising if allegations were not made that the company and its two controlling persons were engaged in a conspiracy to violate the Act. As you know, conspiracy is broadly defined as an agreement between two or more persons to accomplish together a criminal or unlawful act.' And just to make quite sure the law was understood, the memorandum added that a conspiracy to corner a market is also illegal under the Sherman Antitrust Act.

But what the Hunts were paying for (it was certainly not prose style) was information about the ability of the CFTC to make the intentions of the law stick. They called for a supplementary opinion from the same firm. 'You have requested,' it read, 'that I outline for you the parameters of safe conduct in the Act . . . and you have assured me that your intentions are that your activities not be in violation of the Act.

'As you have undoubtedly concluded, the lines are quite ethereal and indistinct. I am unable to say with exactitude "this may be done and that may not."' That was the interesting part. The corollary of the fact that the lines were indistinct and ethereal was, surely, that improper behaviour was equally difficult to define. When Bunker and Herbert and Great Western bought millions of ounces of silver in 1976, the CFTC took notice but actually did nothing. The law could be stretched. But in looking for a big institutional buyer to help him boost the market price, Bunker realized that although it was not absolutely necessary to find one of which he was not chairman of the board, greater anonymity could clearly help.

By the end of 1976 Bunker, Herbert and their corporate fiefdoms owned at least 100 million ounces of silver, worth around half a billion dollars. But the silver price stubbornly stayed where it was. The Hunt brothers seem to have felt it was time for a diversion, because they made a foray out of silver and into the Chicago soybean market. Soybeans are used to make oil and meal to feed livestock, and market professionals can trace an unlikely connection between silver and soybeans. The theory is this: when the price of soybeans goes up, so does the price of food, because the more costly meal affects the cost of meat. Since silver is a hedge against inflation, soybean speculators often invest their profits in silver to protect themselves against the ensuing inflation. There is a certain crazy market logic about the theory, and perhaps Bunker imagined that his soybean ploy would have an effect on the value of his silver. There is another explanation, which, being the more straightforward, is the more probable. Bunker grew soybeans on his farms in the South, so he knew a bit about the market and thought he could make a few million dollars expeditiously.

There is one important difference between the soybean market and the silver market. Limits are imposed on the quantity of soybeans a speculator may buy. This restriction, known as position limit, is put there to curb excessive speculation, and in the case of soybeans the limit is 3 million bushels. Since this amounts to roughly 5 out of every 100 bushels of beans grown in the United States, it ought to satisfy the most rapacious customer. The limit set by the CFTC, also applies 'to positions held by and trading done by two or more persons acting pursuant to an express or implied agreement or understanding.' This clearly meant that if Bunker and Herbert Hunt traded together, they should between them buy no more than 3 million bushels; but this regulation did not exactly conform to the plans the brothers had for their excursion into the soybean market.

We have an unusually complete account of their soybean speculation, since the CFTC revealed it all in a Chicago courtroom. The indictment reads like a family tree, naming not only Bunker but his son, Houston Bunker Hunt (a nineteen-year-old college freshman at the time), and his three daughters, Ellen Hunt Flowers (then a twenty-five-year-old housewife), Mary Hunt Huddleston (same occupation, age twenty-three), and Elizabeth Bunker Hunt (then a twenty-two-year-old student at the University of Alabama). Herbert Hunt was also named, of course, as were his twenty-four-year-old son, Douglas Herbert Hunt, and the family holding company, Hunt Holdings. One of the CFTC commissioners observed that the only member of the family without a position in the soybean market was the dog. The case, stated briefly, was that collectively the Hunts, with the children being financed entirely by their parents, had long positions in the old crop – harvested the previous summer – totalling 23.9 million bushels, eight times the legal limit. Since the crop amounted to 65 million bushels, the family owned 37 per cent of the soybeans in America. If they had chosen to take delivery of the soybeans, as their contracts allowed them to do, the world market would have been severely disrupted.

This threat of chaos sent the price up from a little over $6 a bushel at the beginning of January 1977, when Bunker and Herbert Hunt each first bought 3 million bushels of soybeans, to more than $10 a bushel in April 1977. That appeared to guarantee a hearty profit when the price was going up. But the brothers also gambled on the price's coming down later in the year, by going short in the new 1977 crop. Unselfishly, Bunker and Herbert had decided to cut most of their children in on the deal (some of Herbert's were still a little young). And since none of them had the ready money to play the market, their parents lent it to them. Houston Hunt borrowed over $2 million – a fair sum for an undergraduate – to put up the margin on his 3 million bushels, and the court document states dryly: 'Houston Hunt conducted his soybean trading from a public pay phone at the Phi Kappa Alpha Fraternity House, University of Tulsa, Tulsa, Oklahoma.' The loans to the Hunt girls were more modest – $225,000 each. The cash all went to the same broker, Drexel Burnham in San Francisco, where the accounts were all handled by the same man, a vice-president of the firm named Scott McFarland. This was one of two brokers used by the Hunts, the other being Mitchell Hutchins, in Chicago, where the accounts were also handled by one man, Owen Nichols.

The CFTC's accusation was that the brothers had traded together, and on behalf of the family. Paragraph 142 of the indictment reports: 'N. B. Hunt and W. H. Hunt gave orders for each other for their commodity futures transactions.' Their accountants in Dallas prepared joint position statements that showed the aggregated positions of the children, who knew little of what was happening. A further paragraph reveals: 'On more than one occasion, defendant Houston Hunt found a position statement, setting forth the positions of himself and his sisters, in his father's home.'

The CFTC's case also contains an excellent example of the forgetfulness that can overtake Bunker Hunt when he is giving legal depositions. This one concerned the loans to the children. 'Although N. B. Hunt did not recall whether the loans had been made for soybean transactions, he testified that soybean transactions were a significant percentage of his commodity futures trading from 1 January to 22 April 1977 and these loans could have been used for commodity futures trading.' Bunker clearly had completely forgotten that he had opened the accounts for his children at Drexel Burnham, where Scott McFarland obligingly violated the company policy that requires that the accounts of customers entering orders for one another should be combined for the purposes of speculative limit requirements. Had the rules of Drexel Burnham, the Chicago Board of Trade, and the CFTC been adhered to, the Hunts could have accumulated only 3 million, rather than nearly 24 million, bushels of old-crop soybeans. It was so egregious a contravention of the rule that the CFTC decided it had no choice but to act, although the case would stretch the feeble resources of an understaffed and inexperienced federal agency.

On April 28, 1977, the CFTC asked the U.S. District court in Chicago to order the Hunts of Dallas, Texas, to 'liquidate in an orderly manner all existing positions which exceed speculative limits' for soybean futures. The reason given was: 'The price distortion or manipulative activity that may result from the defendants' positions could cause serious injury to the American public.' The court papers noted that the Hunts' trading 'had continued even in the face of repeated admonitions from the Commission and its staff that violations were serious and a threat to the market.'

Bunker and Herbert Hunt were not well pleased by this attack on their freedom, but one item in the indictment outraged them: the CFTC published confidential details of their positions, showing in which future months they were long and when they were short. Herbert complained later that this information put so much pressure on the market that it turned any paper profits into losses; and, indeed, it did help transform the soybean futures market, since the dealers were expecting that the Hunts would be forced to sell.

Further, the CFTC asked the court to rule that the Hunts disgorge the profits they had made while the position limits were exceeded, despite Herbert's claim that the profits had been turned into losses. Herbert's lament was contradicted by Bunker's son, Houston, however, who boasted to friends in Dallas that he personally had made $7 million in just seven weeks, and by the fate of the largest short seller of soybeans, Cook Industries, which had gone bankrupt in June 1977.

The case was heard in Chicago on September 28, 1977, a preliminary hearing having denied the CFTC's request for an interim injunction to stop the Hunts trading soybeans. The court's judgment was curiously ambiguous: it found that the Hunts had violated the regulations, but it refused any of the remedies the CFTC had sought. The explanation was that the CFTC had instituted the wrong sort of proceeding. 'It is obvious,' remarked the judge, 'that if the Hunts were in knowing and deliberate violation of the position limits established by the regulation, sanctions should have been sought and imposed.' What the judge wanted to know was; why had the Hunts not been charged with squeezing or manipulating the market? A good question, to which the answer could not be given in court. Privately, CFTC staff people explained that to prove manipulation they would have had to demonstrate that the Hunts *intended* to manipulate the market, and the commission's legal counsel was not convinced that the evidence was good enough. The CFTC's own lawyers, in fact, confirmed the legal opinion the Hunts had received in 1976: that the lines were too 'ethereal and indistinct' for the commission to risk a manipulation case.

Any satisfaction the Hunts may have derived from the judgment was diminished a month later, when the CFTC used its powers to refer the case to an administrative proceeding under its own auspices. The brothers cried foul, complaining to a congressional committee that the family's lawyers had already spent 7,200 man-hours on the case – at a cost of more than $1 million – and, as Herbert said, 'It is not over yet.'

Nor was it, because on January 8, 1979, the Seventh Circuit Court of Appeals overturned the lower court's ruling and awarded victory to the CFTC, on a split decision, on all counts. 'The misconduct was systematic and carefully preconceived,' stated the majority decision. The interim injunction to prevent the Hunts trading more than 3 million bushels of soybeans was finally granted; furthermore, the appeals court ruled that the Hunts could be compelled to disgorge illegally gained profits. That was more easily said than done; another two and a half years passed before an out-of-court settlement was announced by the CFTC in July 1981. Bunker and Herbert Hunt had offered $500,000 to end the case, and agreed to stay out of soybean futures for two years – a meaningless concession, since by then, as will be seen, they were already banned from *all* commodity markets. (The CFTC justified the settlement by claiming it would save time and money; the commission did not say whose money, but if Houston Hunt was right about the profits, it was unquestionably the Hunts'.)

Looking back on the soybean caper, the commissioners of the CFTC began to wonder about the Hunts' motives. The Hunt soybean position was so large that it inevitably attracted attention; the classic market squeeze by real professionals is always more discreet, with a smaller potential for profit but a greater chance of getting away with it. The Hunts always wanted to maximize profits, ignoring the market maxim about never trying to get in at the bottom of the market and out at the top. 'There seemed to be a fatal flaw in the Hunts' analysis,' commented Commissioner Robert Martin.

Bunker and Herbert were volubly dissatisfied with the appeal court's judgment, and blackguarded the CFTC in any available forum. Their defence seemed to be that they had only been trying to make a bit of money for their kids, as though that were a justification for a particularly blatant breach of commodities law. But the application of the law in their case seemed to them to be further evidence of the rottenness of Big Government. Predictably, the brothers felt they had been singled out for vindictive action.

In 1978 one of the Hunts' congressional allies made a clumsy attempt to protect the brothers from the CFTC. Steven Symms, an ambitious young Republican from Idaho, introduced a bill to prevent the CFTC from punishing violators of commodity laws whose cases had been dismissed on technical grounds. Symms's bill seemed to have no purpose other than to help the Hunts fight their soybean case. It was too transparent; it did not pass. Bunker Hunt was still paying to learn, and the lesson this time was that no matter how ethereal and indistinct the law seemed, life would be much easier if he were less blatant in his disregard of it.

But the winter of 1978–79 was not a total calamity for Bunker and Herbert Hunt, because the silver price was perking up at last. In November 1978 there was a flurry in the market, which for once had nothing to do with Bunker – though it did involve his old acquaintance Don Dial, one of the men who had inspired his original conversion to silver.

The facts about the events in mid-November 1978 on the Chicago silver market are in dispute. The CFTC has since charged Don Dial and others with market manipulation, after they had bought silver on the morning of November 13, allegedly knowing that later in the day they would be placing substantial orders for a new client, a Pakistani named Nasrullah Khan, whom Dial's associates had met in London and who claimed to have millions of dollars to spend on silver. On the morning of November 13 Khan's cheque for $25 million, uncertified and drawn on a bank in an obscure Caribbean island, was deposited in a Chicago bank to meet his margin payments. With Khan entering the market on that scale, the silver price was certain to rise.

Scott Dial, Don's son, who has inherited his father's passion for silver, claims that the reason he and the family's associates also bought silver in Chicago early on November 13 had nothing to do with Khan's ample investment: he attributes the decision instead to President Jimmy Carter's package of economic measures to support the ailing dollar, introduced on November 1. Anticipation of a stronger dollar and lower inflation had caused the silver price to fall, but after little more than a week, on November 10, the price had begun to rise again. 'A key reversal,' judged Scott Dial, who recommended that his customers buy on Monday, November 13.

Whatever their real motivation, the Dials certainly went on a spree in the Chicago market. Within ten days, 9,300 contracts – 46.5 million ounces of silver – had been accumulated for Khan's account, and the price rose well above $6. Somewhat belatedly, Khan's brokers had begun to worry about his $25-million cheque, and they had every reason to do so, because when it was presented to the Oxford International Bank and Trust Company, on the Turks and Caicos Islands, it bounced. The Dials confessed this mortifying discovery to officials of the Chicago Board of Trade, who were appalled and ordered that Khan's position be liquidated immediately. Dumping such a large holding would normally cause the price to plummet, but in Chicago that November the price of silver did not fall; it was actually up by four-tenths of a cent. Scott Dial observes: 'The whole world knew a big position had been acquired and sold, and the price had not gone down. After that we were insane about silver.'

Bunker Hunt got the message, all right, and it was just the sort of news he wanted to pass on to some new friends, whom he had happened to meet a few weeks earlier at a racetrack in Paris. Bunker had good reason to believe, after four frustrating years searching for Arabian allies, who, like him, counted money in hundreds of millions of dollars, that at last he had found one. And maybe more.

Chapter 5

The Arabian Connection

Saudi Arabia is a forbidding society, and nothing that happens behind its closed doors is properly documented. Public accountability is not a concept familiar in theistic states, and Saudi Arabia is governed by Muslim law, faithfully based on the Koran and administered by its royal family. There are no taped records of important meetings, and articles about the decision-making process never appear in Riyadh or Jeddah newspapers. But Arabs talk incessantly among themselves and swap stories with indiscriminate enthusiasm. Nothing has been written down about the origin of Bunker Hunt's great silver gamble, and he himself is naturally disinclined to discuss it. As for the Arabs, they have a well-developed sense of privacy, on which Western reporters have no permission to intrude. But stories are told nonetheless, and by cross-checking them it is possible to get a convincing outline of the truth.

The story a Levantine merchant named Naji Robert Nahas told his Lebanese friends in Paris was that he met Bunker Hunt in 1978 at the auction of thoroughbred horses that follows Europe's richest horserace, the Prix de l'Arc de Triomphe. If so, that makes it possible to date the conception of the great silver gamble exactly: October 1, 1978. The Prix de l'Arc de Triomphe is the climax of the European horseracing season, and its location is quintessentially French – with a view of the Eiffel Tower, like a toy replica in the distance, from the imposing grandstand at the Longchamp racecourse in the Bois de Boulogne. The meeting is an international occasion – the racing set's last party before the winter. Under the clipped trees on the manicured lawns by the parade ring, Pimms' is consumed as well as champagne, and English is spoken as commonly as French – in the various accents of the British Isles, America, and the Middle East. For Arabs, one of the more harmless pleasures of life in the West is racing horses. Once the Sport of Kings, racing has become the hobby of the newly rich, and fresh money comes from men like Bunker; the only royal family that can afford to participate on this scale is the Al Saud from Saudi Arabia.

Bunker had no runner in his own colours – a check of dark-and-light green squares – in the Arc in 1978, but he did have an interest in a horse called Trillion, running in the name of a friend of his, Ed Stephenson; Trillion came only second, to Alleged. The next day Bunker went to see if he could buy a potential winner at the international auction of yearlings at the Polo de Bagatelle, a sporting club close by Longchamp. Bunker had been dominating horse auctions for years, buying whatever took his fancy, to the despair of less-well-endowed owners; but he was not the only big bidder that year in the large indoor riding school at the Polo de Bagatelle. The horses are paraded before a small, comfortable stand erected for the occasion, and bids are displayed on a screen that quotes the latest offer simultaneously in French francs, American dollars, British pounds, and Japanese yen; that day, the most favoured yearlings attracted the attention not just of Bunker Hunt but of a couple of Arabs as well. One of the Arabs was Mahmoud Fustok, a man in his early forties, who wore his dark hair slicked back in the manner of a character in an old B movie who is never quite to be trusted. The other Arab was taller than Fustok, balding, said by friends to be handsome in a sallow, Lebanese way, and no more than thirty-five at the time. He was Naji Robert Nahas.

Nahas was the son of a Lebanese engineer who, like many of his educated fellow countrymen, had lived comfortably in Cairo before Colonel Nasser's revolution spoiled it all. In Cairo, the cultural thing to do was to watch the racing at the Gezira Sporting Club, and Naji caught the bug as a boy. But when his parents returned to Lebanon shortly after the revolution in 1952, Naji found the atmosphere stifling; he was interested in deals, even as a student, and the opportunities were too small in Beirut. So in his early twenties he emigrated to Brazil, where he began to speculate in land. He bought a great deal of it and held on to it, and then branched out into shipping. Naji was a capable man, steeped in the Levantine merchant tradition – which goes back three thousand years, after all, to the Phoenicians. When the Saudis began to invest some of their new wealth in South America after 1973, Naji was the middleman in a couple of deals. These brought him into the circle of Mahmoud Fustok.

Fustok held a Saudi passport, although he was Palestinian by origin. His father had migrated south into Arabia and ingratiated himself so successfully with members of the royal family that one of his daughters, Aida, became a wife of Prince Abdullah Ibn Abdul-Aziz, the thirteenth son of King Abdul-Aziz Ibn-Saud, the founder of the nation. Abdullah's rotation of his four wives eventually excluded Aida, and they were divorced, but the links between the two families remained strong, and Mahmoud became a close business adviser of Abdullah's, particularly in Europe.

Prince Abdullah was born in 1923, and, dressed as a desert prince, he is an imposing man in his flowing black *mashlah* with its border of gold thread, and his Bedouin headdress, the *ghutra*. With his dark eyes, perfect white teeth, and a barbered black moustache and beard, Abdullah looks more like his father than any of his brothers does, an image that is slightly dented when he opens his mouth, because Abdullah has a bad stutter. Prince Abdullah is third in the hierarchy – behind King Khalid and Crown Prince Fahd – with the title of deputy prince minister, and is also the head of the internal security service, the National Guard. Like his brothers, Prince Abdullah is a very rich man indeed.

Because the wealth of the Saudi state is virtually indistinguishable from that of its rulers, Prince Abdullah's National Guard headquarters in Riyadh is a reliable example of his life of opulence. I was able to tour the building during the visit to Saudi Arabia of the British prime minister, Margaret Thatcher, and was struck first by the fountain shooting water, which was once so scarce, thirty-five feet into the air, then by the gleaming white marble on the floors and walls (the sentry stands on a piece of wood to protect the marble when he jumps to attention), and the glittering crystal chandeliers. At the top of a richly carpeted staircase is Abdullah's office, a large panelled corner room with cream Brazilian leather chairs around the walls, facing his ample desk, on which there is a simple wooden reading lectern and a paperweight, measuring twelve inches by eight, made of solid gold. The carpet I noticed when I glanced up and saw it reflected in the stainless steel ceiling. It was a beautiful multicoloured Nain from Iran, the most expensive carpet in the world.

When Abdullah leaves his office he indulges his great passion for horses in the Riyadh Equestrian Club, which is almost as ostentatious. Fustok was buying for Prince Abdullah at the Polo de Bagatelle on October 1, 1978, and he knew exactly which horse the prince wanted. Bunker wanted the same horse, and as he was finally opposed by someone as rich and as stubborn as himself, he was the underbidder – an extremely rare occurrence. It was so unusual, in fact, that Bunker's curiosity was aroused by the man who had bid more than he had, and he wondered whether Fustok would care to join him for a drink. Both the bidders had friends in common. Both trained their horses in the forest of Chantilly, north of Paris. Bunker actually owned a stable there, which was run by another émigré from Nasser's Egypt, a shrewd and sardonic man named Maurice Zilber. (Zilber's little joke is that his horses run well because he speaks to them in Aramaic, the language of Jesus Christ.) Fustok's horses were trained nearby by a Lebanese named Maurice Seliba. Chantilly is a tight community; everyone knows everyone else; a meeting between Fustok, his friend Nahas, and Bunker would not have been difficult to arrange.

When they met shortly after the auction, the conversation moved easily from horses to business, and from business to silver. Bunker, according to the story Nahas told his friends, said he needed more money to lift the silver price: with a billion or two, he thought he could control it. Fustok and Nahas were intrigued; and Bunker was talking to the right people. They were sure that Prince Abdullah would be interested because the Hunts and the Saudi prince already had much in common – oil as well as horses. That was the grounding for friendship, and friendship is the essential basis for a business relationship in Arabia.

That meeting successfully established one direct line to the royal family, but Bunker Hunt had by now been let down so often in Arabia that he did not intend to rely on a single link. Fustok and Nahas were not the only intermediaries he had interested in a well-financed speculation to push up the price of silver.

In February 1978, Bunker had gone to Washington to meet New Zealand's prime minister, Robert Muldoon – a meeting arranged by the ubiquitous John Connally, who was then back on Bunker's payroll, at $70,000 a year. Predictably, Bunker wanted to complain about the taxes New Zealand levied on his oil exploration there. The story is taken up by Bill Bledsoe, Bunker's former assistant; in the evidence he gave to congressional investigators:

> Shortly after the meeting with Muldoon, we were advised by Governor Connally [John Connally had been governor of Texas from 1962 to 1968] that Khalid bin Mahfouz was at the same hotel where we were, and Bunker and Herbert Hunt had previously told Governor Connally of their desire to meet this wealthy gentleman from Saudi Arabia. Governor Connally was well acquainted with him, and took us to bin Mahfouz's suite, which consisted of the entire floor of this hotel, complete with 30 or 40 security guards. The purpose of the meeting was to enlist not only bin Mahfouz but later another gentleman called Gabe [*sic*] Pharaon into buying silver with the Hunts. Governor Connally has other ties with the Saudis, involving activities in Texas and Georgia, and the plan was to get the Hunts in the front door with these very wealthy Arab sheiks, and the Hunts would sell the Saudis on the value of silver over the worthless U.S. dollar.

Bledsoe's account sounds extravagant, and perhaps there were not quite so many guards as he remembers – though the Saudis were deeply sensitive about security at that time, since an OPEC meeting in Vienna had recently been invaded by terrorists. More important is an omission from Bledsoe's evidence: he does not say Bunker actually *met* Khalid bin Mahfouz or Gaith (not Gabe) Pharaon. Frankly, we do not know exactly when the three men did meet; but that they did, and talked business fruitfully, is clear from later events. The real value of Bledsoe's account of the Washington trip lies in its description of Bunker and Herbert's intentions.

Khalid bin Mahfouz was still in his middle thirties at the time, but the oil boom had made him a very rich young man. The Saudi royal family insists on doing its domestic banking business with Saudi Arabians, and bin Mahfouz was perfectly positioned to take advantage of the rush of oil money after 1973, since his family ran the National Commercial Bank in Jeddah, the largest private bank in the kingdom. He was one of the most powerful group of merchants and bankers in Jeddah, the Hadhrumi, whose families had originated in the Wadi Hadhramaut, on the Indian Ocean coast of what is now known as the People's Democratic Republic of Yemen but which remains better known in the West as Aden. Khalid's father had travelled north to Jeddah and taken a position in the household of the Kaki family, one of the leading money changers in the Jeddah trading centre, the Souk. A Kaki daughter took a fancy to the young man from Hadhramaut, and asked if she could marry him. Her father consented and took his son-in-law into the bank. By the 1970s their sons were running it, and the most able and ambitious of those sons was Khalid. The bank still traded in the scruffy, one-room offices at the entrance to the Souk's arcade, but around the corner the bin Mahfouz worked in the air-conditioned comfort of their new multistory head office building. By the end of the decade, the National Commercial Bank's turnover was calculated in billions of dollars, and Khalid had holdings in banks in Houston, Paris, Luxembourg, the Bahamas, and Brazil, and good financial contacts in all those places. (As with other merchant bankers, it is often difficult to distinguish between investments made on the bank's account and personal holdings. Khalid bin Mahfouz's were a mixture of the two.)

The reason Hadhrumi dominate Saudi banking is that they have a more relaxed attitude toward the Muslim religion than the native Saudis do. Usury is not forbidden to them and they have had the habit of making money longer than the Saudis; moreover, they have a reputation for being hard and mean businessmen, which the Saudis themselves are not. Their skills were rewarded by the gift of Saudi citizenship, and the royal family grew accustomed to using them as middlemen for their own investments.

Khalid bin Mahfouz seemed to have a particularly intimate relationship with the most senior members of the royal family. One clue to this is the status of his bank. In the late 1970s the kingdom's central bank, the Saudi Arabian Monetary Agency, known as SAMA, had decreed that all privately owned banks should sell shares to Saudi citizens. And all did so – with one exception: the National Commercial Bank. Other bankers thought there was only one man in the kingdom powerful enough to grant bin Mahfouz immunity from SAMA's directive, and that was Crown Prince Fahd himself.

The crown prince is a less regal-looking figure than his half-brother, Abdullah. He is taller, but plumper. He loves gambling, and has played and lost fabulous sums of money in European casinos. And Fahd not only had used Khalid bin Mahfouz as a conduit before but was well acquainted with the second of the Saudi businessmen to whom John Connally wished to introduce Bunker.

Gaith Pharaon's relationship with the royal family is inherited from his father, a doctor, who had attended all four kings of Saudi Arabia, as well as the most senior princes. Gaith's father had dispensed advice as well as medicine, and when his son showed ability as a businessman, it was natural that the royal family should help him, out of respect for and gratitude to his father. Pharaon had begun as an agent, taking a percentage on contracts he was able to place with foreign companies, but he was not content to let his business career rest there, as Fustok was. He wanted to run his own operation, and by the end of the 1970s he had achieved his ambition. The company was called Redec, and it owned a range of subsidiaries from construction companies to hotels. He invested heavily in Hyatt International, he owned a share of a Georgia bank, and Redec's real-estate developments included the Plaza of the Americas in Dallas, not far from Bunker's office on Elm Street. Like most other Saudi businessmen, Pharaon is a compulsive borrower, and Western banks have never been slow to lend to him.

John Connally had chosen well for Bunker when he singled out Khalid bin Mahfouz and Gaith Pharaon. For some years Bunker Hunt had been accident-prone in the silver market as well as in the courts, but by late 1978 his luck seemed to have changed at last. He had established links to the real money in Saudi Arabia after almost four years' trying. But he was still not content.

For some months late in 1978 he had been cultivating Arab businessmen by sending fifty or so translated reprints of an enthusiastic report on silver that had been published in *Myers' Finance and Energy Report.* Finally he uncovered yet another potential source of funds in Arabia to help him push up the silver price. In February 1979, the arrangements were complete and Bunker took a flight to Dubai, on the Arabian Gulf. He had already met the leading bullion dealer in the port, Haji Ashraf, and done business with him in

London, but there was someone else he wanted to meet – Dubai's leading young entrepreneur, Abdul Wahab Galadari, whose name is to be seen everywhere around the town, as the owner of construction companies, automobile dealerships, a bank, a travel agency, a commodity brokerage house, and the local Hyatt hotel. Galadari is in his middle forties, and is a very single-minded businessman. 'If you ever see him nod off,' says one of his associates, 'you'll know the conversation has turned to politics.'

I met A. W. Galadari two years after Bunker's visit to Dubai, in his lavish office, which is in itself worth a detour. At the risk of dwelling on the subject of Arabian interior decor, Galadari's office is as well worth describing as Abdullah's because it is a symbol of the wealth of Arab businessmen, which was their heady attraction for Bunker Hunt.

Galadari's office suite is in the Hyatt Regency Dubai, which he built and in which he owns a large majority holding, and the suite is approached by passing the hotel ice rink (the daytime temperature in Dubai rarely falls below 95 degrees). The door is wooden, heavy, and intricately carved, and opens onto an anteroom with a salmon-pink marble ceiling, Persian carpets hung on the walls, and sofas covered in suede with leopardskin trimmings. Suede covers the walls, too, a decorative theme carried through into Galadari's office, where he sits behind a desk composed of a thick sheet of glass mounted on two seated lions, which are covered by thin sheets of gold. The Hyatt Regency, like many more of Abdul Wahab Galadari's enterprises, was financed mainly by money borrowed from the banks. Since the man had such generous lines of credit, it is not surprising that Bunker should have wanted to meet him.

Bunker arrived in Dubai in the comparative cool of an early February evening in 1979; he was met by Galadari at the airport and driven to the Intercontinental Hotel, newly built on the Creek, with a good view of the dhows from the bedrooms. (That view is the only attribute that distinguishes the Intercontinental from any hotels newly constructed in Dallas; otherwise they are practically identical, right down to the rib of beef served in the rooftop restaurant.) Bunker, not being interested in views, went right away with Galadari farther down the Creek to Haji Ashraf's poky little office on the rooftop of a low building by the Souk. There Bunker launched into his well-rehearsed lecture about the inevitable forthcoming rise in the price of silver. Although both Galadari and Ashraf speak English, the accompanying four-page pamphlet had been thoughtfully translated into Arabic. 'If you believed his manifesto, you would have believed that the silver price was going to eighty-five dollars,' says Galadari.

But Galadari and Ashraf have differing recollections of Bunker's business in Dubai. Each describes a deal that is, in technical terms, the opposite of the other's.

Haji Ashraf's story is that Bunker offered to exchange 5,000 future contracts for 25 million ounces of silver bullion. Presumably, in that case, Bunker hoped that a large holding in the futures market by a Dubai merchant would cause the market professionals to suspect that the Arabs were indeed moving into silver in a big way. The consequence ought then to be a rush to buy. The advantage to Ashraf would be that these purchases would increase the value of his futures contracts, which he could then sell at a profit.

Abdul Wahab Galadari, on the other hand, recalls taking Bunker to his beach house outside Dubai the day after his arrival, and he is in no doubt what Bunker suggested to him there. 'He said he had between twenty and thirty million ounces of bullion which he would sell to me. With the money he received from that sale, he said, he would go into the market and buy, forcing up the price. I knew what he was talking about, and he knew that I knew, but, very frankly, I don't like to manipulate the market. It's not a question of disliking Hunt, but we don't like to manipulate the market. We like to make money, definitely, but not by means of the sort of plan Mr Hunt offered. He's a likeable man; I don't think he's a bad man. It's just that his way of doing business is not ours.' The attraction of the scheme Galadari describes is not difficult to fathom. The silver price, at the time of Bunker's visit to Dubai, was $7.44 an ounce. (Ashraf's memory for the daily silver price is as phenomenal as Bunker's.) The sale of 20 million ounces, to take the lower figure, would have raised nearly $150 million – quite enough to enable Bunker Hunt, buying on margin, to drive up the silver price. Profit to the Dubai merchants would have accrued rapidly through their holdings of more valuable bullion or futures contracts.

Neither Galadari nor Ashraf wanted to do a deal with Bunker, but, at the end of his fruitless two-day visit to the Arabian Gulf, Bunker nonetheless placed orders for his own account in the Chicago market for 4 million ounces of silver. Ashraf remembers thinking that Bunker must have been hoping that dealers would infer: 'Ah, the Hunts have fixed their manipulation with the Arabs.' The silver price did actually rise by 50 cents, but only briefly, and Bunker left Dubai to try his luck elsewhere. After his successful meetings in Washington and Paris in 1978, he knew exactly where to go. 'He told me that if he did not succeed in Dubai, he'd do it in Saudi Arabia,' says Abdul Wahab Galadari emphatically.

Saudi Arabia is a family business. The country is actually named after the family that runs it, the Al Saud, descendants of Abd-al-

Rashman, sultan of Nejd, whose third son, Abdul-Aziz Ibn Saud, became the first King of Saudi Arabia, having united the country by conquest before World War II. Ibn-Saud, beside being a mighty man of war, had an instinct for paternity that makes H. L. Hunt's appear modest: in a period of some fifty years he fathered forty-four sons and seventy-two daughters – at least, that is the number he legitimized as members of the royal family. By 1980 the princes of the royal family numbered between three thousand and four thousand. Like many other statistics in Saudi Arabia, that figure is inexact.

Three of the sons of Ibn-Saud succeeded him as King; first, Saud (who was deposed and spent his last years in exile in Greece and Egypt sipping Cointreau); then, Faisal (who was assassinated in 1975); and finally, the present King, Khalid. All the significant posts in the administration are held by sons of Ibn-Saud, and all but one of these sons are full brothers, sharing the same mother. Prince Fahd is the oldest of these brothers, and he is the prime minister; Sultan, Naif, Mitab, and Salman are, respectively, the ministers of defence, interior, and public works, and governor of Riyadh. Prince Abdullah is the only one of their half-brothers to have a place in the most senior echelon of the hierarchy. (Better-known personalities, such as Ahmed Zaki Yamani, the oil minister, and Prince Saud Ibn Faisal, the foreign minister, are more influential outside Saudi Arabia than inside it.)

There is no parliament. Saudis do not vote, and the money that comes from the sale of oil is the property of the royal family. A proportion of that is spent on the royal family itself – each legitimate member receives a monthly stipend – and there is no question about the exchequer's ability to afford it. Since the oil price was quadrupled by the Organization of Petroleum Exporting Countries (OPEC) in 1973, there are tens of billions of dollars in the currency reserves of the central bank, the Saudi Arabian Monetary Agency, or SAMA. Within five years of the oil-price explosion, the Saudi administration had initiated a remarkable range of industrial projects, including new chemical plants to use the oil at home, new ports, desalinization plants to bring water to the desert, new roads, telephone systems, and social facilities such as hospitals, houses, and schools. (And no expense is spared. I have visited a hospital in Riyadh where the walls are carpeted, and the outside courtyards are carefully covered with Astroturf to make it more agreeable to kneel in prayer, facing toward Mecca.) The contracts for all these projects were prodigious, and most of them were awarded by senior members of the royal family, acting in their ministerial capacity. The boom led to an astonishing business bonanza for Saudi Arabia's small merchant class.

One reason why the merchants worked closely with the royal family was the insistence by Muslim kings that family members should not be seen to be involved with commerce. This view was pronounced under King Faisal, who was particularly devout and would not countenance any public deviation from the faith by his brothers and their children. Large palaces in Riyadh and Jeddah, villas in the south of France or on the Costa Brava in Spain, and apartments in London and Paris were perfectly respectable, because real-estate speculation was not anathema. But commerce was to be left to the merchants, who consequently became prominent in the West as the Arab oil sheikhs. (Most of them are not actually sheikhs. Brian Lees, a British genealogist whose speciality is the Saudi royal family, writes: 'The title sheikh is a mark of respect to any mature man whose wealth, social standing, and personal qualities are thought by the speaker to merit it. It is regrettably as much abused as Esquire in English: Western businessmen are according the title to Saudi business colleagues indiscriminately, and often when it is patently not merited.')

A Saudi banker of my acquaintance divides the money men in the kingdom into two classes. The first he calls the 'Rockefellers', because they built their fortunes by careful capital accumulation in the West. The best-known example of this class is Adnan Khashoggi, whose company, Triad, has acquired, among a multitude of other companies, the charmingly named Bank of Contra Costa. Khashoggi is notable because of his life-style, which includes his own Boeing and a noisy divorce. A better example of the 'Rockefeller' class of Saudi businessmen is Suleiman Olayan, who started driving trucks for the oil consortium Aramco in the eastern sector of the kingdom, and has built a business empire with a financial base that, the Chase Manhattan Bank reports, 'has awed bankers.' Unlike Khashoggi, Olayan has such a strong desire for privacy that he decided to buy no more shares in American banks after attracting the attention – even though it was most sympathetic – of *The Wall Street Journal* and *The New York Times*. These men – Khashoggi and Olayan – may be more flamboyant in their method of acquiring new business than most of their Western counterparts, but neither of them is a speculator by nature, preferring on the whole to accumulate wealth more cautiously than some of their Saudi contemporaries.

The 'Rockefeller' class was not likely to ally itself with Bunker in the silver market. His allies were much more likely to come from the second class of Saudi businessman, which my banker friend refers to as the 'Maharajahs'. They are men who, having procured contracts in the West by means of their contacts with senior members of the royal family, simply spend their share of the abundant commissions taken by the princes on fast horses, grand houses, and comfortable private jet aircraft. Mahmoud Fustok is an excellent specimen of the 'Maharajah'.

In the late 1970s, as the puritanism that had characterized King Faisal's regime began to weaken, the 'Maharajahs' were joined by young princes, who started to act openly as agents for companies seeking contracts from ministries run by their fathers and uncles. One of Prince Abdullah's sons, Faisal Ibn Abdullah, became a 'Maharajah', but the most prominent among the princely members of this class is Mohammad Ibn Fahd, the fifth son of the crown prince, whose commission for a new telephone system was so immense that he was forced to repay it. Still, he retained many more from large construction projects worth billions of dollars. Prince Mohammad's normal rate of commission is between 20 and 30 per cent, and one might think that this provides him with a sufficient income. Not so; Prince Mohammad has a very substantial entourage to keep in the style to which it has recently become accustomed. When the prince discovered the projected overland route for the pipeline to bring desalinated water from the Red Sea to Riyadh, he immediately registered ownership of large tracts of land over which the pipeline would be laid. (It is, apparently, fairly easy for the son of Prince Fahd to do this; the land belongs to the royal family, after all.) Next, Prince Mohammad presented a bill to the relevant ministry, demanding compensation for the inconvenience the pipeline would cause him. When the bill was paid, the 'compensation' amounted to $80 million.

That is the kind of story which does not appear in print; its dissemination begins in Riyadh and Jeddah and filters west by word of mouth, reaching London, Paris, and New York some months later. But stories like this make it possible not only to assert that Prince Abdullah is very rich but even to describe some of the ways in which he acquires his wealth.

Another story about just one of hundreds of Saudi government contracts accurately indicates how the wealth of the princes accumulates. The tale begins in 1976, when a Belgian company named Eurosystem Hospitalier won a contract to build two five-hundred-bed hospitals, one in Riyadh and the other in Jeddah, for the National Guard. (The National Guard was not necessarily expecting heavy casualties; the hospitals were for wives and children as well.) The contract was worth $1.2 billion to the Belgian company, which had been able to parade one of their nation's own princes – Albert, the king's brother – to help beat strenuous international competition. In Brussels the deal was known as 'the contract of the century'.

Some of the competitors were surprised by the success of Eurosystem Hospitalier. The company had never actually built a hospital; furthermore, it did not exist before the National Guard tender had been announced, although it was backed indirectly by Belgium's largest holding company, the Société Génerale. So the competition was not exactly astonished when Eurosystem Hospitalier ran into serious difficulties; the Mexican subcontractor doing the construction work showed a great lack of urgency about the job, and the irregularity of payments from the National Guard reflected the poor progress on the sites. In July 1979, Eurosystem Hospitalier went bankrupt, causing great distress to the Belgian government, especially when Belgian newspapers began to hint at the real reason why the contract had collapsed. Eurosystem Hospitalier had been bankrupted by the enormous commissions paid to win the contract. Various sums were mentioned, and the best estimate was the largest: no less than $360 million. But none of the Belgian newspapers was able to name the recipient of this fortune.

Naturally, the contract had been awarded by the head of the National Guard, Prince Abdullah. And a year later, in 1980, the prince, as a senior member of the royal family, came under the scrutiny of a rare group of radical young Saudis who reject the rule of the princes. The members remain individually anonymous, but the group calls itself the Young Revolutionaries and publicizes its cause by sending litanies of complaint about the behaviour of the royal family to a number of Western newspapers. In the summer of 1980 one of these arrived at the *Financial Times* in London. The document was inspected by Saudi specialists in London, who declared that, while a few of the charges seemed extravagant, most were thought to be perfectly credible. Among the list of 'credibles' was the statement that the $360-million commission on the Eurosystem Hospitalier contract had been paid to Prince Abdullah, to his brother-in-law and business partner Mahmoud Fustok, and to Prince Abdullah's henchmen. 'We have knowledge of the banks involved and we have copies of the statements which show the funnelling of funds to Prince Abdullah,' the Young Revolutionaries claimed.

Commissions on such contracts are only one way of amassing a fortune. Oil was a much more promising medium for making a few hundred million dollars, especially when it is in short supply. There are always countries like Italy, Japan, and Thailand that want oil badly enough to be willing to pay a little extra for guaranteed supplies. In 1979 Saudi Arabia established a two-tier pricing system for oil. The official Saudi price was fixed at $32 a barrel, some $4.50 less than the then-prevailing world price. The declared object was to protect the industrially depressed economies of the West from the worst excesses of OPEC's price increases – a laudable goal. But the effect was further to enrich some of the royal princes. Since 1978 select members of the family had been able to receive allocations of oil from the Saudi Petroleum Ministry at the official price, and after 1979 none of the oil received in this manner was sold at $32 a barrel. The difference between the official price and the price this oil fetched on the open market was commission, and it is difficult to imagine an easier way of making large sums of money. After establishing a few initial contacts, all that is needed is an oil allocation and a telex machine. The evidence that Prince Abdullah took his share is the existence of a Spanish company marketing oil that is run by his son, Prince Faisal Ibn Abdullah.

In the spring of 1979, Bunker, having left Dubai empty-handed, needed to divert some of the great wealth of the royal family into the silver market. The exact process by which he did so is not described in any of the stories told by Arabs about the silver affair, but one émigré Lebanese explained to me in Paris that the translation of a show of interest into an active participation would, if it followed the customary form, have been delightfully informal. I suggested to the Lebanese that Prince Abdullah must surely have been influenced by Bunker's argument about silver's being a shrewd way of protecting wealth during a period of inflation. 'No,' he replied, 'Prince Abdullah has no very sophisticated notion of inflation or silver. If it hadn't been for horses and oil, I don't think he'd have gone in with Bunker Hunt. They go in because they like you.'

So how would the decision have been taken?

'Fustok would probably have looked at a file and then taken it to Prince Abdullah and said, "You remember Mr Hunt; he knows a lot about silver and suggests we go in with him." Abdullah would only ask whether it was a good deal, and if the answer was "Yes", Abdullah would simply say, "Go ahead".'

There was just one other thing. Prince Abdullah would have wanted to know that the deal was not illegal. The most senior princes, unlike some of their sons, feel the dignity of their political stature threatened by financial scandals. Prince Abdullah had already been embarrassed by the Eurosystem Hospitalier incident, and the Saudi information minister had obligingly denied his involvement: one incident was quite enough. Judging by Arab protestations of shocked innocence after the silver price collapsed in March 1980, there is every indication that Bunker assured the prince that everything he proposed was entirely above board. And Abdullah would not have had the expertise to question that advice. He was surrounded by

'Maharajahs', whose inexperience led them into errors that the 'Rockefeller' class would not have made. And their inexperience was compounded by greed. Bunker was not just offering to secure their investment. His plan sounded as if it would double their money – at least double it.

Naji Nahas could hardly believe his luck when he found himself involved with Bunker's scheme, particularly as he needed the money. In the winter of 1978–79 Nahas had been suffering from a mild business recession of his own, paying heavy interest on the bank loans he had taken out to buy land in Brazil. He was not broke, exactly, but he could certainly do with the money he hoped to make in the silver market.

As a front man for the Saudis, Naji Nahas was the first of the colleagues to surface in 1979, looking for a clever commodities dealer to transact the Saudi silver business in New York and Chicago. In Geneva, Nahas asked an ex-employee of the Continental Grain Company, the giant wheat dealer whose subsidiary set up especially to take advantage of the bonanza in commodities outside the grain trade – such as precious metals – had become one of the fastest-growing firms in the futures markets, whether he knew a good man in New York. Nahas was given the name of Norton Waltuch, who ran the New York office of Conti Commodity Services, and in January 1979 the two talked on the telephone for the first time. According to Waltuch's own account – dragged out of him by Senator Donald Stewart during his investigation eighteen months later – the two men spoke in a desultory way about orange-juice futures. (Waltuch had made a killing in orange juice a couple of years earlier.) Then Nahas asked Waltuch: 'What do you like now?'

'I said at that time I was very, very bullish on silver, and that is how it developed,' Waltuch told the senator. Nahas promptly agreed, with quite remarkable prescience, to invest half a million dollars in the silver market.

Mahmoud Fustok had no need to seek out men to attend to the money he and Prince Abdullah were about to spend in the silver market. He had formed an attachment with an investment advisory company even before he met Bunker Hunt in Paris in the fall of 1978. Fustok's main investment account was at the Chase Manhattan Bank's Geneva branch, which sensibly invested his money in foreign currencies and short-term commercial loans. Among the bankers he had met at the Chase were a group of its employees who had quit early in 1978 to form an investment company that was to be sponsored by the fourth-largest bank in Switzerland, the Banque Populaire Suisse. The company was called Advicorp Advisory and Financial Corporation SA, and its three main partners – Pierre Alain Hirschy, Jean Jacques Bally, and Antoine Asfour – persuaded Fustok to open a second investment account with them. By the summer of 1978 Fustok's deposits with Advicorp were $17 million, but that was small beer compared to the sums he would need to play the silver market. So, in February 1979, Fustok closed his account at Chase Manhattan and transferred all his funds to Advicorp. They were worth more than $50 million; and Fustok was not Advicorp's only Saudi customer.

The last organizational link was the introduction of Fustok's Swiss friends to the New York broker whom Nahas had found to transact their business, and in May 1979 Norton Waltuch visited Paris and Geneva to meet his new clients. In Paris, Nahas introduced Waltuch to Mahmoud Fustok. In Geneva, he took Waltuch to the office where Advicorp's operation would be conducted – situated on the second floor above a restaurant in a pleasant cobbled market, conveniently near the financial district, at 7 Place du Molard. There Nahas spelled out a bewildering array of company and account names. The plate on the door outside the office read IMOVEST INTER. The plate downstairs at the street entrance said ADVICORP. There would be a nominee account in the name of the Banque Populaire Suisse, and another for Gillian Financial. The dealers for these accounts would be Jean Jacques Bally and Pierre Alain Hirschy.

Once Waltuch understood that the business was not going to be limited to Nahas's original stake of half a million dollars, he ceased to be the New York manager of Conti Commodity Services and in May 1979 became a vice-president in charge of a new Conti operation called Conti Capital Management, with authority to run a special commodity fund as well as individual accounts. One of these funds was registered in the Bahamas under the name of Conti Capital Limited, and among its shareholders were Waltuch himself, Naji Nahas, and two Saudis named Ahmed and Mohammed Kaki (members of the same Kaki family into which Khalid bin Mahfouz's father had married, which meant that he had married into the National Commercial Bank of Jeddah).

The web Bunker Hunt helped to spin in the spring of 1979, after his return from Dubai, was fine, complex, and not anchored only to Prince Abdullah's inexperienced front men. The presence of a name like Kaki in Waltuch's operation indicates that the Jeddah merchants had now been persuaded to play Bunker's game, too, and they were men who acted as conduits to other members of the royal family, including Crown Prince Fahd. A more sophisticated man than Prince Abdullah, Fahd would have wanted a camouflage screen between himself and his gamble in the silver market. A banker like bin

Mahfouz and a businessman like Gaith Pharaon offered better protection than the naïve men around Abdullah. Moreover, the merchants were less casual in their business methods, and, showing some 'Rockefeller' type characteristics, they insisted on establishing a formal relationship with Bunker.

Khalid bin Mahfouz wished to be discreet, too, and the operation was organized so that his name would not appear in public. The public positions as directors of a company that was established to conduct a joint silver business with Bunker were taken by two Hadhrumi merchants who were less well known than bin Mahfouz, and who would attract less attention than he might do. Mohammed Aboud al-Amoudi was from a family of money changers and bullion dealers whose name was familiar in the Souk. Ali bin Mussalam was a member of another substantial merchant family. Bin Mahfouz's interest was taken care of by his man in London, yet another émigré from Aden, Mohammed Salah Affara. Affara was named president of the company that was formally established on July 15, 1979, in Bermuda with the object of dealing in precious metals, and registered under the name International Metals Investment Company; it became known as IMIC for short. Its shares were divided equally between the Saudis – al-Amoudi and Mussalam, with Affara taking one nominal share – and Bunker and Herbert Hunt, whose holding was in the name of a Delaware corporation hopefully entitled Profit Investment Company.

A month before IMIC was formally established, Mohammed Aboud al-Amoudi sent one of his employees to New York to learn the futures business. It is said in Paris by Lebanese businessmen who know Naji Nahas that Bunker Hunt taught Naji all he knew about the futures market, but the Jeddah merchants were unwilling to leave such an important education entirely to Bunker. Al-Amoudi's man sought professional advice.

On his way back to Saudi Arabia this man stopped off in Europe and there confided to a friend that a new company was about to take a plunge in the silver market and drive the price up. And what, asked his friend, was the ultimate objective of the operation? What would they do when the price was driven up? Al-Amoudi's man replied that he believed the Jeddah merchants and their princely clients hoped to persuade the Saudi Arabian Monetary Agency to convert a portion of its reserves into silver. Since SAMA's reserves at that time were some $60 billion, there was clearly enough money to finance such a deal. And what was really seductive about *that* idea was the implication of SAMA's using silver as a reserve asset: it would give silver a monetary value again, just like gold's, and it would legitimize a new, high price.

The SAMA connection sounds farfetched, since SAMA is more independent of the royal family than any other agency of the Saudi government. The United States and European governments had consistently warned the family of the harm they would do to the kingdom's international financial reputation if they started to plunder SAMA's immense reserves. But the idea could have been rationalized: persuading SAMA to hold some of its reserves in silver would not be plunder, as such. And of the tiny group of men in Saudi Arabia who could influence SAMA's policy by direct intervention, the most influential was Crown Prince Fahd; another member of that group was Prince Abdullah.

The evidence linking Prince Abdullah to the silver game is sound enough, but Crown Prince Fahd's name surfaced much later, and the links were more circumstantial. I had first heard of his involvement in Jeddah, then in London and New York, but it was not until I heard a story in Washington that I believed that the crown prince had indeed been one of the players.

I had heard a version of the same story in London, which was that in the summer of 1980 Crown Prince Fahd had publicly humiliated Gaith Pharaon in the prime ministerial majlis, or palace, by slapping him on the face three times and dismissing him. The cause of Fahd's anger, according to the London account, was that Pharaon had criticized the commercial morality of the rule of princes, and singled out Fahd's own son, Mohammad. When I repeated this version to other bankers and businessmen they thought it an unlikely tale, not because of the violence but because of the cause: Pharaon is not given to lecturing others about commercial morality. In Washington I heard the second version, which my acquaintances found much more convincing. The reason Fahd had slapped Pharaon three times was, it was said, not because he blamed Pharaon for the failure of the gamble in the silver market but because the crown prince had discovered that Gaith Pharaon was taking a commission on all his, the prince's, silver purchases. The story leaves the case not proven, and the absence of documentary evidence would not satisfy a court of law; but it rings true.

Meanwhile, in Dallas, Bunker and Herbert Hunt carefully established their own large position in the silver market. Before the registration of IMIC, both wished to be able to withdraw from the market for a while and leave the action to the new company. So, beginning in the middle of June, Bunker began to buy what are known in the market as straddles: he acquired similar quantities of long contracts to buy silver and short contracts to sell it. Theoretically, as we have seen, the purchases cancel each other out, since the gains on one side of the market cancel losses on the other, and normally they are bought by speculators for tax reasons, but Bunker's purchases had a different purpose. By July 11 he had bought 5,790 straddles through Cargill Investor Services, a dealing subsidiary of Cargill Inc. another huge, private grain company, thus cleverly concealing his tracks because Cargill was not a dealer he commonly used. Even dealers as expert as Theo Hook had no idea who the buyer was. Moreover, the transaction was conducted so that it would not attract undue attention from the Commodity Futures Trading Commission. Because he bought short contracts as well as long, Bunker's net position – the one inspected by the CFTC when they look for a potential squeeze – was virtually unchanged.

In the first week of July, Herbert Hunt enlarged his own position in exactly the same way as Bunker had, buying 4,544 straddles, and both the brothers' contracts to buy silver were due for completion before their contracts to sell. By the time IMIC was established, Bunker and Herbert had purchased straddles that, if they took delivery of the long side, would enable them to demand 50 million ounces of silver in two future months – the February 1980 contract in Chicago and the March 1980 contract in New York. Simultaneously, Bunker and Herbert rolled over their existing positions, which were for another 75 million ounces of silver. But instead of rolling them into nearby contract months, such as October and December 1979, which had for years been their normal practice in the market, they moved them all into two months in 1980 – the February in Chicago and the March in New York. Their total long position in those two months was now 125 million ounces – the most they had ever held in the futures market – already worth more than $1 billion. Without being aware of what was happening, the market was now desperately vulnerable to the Hunts.

By the end of July the web was fully spun. On July 24 the final division of the shares in IMIC was registered in Bermuda, and the next day Bunker had time to attend to his hobby. At Joseph E. Johnson III's Kentucky Horse Center, Bunker held a sale of his own yearlings, a most satisfactory affair, since a new world-record price of $1.45 million was paid for a yearling filly. In all, sixty-nine horses were bought, for a total of $12,260,000. One feature of the sale was that the two biggest buyers had never purchased racehorses before. Both were from Los Angeles – one a Hollywood executive named Seymour Weintraub, recently deposed by Columbia Pictures, and the other a dealer in rare old coins, Bruce McNall.

The account of the auction by Joseph Pons, Jr., in *The Blood Horse* not only was mildly incredulous about the scale of the buying; furthermore, Pons reported the presence of another newcomer at the sale. 'In addition to Weintraub's and McNall's, frequent purchases were made by Naji Nahas, a leading racing figure in Brazil. Nahas was being advised by Maurice Zilber, who had trained Dahlia, Youth, and Exceller to major triumphs carrying Hunt's green block silks. Nahas signed for 11 yearlings for $1,100,000,' Pons reported.

His account continued: '"Mr Nahas handles the Arab money in horses," said Mr Hunt. "Zilber will do the training. I understand Mr Nahas bought an Argentine horse for $1 million recently. I appreciate the patronage of my friends at the sale," Hunt added. They included Zilber, Hunt's cousin Stuart Hunt, and his long-time friend Ed Stephenson, who races Trillion in Partnership with Hunt.'

Pons reported that Nahas had bid a further $1.3 million for the filly that eventually broke the world-record price. For a man who claimed to have been short of money only a few months earlier, Nahas was spending with abandon – or perhaps it was just that his credit was especially good, since Bunker knew more about his prospects than anyone else at the sale. That might have applied to Seymour Weintraub, too, because he was about to invest heavily in silver as well as in horses.

There was one other man who would have known about Nahas's prospects at that sale in Kentucky on July 25, 1979. He admitted his presence there to Senator Donald Stewart in the following exchange eleven months later, on June 26, 1980.

SENATOR STEWART: Did you talk to [Hunt] at all?
NORTON WALTUCH: Well, he came over and asked me what I thought about silver.
STEWART: So you discussed silver and the purchasing of silver?
WALTUCH: Not the purchasing of silver. He asked me my opinion of silver.
STEWART: What did you say?
WALTUCH: I said I was bullish in silver. I thought the silver market would be significantly higher.
STEWART: Did you have an extended conversation or a brief conversation?
WALTUCH: Ten or fifteen minutes perhaps.

The game was about to begin. There was, however, one problem. Far too many people had been let in on the secret. A banker in London told me months later that during the first week of August 1979 he had been talking to his wife, who added some intriguing information to a story he had already heard a snatch of. The banker knew that there was something about to happen in the silver market involving some Lebanese and the Hunt brothers from America. His wife added piquant details about the involvement of the Saudi royal family. The banker was curious to know how she had found out. She replied that she had heard the story from Mahmoud Fustok's brother's ex-wife.

Chapter 6

How to Corner the Silver Market: A Simple Guide

By the end of July 1979 the players had taken their positions on the board without even having notified their opponents that they were about to become involved in a game. At the beginning of August, positions of bewildering complexity were established with remarkable speed and ruthlessness, so this is a good moment to pause and reflect on the process that now becomes the centre of our story: the manipulation of the silver market.

There is no more or less mystery about this than about any other recondite activity, like rolling craps or computer fraud, and, indeed, a strategy for manipulation was discussed quite openly in March 1979 in the magazine *Euromoney*. The author was Dr Henry Jarecki, chairman of Mocatta Metals in New York, and he wrote: 'If 150 million ounces of silver were owned by parties who intended to hold it for a 30–40 per cent appreciation after interest cost, those parties would have a major impact on supply and might well succeed in achieving the price they ask. Someone who wanted to buy that much silver could do so with a billion dollars, which sounds a lot, but since he could borrow 80–90 per cent of the funds to do it with, a silver squeeze could be financed for $100 million. Whether it will really happen is hard to predict; most people with $100 million to spare have better things to do.' But Bunker and Herbert Hunt and the princes of the Saudi royal family are not 'most people'.

With the assistance of Dr Jarecki's article, and of conversations with some indulgent dealers, I have compiled a guide to a silver market manipulation that will allow us to compare the theory of market squeezes and corners with the actual behaviour of our characters as it has been, and will be, described in these pages.

The ideal silver manipulation leading to a corner, or perhaps something even more ambitious (like a cartel), comes neatly packaged in ten separate stages. And since this is a consumer's guide, I shall assume that you, the reader, rather than any character in this book, are undertaking the manipulation. There are just two preconditions to the manipulation: you must be willing to keep your motives strictly secret; and you must have a great deal of money – more, probably, than Dr Jarecki's estimate of $100 million.

Stage 1: do not try to sneak into the silver market undetected: announce that you are in business, and that you intend not merely to speculate in the silver futures market but to take delivery of silver bullion. Naturally, though, you will be much less open than this about the actual alliances you make. You need partners, not only to raise some of the original capital but also to distract attention from yourself. Further to this end, it is sensible to distribute the accounts held by you and your partners among a number of brokerage houses and bullion merchants. Placing them all with a single dealer might lead him to suspect collusion – a clear tactical error. By the end of stage 1 you will be a familiar figure in the silver markets, having acquired a position in the futures market quite openly, buying on modest margins and pyramiding your holding by reinvesting all your profits. It is perfectly possible that, at this stage, market professionals will think you are a sucker, ripe for the picking.

Stage 2: it is now essential to make sure that your partners, the biggest of them at least, cannot betray you, for they might not be so ambitious or so greedy as yourself. Since you wish to dictate the price of silver, you cannot risk their spoiling your game by selling their silver in the market before you are ready to do so. (This form of betrayal is known as being backdoored, since your partners will have left the game by the back door.) One way to insure yourself against this is to establish a company in which *they* will own shares and provide capital but *you* will take the decisions.

Stage 3: now is the time to arrange to use other people's money instead of your own to finance the last big push. Approach banks and ask them for loans based on the value of the silver you already own. They will not give you 100 per cent of its value; 90 per cent is as much as you can expect to get. But as the price of silver rises, you will need less and less bullion to raise the same sums of money. Normally, commercial banks will lend as much as 90 per cent of the value of silver used as collateral only to the bullion dealers, because the banks know that the silver is hedged in the futures market and that they can always get their money back. Persuade them to extend a similar privilege to you by appealing to a banker's fundamental instinct – to make money as quickly as possible – and by showing total disregard for the price they will ask you to pay for their money. When the banks ask for 1 or 1½ percentage points above their prime, or basic, lending rate, do not quibble as an everyday commercial borrower would. You are going to make so much profit with the banks' money that you can afford to appear nonchalant. The loans are used to build up your basic holdings of bullion: 75 million ounces or so will do.

Stage 4: it is time quietly to undermine the ability of the competition – the short sellers of silver – to fight back, by making it difficult for them to buy the silver they are contracted to deliver to you. There are two methods of doing this. First, you book and pay for space in the refineries that transform scrap and coins into deliverable bullion bars. You do not need to use the space; just ensure that the shorts cannot do so. Second, visit the main silver-producing nations – especially in South and Central America, where major decisions are taken by a few people – and persuade them that since the price of silver will be going up (they will understand), it would be prudent of them to withhold their new silver production from the market until the price has risen. This, as a blatant appeal to national self-interest, is well worth trying.

Stage 5: you are now in a position to decide exactly when you will squeeze or corner the futures market. Choose a delivery month, some months ahead, in which you will apply maximum pressure. February in Chicago and March in New York are particularly suitable, for your position will not be muddled by competition from speculators who are adjusting their year-end tax liabilities. Your biggest positions will now be concentrated in those target months; you and your allies ought to be long by some 50 to 75 million ounces, bringing your total potential holding close to 150 million ounces.

Stage 6: in the months before you corner the market, add to the confusion, and to your market power, by buying straddles. This means that instead of just increasing your long position, which might attract the attention of nosy federal regulators, you buy and sell an equal number of contracts, just as many ordinary speculators are doing. But since you know something they do not, *you* buy all your long positions in your target months, and sell contracts only in the following months. Your large holding of short contracts thus in no way relieves the pressure you are applying to the market, and you can demand delivery on any long contracts that fall due before your target month. Now you effectively control nearly 200 million ounces of silver.

Stage 7: start to manipulate the price upward. One expeditious method of doing this is to make occasional heavy purchases of silver in the London metals market. You choose London because its market is smaller than New York's, so one big order there will move the price up by a larger sum than a similar order would do in New York or Chicago. And although the New York and Chicago dealers are perfectly well aware of this technicality, your secrecy means they do not automatically suspect you, and their markets will tend to follow the London trend when they open, later that day. These tactics push your holdings over 200 million ounces.

Stage 8: so far, you have been operating covertly, hoping that the market professionals will not have noticed what is happening to them, but now you engineer a drama in the marketplace. You do not do it yourself, of course. A compliant market professional must do it for you, and one will not be difficult to find, since he will be able to make money himself by knowing your intentions. The dealer will deliberately cause a stir by loudly bidding the maximum possible price for silver futures. (This process is known as bidding limit up, since the markets limit the sum by which the price of a futures contract – as opposed to the price for immediate delivery, or the spot price – can move in a single day.) This will disturb the professionals and reduce the volume of business; you – or, better still, your partners – might have to make some expensive purchases, but never mind, your existing position is already showing a massive profit. A second, more technical method of creating drama is to remove the silver bullion you have bought from the Comex and Board of Trade depositories; this reduces the stocks of deliverable silver and makes the shorts even more nervous that demand may outstrip supply.

Stage 9: by this time the embarrassment of the bullion dealers (who hold large short positions in the futures market to hedge the value of the bullion they own) will be acute. They will be asked for heavy margin payments, and will, in turn, be calling for action against speculators like yourself. Now you disarm criticism by making deals known as EFPs – exchanges of futures for physicals. When you commit yourself to taking delivery of bullion before your long contracts fall due, your long positions in the futures market for the same amount of bullion are cancelled, as are the dealers' short positions. This relieves the strain on some of the shorts – and it also further reduces the supply of deliverable silver.

Stage 10: now you are ready to squeeze, or, better still, to corner the market. You own so much bullion that stocks have fallen drastically, and you own so many long futures contracts that there is not silver enough in the warehouses to meet your demands for delivery in your target month. The shorts have nowhere to turn to buy silver – except to you. They are entirely in your power. All are desperate to know how you propose to get out. You may do so in a variety of ways. The most traditional is to find the unfortunate known as the naked short, who must pay whatever price you ask to cover the contracts he has made with you. But that does create the danger that the company that owes you money will go bankrupt. Depending on your subtlety or ruthlessness, you might wish to force such a bankruptcy, hoping that it it will create such panic that the market will be closed, and all contracts – not just those you have with the naked short – will be settled at the high price you have yourself created. This option limits you to a one-time gain, since you cannot speculate in a market that has been closed. But if you are satisfied with a 30 to 40 per cent gain on your investment, you will be well pleased, and much richer – by a few hundred million dollars – on the completion of your successful corner.

There is one further option, however, and that is to use your market profits to raise even more money on the mass of bullion you own, and spend it achieving control of the sources of supply: the mines themselves. You need not own them all effectively to dictate the price of silver. In this 100 per cent solution, your corner ceases to be an end in itself, designed to secure only short-term profits, and becomes the means to the end. For once you control the silver price through your purchase of a number of silver mines, the futures market becomes irrelevant. You can create a cartel to market silver, and at that stage you and the market are indivisible. You have not cornered the silver market: you have cornered silver.

To attempt to corner the silver market means, I suppose, that you are greedy enough to be quite unconcerned by the disruption of a world-wide market. To wish to corner silver itself suggests a new dimension to our concept of greed.

Chapter 7

The CFTC: Stepchild Among Agencies

Bunker Hunt was never in any doubt that corners in commodity markets are illegal. The duties of the Commodity Futures Trading Commission – more commonly known by its initials as the CFTC – specifically include busting manipulations, squeezes, and corners. The whole Hunt family had come up against the CFTC during the soybean caper in 1977. As we know, a year earlier, Bunker Hunt had purchased some expensive legal advice about its actual powers, which the lawyers had judged to be 'ethereal and indistinct'. Nevertheless, the CFTC could not be ignored; it was an umpire in the game that was about to begin.

The emblem of the Commodity Futures Trading Commission, an American eagle with the scales of justice balanced in its claws, hangs outside an anonymous modern concrete building on the corner of K and Twenty-first streets in Washington, D.C. Inside, each of the commissioners inhabits one of those comfortable and well-designed office suites that have become characteristic of the federal bureaucracy; Bunker's office in Dallas looks shoddy by comparison. Every couple of weeks the commissioners take their business into the boardroom, but their discussions rarely grip those few spectators who turn up. As one staff man observes: 'Eight days' notice is required before anything is agenda'd at a board meeting, so not much comes up.' (The use of 'agenda' as a verb is another characteristic of contemporary bureaucracy.)

The significant business of the CFTC takes place on Friday mornings, behind closed doors, in a gloomy, top-floor back room. The room is dominated by a large, round, laminated table, cluttered with pencils, pads, and microphones – which are there not to make the conversation audible but to tape it for the record. The commissioners listen to the weekly surveillance briefings, in which the staff discuss price fluctuations and reveal any substantial changes in the positions of market traders and big speculators, which must be reported confidentially to the CFTC each day.

Sitting opposite the commissioners at the round-table briefing are the directors of enforcement and of economics and education; the general counsel; the executive director; and John Meilke, director of markets. And on July 27, 1979, the subject of the Hunts had been raised, out of curiosity, by the newest of the commissioners, David Gartner. It was an unusually lighthearted discussion, and the commissioners – Chairman James Stone, Read Dunn, Robert Martin, and Gartner – had no reason to know that a transcript of their words would be revealed the following spring by congressional investigators. But it was, and it reads:

GARTNER: Can I ask one general question? The Hunts. Every week we see them in something, silver, soybean oil, livestock, whatever. Do you think there's any possibility these guys are just having fun, just horsing around. Like playing Monopoly like you and I might do, or nickel and dime poker [laughter]. Is this a little game they're going through?

MEILKE: Well, they're playing with some awfully big bucks. I was looking at their silver position and on Chicago and New York combined – and I'm talking basically about the two brothers, Bunker and Herbert – their position is roughly 20,000 contracts long and 10,000 contracts short. The net of that position, 10,000 contracts at $9.50 silver, is worth 475 million dollars.

GARTNER: That's a lot of money.

MEILKE: That's a lot of money.

[SPEAKER UNCLEAR]: . . . even by their standards.

DUNN: . . . for you maybe [laughter].

[UNCLEAR]: Certainly it is!

MEILKE: Herbert Hunt has limit positions in meal, oil and beans. Bunker has got 1,200 contracts long in October cotton.

STONE: Following Commissioner Gartner's curiosity, do we have any idea whether on balance they make substantial profits from all this activity?

MEILKE: I'm sure they have in silver, the way the silver market has moved, and that may be financing ventures in other markets. They have been net long on silver all along and they've built some positions and silver has moved dramatically. Other than that I really don't know – I don't think they made any money on that June cotton deal.

STONE: Are their positions in silver big enough to have moved the market?

MEILKE: No, I don't believe so; normally, their posture is they'll be long in nearby futures with some short spreads out in future months, and as the delivery month approaches they'll roll it forward. Right now they're in 1980 futures, they're not in 1979, which is further advanced than they normally are.

GARTNER: It just seems to me there are people with a hell of a lot of money and not a lot to do with their time, fiddling around like you and I might play a game of checkers [laughter].

DUNN: General feeling of the trade is that these are often actions for tax losses.

MEILKE: Could be, I don't know.

[UNCLEAR]: I don't have that, not that much Monopoly money.

The transcript displays a lack of urgency that, to be fair, seems more reprehensible in retrospect than it could have done at the time. The reasons for the absence of robustness were a combination of inexperience, a lack of bite in the law the CFTC administered, and a bitter clash of personalities. These factors became more important as the months went by, and since they are so influential in the story that follows, the CFTC is worth examination.

The CFTC was once described, by Senator Adlai Stevenson III, as 'a stepchild among regulatory agencies' – a metaphor that is accurate in the sense that the CFTC does give the impression of being somewhat insecure, and even lost. But there is no doubt about its parentage. The pretext for the creation of the CFTC was the brilliant covert raid by the Russians on the grain futures markets in 1973, when the Russians played capitalism and bought millions of tons of grain cheaply enough to compensate for the disastrous Soviet harvest. Since Midwestern farmers had not shared in this bonanza, their representatives in Congress supported the foundation of a new agency to prevent such a raid happening again. But there was a further justification for congressional action, because the futures markets were rapidly becoming a playground for speculation and tax evasion.

The futures markets had not been unregulated before. The Commodities Exchange Act of 1936 had reflected President Franklin Roosevelt's distaste for 'ignoble speculation' in commodities, but regulation had been delegated to a section of the Department of Agriculture, and enforcement was the responsibility of the Justice Department, which lacked the experience or the will to harry market manipulators. Moreover, that legislation embraced only agricultural commodities, such as grains and soybeans, but by the 1970s there were new futures markets in gold, pork bellies, timber, and foreign currencies, including the pound sterling and the Japanese yen – not to mention silver, which by 1976 was the most heavily traded commodity of all. The CFTC was given responsibility for the whole lot.

The text to which the new commission addressed itself was issued by the Senate Agriculture Committee in November 1974: 'The proper regulatory function is to assure that the market is free from manipulation and other practices which prevent the market from being a true reflection of supply and demand.' Consequently, the new law made it 'a felony for any person to manipulate or attempt to manipulate the price of any commodity whether in the cash or the futures market.' The CFTC was given power to react to the 'threatened or actual manipulations . . . or any market disturbance which prevents the market accurately reflecting supply and demand' by declaring a market emergency, after which there is virtually nothing the CFTC cannot do: as long as the CFTC is seen to be 'market neutral' – to take no action that would assist either buyers or sellers – the markets can be closed, the commission can impose a price for settling contracts, and individuals can be indicted on charges of manipulation. The language of the law suggests that a regulator with experience, determination, and ambition could represent an awesome threat to the commodities industry.

There is just one drawback to this panoply of regulatory power: the act omits any definition of 'manipulation' or 'squeeze' or 'corner'. Moreover, the CFTC is committed to show intent to manipulate – a difficult thing to do even in so apparently straightforward a case as Bunker and Herbert's excursion into soybeans in 1977. This is the Catch-22 of commodities regulation: the law gives the CFTC immense power, and makes it almost impossible to deploy it.

When the CFTC began to work in April 1975, the first chairman was a California politician named William T. Bagley, an anti-Reagan Republican who was compensated by President Gerald Ford with the chairmanship of the CFTC after he lost an election for the California state controllership in 1974. Bagley had left barely a mark on the commission when he returned to the bar in Sacramento after three and a half years in the job.

Four years after its establishment, only two of the original five commissioners still held office, and this unusually rapid turnover was because of the rule that the composition of the CFTC should reflect the political balance in Washington. Of President Ford's appointments, three were Republicans and two Democrats, and when President Carter came to Washington the pattern shifted as commissioners' terms expired. Two Republicans departed, but so did a Democrat; and the White House found it remarkably difficult to get replacements who wanted the job and were acceptable to the Senate Agriculture Committee, whose consent is required. By the summer of 1979, two Democrats – including the chairman, James Stone – had been appointed, but the Republican vacancy proved impossible to fill. The absence of a fifth man gave the Democrats a three-to-one majority on the CFTC which should have created a decisive and harmonious working majority. It did not.

As chairman, James Stone is not an entirely convincing figure, largely because his appointment failed to invest him with much authority. He is obliging, making instant coffee for a visitor like myself before sitting down in a wicker rocking chair; next to him is a tape deck and a drawer of tapes of Mozart and Schubert. The atmosphere is pleasant and relaxed, not unlike that of a seminar with a promising young professor.

To look at, Stone is a pale-faced slip of a lad, and the only indication that he has reached his early thirties is a small bald patch on the crown of his head of curly auburn hair. At first glance, it seems frankly astonishing that this is the chairman of the Commodity Futures Trading Commission. Admittedly, it is not the grandest job in Washington, but it suggests, nevertheless, that there is more to Stone than meets the eye.

James Stone was born in November 1947, so he was only thirty-one years old when his appointment was announced. He is a New Yorker by birth; his father is a lawyer and his mother a romantic novelist whose work is published under the pseudonym Babette Robinson. The family moved from the Upper East Side to suburban Pelham, New York, when James was four, and he was bright enough to be a National Merit Scholar, before leaving Pelham High School to become a Harvard man. His secure middle-class upbringing can hardly have prepared him for the greed and rapacity that motivate speculators. Stone never had any need to gamble. He was graduated Phi Beta Kappa and stayed on at Harvard as a fellow in economics, becoming Dr James Stone, a Harvard lecturer in the economics department, specializing in the securities industry. He worked briefly on Wall Street, and decided that the stock market would be much more efficient if the exchanges and the brokers were all swallowed up in one vast computer. 'The entire process would be free,' he wrote, 'and fraud would be next to impossible,' though he did not explain what would happen when the computer broke down. But his was a classic establishment education for a job in a Democratic administration.

In 1975 the idealistic young technocrat attracted the attention of the governor of Massachusetts, Michael Dukakis, who appointed the twenty-eight-year-old Stone state insurance commissioner. 'I always thought of public life as a possibility,' Stone said; and he described himself as a representative of a new breed of 'public interest-type regulators,' although the files of Boston newspapers suggest that his insurance commissionership had not been an unqualified success in the public interest. Loopholes in insurance regulations were inadvertently created, which led to large premium increases, and Stone confessed unhappily that 'sweeping changes came too quickly.' In May 1977 the *Christian Science Monitor* reported: 'Rumours are rampant that Mr Stone will be fired, or will resign to take a job in the Carter Administration' – a singular commentary on the reputation of Carter's Washington. In fact, the report was only slightly premature, because Stone arrived in Washington two years later, some months after the defeat of Governor Dukakis and Stone's subsequent resignation.

Stone had qualified as a regulator, and the Carter administration clearly believed that the absence of any deep knowledge of the commodity futures markets was no bar to his appointment. Anyway, he said, he had taught a course at Harvard about securities, which included commodities. Stone officially became chairman of the CFTC on May 4, 1979, and within months his chief preoccupation was Bunker and Herbert, who never had much time for professors.

The most senior commissioner in 1979 was Read Dunn, a sixty-five-year-old Southerner from Greenville, Mississippi, whose drawl had survived decades spent in Washington, London, and Brussels. A kindly, avuncular figure, he speaks softly without carrying a big stick. Dunn worked briefly as a reporter on the Greenville *Democrat-Times* after graduating from Millsaps College in 1936. By the end of the decade, Dunn, a New Deal Democrat, was spokesman for the Commodity Credit Corporation, and, after three years in the Navy, became a national and international lobbyist for the cotton trade, as executive director of the International Institute for Cotton. The decorations on the walls of his office at the CFTC are large, colourful collages cleverly made by his daughter from the patterns for cotton shirts. There is not much Read Dunn does not know about cotton; it is a pity that cotton has become so insignificant a subject of CFTC oversight. Compared to the days in the flamboyant New Orleans market early in the century, when old H. L. Hunt took a bad beating, the cotton futures market has fallen on hard times. But it meant Dunn and Bunker Hunt had something in common when they met. Greenville was not far from El Dorado, to which H.L. moved after the cotton debacle, and when they met, Dunn and Bunker were able to chat about old times. 'My daddy knew his daddy', says Dunn.

Dunn's sociability was not innocent: he remembered the Hunts being the subject of surveillance briefings in 1975 and 1976. 'We'd been watching them for a long time, and we were never satisfied that we understood their game plan.' But Dunn does not speculate. He is the least ideological member of the commission, and his attitude is pragmatic: show him the facts, and he will decide whether to act on them. For Stone, Dunn's greatest virtue was loyalty; Dunn was to be the chairman's only ally.

The other founder member of the commission was Robert Martin, the only commissioner with an intimate knowledge of commodity markets. Martin had learned his trade with the Standard Milling Company in Minneapolis, and, apart from three years in the Army Air Corps in World War II, he had spent his life in the Chicago grain market before joining the commission in 1975. Martin's experience, deep and narrow as it was, convinced him that the best defence against market manipulation was the rule that no one is bigger than the market. Like Dunn, Martin fondly repeats the hoary market adage: there is something for the bulls, something for the bears, but nothing for the hogs.

Like Dunn, Martin recalled the Hunts' excursion into the silver market in 1976. He remembered that on one occasion in 1976 he had told an old Chicago colleague that the Hunts were predators. It was not a bad description, but Martin learned later that it had been reported back to the Hunts within three days of his having said it. It was the sort of phrase that could be used by the brothers to suggest that the commission was not 'market neutral', as the law laid down it should be, and although Martin did not feel intimidated, he watched his tongue more carefully after that.

Discretion does not come easily to him. Martin is a portly figure, generously frank, full of homely analogies, and brutally critical of his colleagues. By the summer of 1979 Martin had grown disenchanted with the CFTC, which, he felt, spent too much time fighting fires while failing to ask basic questions about the commodity market.

Martin was distinctly unimpressed by James Stone and became convinced that the chairman regarded the CFTC as a stepping-stone, as it were, to greater things in Washington. As for Dunn, Martin was contemptuous of his loyalty to Stone, believing it had no firmer grounding than a feeling that *someone* ought to be loyal. 'Either you believe things or you don't,' says Martin sharply. Perhaps he was angered by the effect of Dunn's loyalty, which was to split the commission two votes to two on many important issues – because, despite having been nominated as a Democrat, the fourth commissioner, David Gartner, developed an antipathy to the chairman that was even deeper than Martin's.

There was a basic ideological conflict between the two men: Stone enthusiastically supported the concept of consumer protection in commodity markets; Gartner believed in the contrary principle of *caveat emptor* – let the buyer beware. But Gartner's antipathy went further than that. Martin observed: 'If Stone proposed that it was Monday, Gartner would have voted against. It was nonsensical and immature. Trouble is, there are too few of us who have worked for a profit.' What Martin meant was that he alone among the incompatible quartet had actually been in business.

When David Gartner joined the CFTC in 1978, at the age of forty-two, his adult life had been spent entirely in politics; all but four years of it on the staff of Hubert Humphrey during his terms as senator and vice-president. That experience had won Gartner a commissionership, and almost lost it for him, because he had developed a close personal relationship with one of the biggest men in the grain trade, Wayne Andreas (a man remembered for his campaign cheque to Richard Nixon, which was laundered in Mexico to pay for the Watergate break-in). That relationship with Andreas caused President Jimmy Carter to state publicly that he thought Gartner should not take up his new job. But Gartner insisted that he had done nothing wrong, and stubbornly took the job in spite of presidential disapproval.

Gartner's deep-brown eyes stand out behind his spectacles in a pale face, and he smokes nervously, but he is, nonetheless, an assertive man. By the time he joined the CFTC, Gartner had edged away from the liberalism of his mentor, Hubert Humphrey, and become as convinced a believer in the virtue of free markets as any propagandist for Comex or the Board of Trade. This conviction provided the ideological basis for his disputes with James Stone. 'Stone is so consumer-oriented,' Gartner charged, 'that he'd probably like to see individual market positions disseminated on a daily basis. That is almost a mortal sin to me.' Gartner distinguished between regulation and oversight, and vastly preferred oversight. 'I would like to see us have less power, because I'm for a responsible industry. I'm satisfied that the very fact we're here causes the markets to think twice.'

But Gartner, like Stone, had no experience of the Hunts, which is not unlike obtaining a master's ticket without having experienced a storm at sea. Gartner's attitude toward manipulation was so innocent as to be touching. 'If Joe Schmoe is going to corner the market in widgets, and he happens to have five billion dollars, is there a law to stop him?' Gartner asked. (There is the Sherman Antitrust Act.) Less theoretically, Gartner continued: 'If the Hunts have some paranoia about the dollar and want to leave some money to their children, what do you do about that?'

Indeed, the commission as a whole seemed to be obsessed by what it could not do. The staff was inexperienced, and since the CFTC lacked glamour, there were no lines of bright young lawyers clamouring for work with the commission. The enforcement department was a poor thing and grossly understaffed compared to the elite group at the Securities and Exchange Commission, headed then by the intimidating Stanley Sporkin. The intellectual standard of the CFTC's research was notably inferior to that at the Federal Reserve Board. Comparisons are unfair, of course, since the CFTC had not existed long enough to develop similar traditions of inquiry and research. But there was a fundamental difference between the three regulatory agencies. The SEC and the Federal Reserve were conscious of their authority and eager to preserve it. The CFTC was conscious of its lack of authority and appeared to have little desire to establish any.

This was a crucial flaw, and one example of the CFTC's indecision greatly influenced what was to happen in the last five months of 1979. It concerned position limits, which were imposed on commodity trading in agricultural products, like soybeans, but not on precious metals, such as silver. In 1977 the commissioners had asked the staff to prepare a paper on position limits for commodities, including silver, and that document recommended a new rule that would prohibit a single speculator's holding more than 25 per cent of the contracts in any contract month; its practical effect would have been to prevent Bunker and Herbert Hunt from buying more than a quarter of the silver contracts on the market. Because of the greater expertise of the exchanges, the CFTC's chief economist also recommended that the limits should be enforced by Comex and the Board of Trade. But the exchanges were unenthusiastic and raised objections that the staff were incapable of demolishing. Consequently, the commissioners dropped the proposed limit rule. It was a decision they were to regret.

Position limits are exactly the kind of customer protection that appeals to James Stone, but he had no opportunity to raise the matter after July 27, 1979, when the commissioners had jocularly discussed the size of the Hunts' silver holdings. Early in August, James Stone announced that he was unwell and, on medical advice, was taking a few weeks' leave. From the evidence available to them, his fellow commissioners believed that Stone had suffered a mild nervous breakdown. In Stone's absence the most senior of the three remaining commissioners took responsibility for an increasingly volatile silver market. It was not a role Read Dunn would have chosen for himself. 'I felt I had to give a lead to the commission, but I sure didn't know a hell of a lot about silver,' he said later.

Chapter 8

August–October 1979: The Price Goes Wild

On August 1, 1979, a new name showed up on the CFTC's daily reports of silver purchasers. The buyer was International Metals Investment Company – IMIC for short. That day its brokers, Merrill Lynch, in Dallas, reported its purchase of 603 silver contracts in Chicago and New York; this represented 3,015,000 ounces – a sizeable amount, but not so large as to attract attention. Anyway, August is getaway month for most commodity dealers. The agricultural specialists need to keep a weather eye on the harvest, but it is normally time for the precious-metals men to redistribute some of their gains or morosely contemplate their losses.

Two other new buyers also entered the market in the first week of August without being noticed. Naji Robert Nahas bought 345 contracts on August 1. The Banque Populaire Suisse, on behalf of a group of speculators based, like Nahas, in Geneva, Switzerland, bought 195 contracts during that week. The existence of these two new accounts began to filter into the collective consciousness of the markets only in the second week of August. By the fifteenth of the month, IMIC had bought 4,491 contracts, and the silver price had moved up a few cents.

In the third week of August, any brokers spending quiet days on the beach were rudely interrupted by telephone calls from New York; the message was that the silver market was currently being dominated by one man, a dealer named Norton Waltuch, an account executive for Conti Commodity Services, the broker for two new buyers, Nahas and the Banque Populaire Suisse. Waltuch was snapping up anything he could buy; at the end of August, the Banque Populaire Suisse had 3,385 contracts, and Nahas, 1,784.

Experienced market professionals like Theo Hook, observing Waltuch's activities from their trading desks, judged that the last two weeks of August were an opportune time to make a quick killing. Theo Hook sold short contracts to balance Waltuch's long buying. 'I thought Norton was full of crap,' says Hook. 'I kept on saying to myself: How's he going to get the price over ten dollars?' But Hook, like most other dealers in New York, was so mesmerized by Waltuch's performance in Comex pit that he failed to notice IMIC's heavy purchases. By the end of August, IMIC had bought 8,085 long contracts – more than 40 million ounces of silver. That was enough to push the silver price to $10.61 by August 31 – up by more than a dollar in a month. It was unnerving, especially to Theo Hook, who decided that he had better take his loss before it grew any greater; the cost of covering his short position by buying offsetting long contracts was $400,000. It was his own money, too; more than he could afford. Hook realized too late that his attention had been drawn away from IMIC by Waltuch's frenetic behaviour. 'It was so well done,' he admits. He had learned from the experience that the market was dominated by bigger men than himself; he retired with as much dignity as he could muster.

This rush of big new bulls into the market was disorientating, not just because they were forcing the price up, but because only their brokers had any idea of their exact identity. All that the CFTC knew about IMIC was an address, which did not help much, since it was a post-office box number in Hamilton, Bermuda, where the commission's writ did not run; the only additional information was the name of the company secretary, Robert Guinn. The commission had its suspicions, but these did not provoke an energetic reaction. At the meeting on September 7, there was laughter at the staff's report that they were checking the Hamilton post-office box number; the director of markets, John Meilke, had to explain to the commissioners that it was important that they establish the magnitude of IMIC's position.

James Stone was back now from his medical leave, though his ally, Read Dunn, remembers: 'Even after he got back, he wasn't up to speed.' Stone asked Meilke at that meeting whether he suspected manipulation, and if so, what kind?

MEILKE: If the position is large enough, it might affect the world price.
STONE: I'd be very skeptical that something going on in these markets could affect the world price.

The staff had picked up some gossip about Saudi involvement with the Hunts, but even this news failed to arouse all the commissioners. 'We're either going to get a non-answer when we ask or the right answer, but even if we get the right answer – that it's the Hunts or the government of Saudi Arabia – what do we do?' asked one commissioner. Only David Gartner was badly shaken by the possibility that the Saudis might be involved. 'This is economic warfare. Is Saudi Arabia trying to corner the market? They should get out of the market if they don't give us the information,' Gartner charged.

The CFTC's public response was more measured. A letter was sent to Robert Guinn in Hamilton, asking him to divulge the names of his principals. (Had they known that Robert was the son of Ed, the man with the *Manneken-Pis* tiepin in Libya, there would have been no need to ask; it could only have been the Hunts.) The CFTC staff was unwilling to rely on a letter to a box number in Hamilton, and asked the U.S. consulate in Bermuda to conduct a company search there as well. Even that was a slow process, but when the commissioners met next, on September 21, they had some information to work on. The consulate's search had revealed that half of the IMIC was owned by Bunker and Herbert Hunt through the Profit Investment Company, and that their Arab partners were Mohammed Aboud al-Amoudi, Ali bin Mussalam, and Mohammed Salah Affara. This was information that the Hunts themselves should have supplied to the CFTC, whose rules state that if a trader has an interest in more than one account, all the accounts should be considered as one for reporting purposes. But that was a detail; at least the commissioners now knew whom they were dealing with, and the information had concentrated John Meilke's mind. 'This is not a classic market squeeze. This is one done by big money and market psychology,' he told the commissioners on September 21. The staff did not actually speak to either of the Hunts until September 24, when Herbert confirmed the brothers' involvement in IMIC, and added weight to Meilke's fears by informing the staff that IMIC proposed to take delivery of the silver in some of its futures positions – a breach of the market's unwritten rule for speculators.

After that, the CFTC could have had few illusions about IMIC; but the other new accounts, held by Nahas and the Banque Populaire Suisse, were much more perplexing, largely because of the fundamentally secretive nature of the ebullient Norton Waltuch. He had been telephoned by the commission's surveillance staff as early as September 4 and asked if there were any connection between Nahas's account and the Banque Populaire's. Waltuch replied that he knew of no connection, and added that he neither directed nor controlled the Banque's trading. Unsatisfied by Waltuch's assurances, the CFTC's executive director, Donald Tendick, ordered that a special inquiry be undertaken by his special assistant, Britt Lenz. Lenz went to New York City on September 17 to inspect the accounts at various brokerage houses, to see if he could find any relationship between the new, Swiss-based accounts. What Lenz uncovered was an extraordinary web of interlinked accounts that appeared to have been woven deliberately to confuse the CFTC.

First, Lenz discovered accounts in two more unfamiliar names, Gillian Financial and Litardex Traders, which shared a mailing address with both Naji Nahas and the Banque Populaire. Monthly statements for all four accounts were to be sent, care of Advicorp, to 7 Place du Molard, Geneva, Switzerland. Advicorp was ostensibly run by two Swiss traders, Jean Jacques Bally and Pierre Alain Hirschy, whom Norton Waltuch had met in Geneva in May, and who claimed to control the account of the Banque Populaire. Or, at any rate, so said Waltuch when he spoke to the CFTC staff on September 4. But Britt Lenz discovered documents at the Conti Commodity offices in New York that flatly contradicted Waltuch's assertion: internal memoranda made it clear that the Banque Populaire and the Gillian Financial accounts were run by the director of a subsidiary called Conti Capital Management – and the director was none other than Norton Waltuch himself.

Waltuch had also informed the CFTC that Naji Nahas directed 99 per cent of his own trading – so it seemed strange that Nahas should have given power of attorney over his trading activities to an old acquaintance of Waltuch's who knew Geneva well, Robert C. Ramsey. Nahas also had a shareholding in Conti Capital Limited, Waltuch's offshore trading company in Nassau. As for Litardex Traders, Linz discovered its account was with another large New York broker, ACLI, and that its president was the same Naji Robert Nahas.

Suspicion that there were links between the Swiss accounts had therefore ceased to be based on circumstantial evidence, and Linz reported in a memorandum to Tendick (which turned up on Capitol Hill that following summer): 'It was very clear that the accounts should be combined for market surveillance purposes, as in fact they were, early in October.' Linz's report referred to 'deliberate errors, misleading information, and late filing of reports' by Conti personnel, which had been referred to the division of enforcement. The curious thing is that the investigation stopped dead, then and there, at the beginning of October 1979. The CFTC, though it knew that the Banque Populaire Suisse and Nahas accounts were related, still had no idea who was involved in the Banque Populaire account, although it was quite certain that it was not a speculation for the Banque itself. When the Banque was asked to reveal the names of the clients, it hid behind Swiss bank-secrecy laws and continued to do so throughout the winter, to the CFTC's growing irritation.

The CFTC ought to have been more than irritated by the Geneva traders; it ought to have been suspicious, because the traders' behaviour in September had been so peculiar. Having called for delivery of 1,184 contracts – 5,920,000 ounces of silver – the Banque Populaire insisted that it be flown to Switzerland. This made no sense, because they could simply have exchanged warehouse receipts for silver in New York for receipts for the same amount of silver in London. It is a common method of transferring ownership from one side of the Atlantic to the other, and saves the transport costs of 7 cents an ounce (or $414,400 for 1,184 contracts). The transfer made even less sense at the time it was done, because silver was then selling for 10 cents an ounce more in London than in New York, and an exchange of receipts would have netted a further profit of $592,000. But sums so small were clearly of no interest to the men behind the Banque Populaire accounts. The only explanation for their behaviour is that they wanted to create an atmosphere of uncertainty and fear by removing the silver from the warehouse and thus diminishing the Comex stocks.

A few Wall Street investment bankers, including Salomon Brothers, reacted as Theo Hook had done, and decided they would not play the game anymore after September. They were free to act boldly, and a few believed that the CFTC should have been equally decisive and closed the market right then, in September 1979. But that was never on; although some of the commissioners were later to change their minds, the CFTC's first reaction was that of a frightened rabbit. It was paralyzed by the prospect of legal actions brought both by the exchanges and by the big speculators like Bunker Hunt, which the commissioners assumed would be the consequence of an arbitrary decision to close the market. As for the exchanges, a majority of their board members were still deterred from boldness by the prospect of all those lost commissions. In the circumstances, the only weapon Comex was willing to deploy to cool the fevered speculation was to increase the cost of playing the game.

On September 4 the margin payment – the cost of playing – had been raised from $2,000 to $3,000 for each contract; two days later it went up again, to $5,000. But these actions were not going to deter the bulls when the silver price was rising, because they had no margin payments to make and they had even more money from pyramided profits with which to finance their new purchases. Comex's tentative moves had had no restraining effect on the silver price at all. By mid-September, silver was traded at $13.35 an ounce, an unprecedented level. On September 17 the margin was raised yet again, to $7,500, and the price still went on rising. That day, for the first time, the Comex board discussed the real concern of its members: that there would not be enough silver in the warehouse if the myserious new buyers insisted on delivery of the massive number of contracts they had bought in the December 1979 future. Comex contacted the Chicago Board of Trade to discover how quickly bullion could be transported between the two markets if it became necessary to break up a squeeze or corner. The price went on up regardless, even after Comex's margin had been raised once more, to $20,000, on September 18.

In London on September 18 the bullion dealers, reacting to a large, anonymous order from the Continent, had fixed the price at $18.30. Who placed that order remains a mystery because there are no regulators in London to whom such deals must be reported and the London Metal Exchange prides itself on the confidentiality of its customer relations. It would not be surprising, however, if the order had come from Geneva, and if it did, it had the desired effect, because the high London price on September 18 pulled up the price in the American markets. There was only one way to describe the markets now; they had gone stark, staring mad.

The game had become so different that some of the major dealers decided that they would also rather watch than play. George Lamborn, senior managing director of Shearson Loeb Rhoades, who thought he had rid himself of the Hunts' commodities business once and for all in 1975, discovered that Shearson had inherited some new Hunt accounts when the firm took over Loeb Rhoades Hornblower Weeks, a smaller brokerage house in San Francisco. Another inheritance of that deal was a broker named Scott McFarland, the same man who, when working for Drexel Burnham in 1977, had so helpfully distributed those soybean contracts among members of the Hunt family. McFarland was now responsible for a Hunt account of 2,600 silver contracts – 13 million ounces' worth. It was 2,600 more contracts than Lamborn wished Shearson to handle.

Lamborn felt too strongly about the Hunts' behaviour to keep it to himself. On September 24 he had met three of his most senior colleagues in the New York commodities market at a Futures Industry Association lunch. They were John Conheeny, from Merrill Lynch; David Johnston, from E. F. Hutton; and Eliot Smith, from Bache. Lamborn told them that he considered the Hunts a danger to the stability of the market. He personally had decided to deny them the huge incremental payments each daily price increase placed in their account when the shorts met their margin calls and their money was transferred via the clearinghouse to the accounts of the longs. Lamborn had told the Hunts that Shearson would pay interest on their gains but the firm would retain the money in order to meet margin calls if the price should go down. The Hunts got the message and removed their account from Shearson, for the second time in four years.

Lamborn's lunchtime story was bloodcurdling enough to persuade Merrill Lynch to start asking the Hunts for more collateral than the firm had done before, and E. F. Hutton decided not to take any new business from them. The only person who was obviously unimpressed was Eliot Smith, from Bache; in fact, he hired Scott McFarland from Shearson's San Francisco office and absorbed the 2,600 Hunt contracts McFarland brought with him into the large position Bunker and Herbert already held at Bache.

When the silver market is unhinged, as it was in September 1979, speculation comes in two separate varieties. The first is futures contracts; the other is gossip – 'Rumour doth double, like the voice and echo . . . Stuffing the ears of men with false reports.' That month, rumour, as if magnified by a zoom lens, concentrated on the substantial figure of Dr Henry Jarecki, chairman of Mocatta Metals. A friend of his began to list the rumours about Jarecki that month and was able to add a new one almost every day: it was whispered that the Mexicans had defaulted on a delivery of silver to Mocatta; that Jarecki was short in the market and the price was rising so fast that he was having to meet some horrendous margin calls; worst of all, that he was running out of credit. This particular rumour reached the august halls of the Federal Reserve Board in Washington and the Bank of England in London. 'It was when the rumours ended up in the various banks that it all became terribly worrying,' says one of Jarecki's associates. That affects a man's credit-worthiness, and indeed, that September Jarecki was in greater need of credit than he had ever been before.

Henry Jarecki is a natural target for gossip. Even in a business with a fair share of ample *personae*, Jarecki is highly visible. He has physical presence – he stands about six feet two inches – a boyish face, and a figure that dieting manages to keep into a controlled pear shape. His conversation is quick and excitable. I have watched him leave his desk while a dealer in Zurich was talking German on the telephone, make a quick decision in English, and return to the German conversation before the Zurich dealer had finished his paragraph.

Jarecki's company bears the name of the oldest and best-known bullion dealer in the world. The London firm of Mocatta and Goldsmid had been bullion dealers to the Bank of England since the late seventeeth century. The name was synonymous with precious metal. In the late 1960s, when Jarecki decided that he preferred bullion dealing to teaching (he was then a professor of psychiatry at Yale), he persuaded Mocatta to let him be their New York representative. He is particularly fond of the Mocatta name, suggesting as it does continuity and stability, but the New York operation is actually his. Jarecki controls it and owns a majority shareholding. The only sizeable minority holding – 30 per cent – is owned in London by the Standard Chartered Bank, which has a long imperial record in Africa and India. Standard Chartered also owns 55 per cent of Mocatta and Goldsmid, and half of Mocatta's Hong Kong operation, but Jarecki's London partners were happy to let him get on with the business in New York by himself.

Mocatta grew remarkably quickly in the 1970s. Jarecki spent millions of dollars installing the latest computers and communications gadgets to equip his market operations, which make millions of dollars out of the arbitrage business. Jarecki had always been intrigued by arbitrage. While he was a medical student in Switzerland he bought gold coins there and sold them for a profit in Germany. The transaction was the opposite of speculation because Jarecki knew he could not lose. And that was the theme of his bullion operation; in a high-risk business, Jarecki's objective was to minimize risk as much as possible. His risks had to be better calculated than anyone else's, and the investment of money and energy paid off so well that Jarecki was soon defined as a phenomenon in the precious-metals market. The judgment was made not entirely without envy and suspicion; Henry Jarecki was, after all, a newcomer to the business, and a Yale professor, to boot. And then, he is not a modest man. Arguably, Jarecki has a lot to be immodest about, but it is easy to imagine the malicious pleasure with which the rumourmongers went about their work in the fall of 1979. By September 21 the gossip had even reached the CFTC. 'How did Henry get caught short?' said one commissioner. 'Usually he's a little smarter than that.'

Jarecki's concept of risk management had been horribly upset by the price explosion. Mocatta owned 30 million ounces of silver, in the form of bullion and coins, and in metal that was leased to industrial silver users. Jarecki insured against a fall in the value of his silver by hedging on the futures market. He acquired a short position of 30 million ounces on the New York and Chicago markets to balance the 30 million ounces he actually owned. This was a classic use of the market, but it meant that Jarecki was long outside the exchanges and short on them, and, unfortunately, the action was on the exchanges. With the price rising, Mocatta had to meet margin calls on its short position. Each time the price rose by $1, Jarecki had to pay $30 million in margin to the longs. The size of these margin calls caused the gossip.

Inevitably, the rumours reached Dallas, and since the Hunts had a particular interest in Mocatta, Herbert decided to find out what was happening in New York. On September 14 Henry Jarecki was sitting at his desk in his glass-walled office three floors below the Comex trading floor in the World Trade Center, talking to a friend in London, when he blurted out: 'My God, the Hunts have just walked in.' It was Herbert, accompanied by his lawyer, Bart Cozzens.

The principals were not unknown to each other; Jarecki had visited the Hunts in Dallas, and the relationship had been amicable, though guarded. Jarecki was from Wall Street, which was one strike against him in the Hunts' view; his being a Jew was another. But that had not prevented them from doing business together. For example, the Hunts had borrowed $50 million from Mocatta to buy more silver, and as collateral for the loan they had deposited 10.7 million ounces of silver. This belonged to the Hunts, but Jarecki had absorbed it in his own bullion holding, using Hunt silver as collateral for his own borrowing. There was no law against this, but it was not necessarily what a traditional banker would have regarded as prudent.

Herbert Hunt's first point was sound enough. The $50-million deal, he said, had reflected the silver price – around $5 an ounce – when the deal had been made. Now, as silver was over $15 an ounce, the loan ought to reflect the increased value of their collateral: Herbert presumably wanted money to buy more silver, because the Hunts had no margin calls to meet. Jarecki could hardly refute the argument and duly offered to increase the size of the Hunt loan, but not by a sum large enough to satisfy Herbert, who said that, in that case, he and Bunker would pay off their loan and use the 10.7 million ounces of collateral for a loan elsewhere.

Henry Jarecki replied that the terms of the loan did not allow for repayment until the loan became due; that was what the contract said. But whether it was the contract or not, Jarecki's reaction only confirmed Herbert Hunt's prejudice against smart Wall Street money. Herbert felt cheated and angrily telephoned Bunker to report that he had an investment to protect; he had better fly to New York, too, because Jarecki's behaviour suggested Mocatta must be in bad trouble.

When the talks resumed, Bart Cozzens, feet shod in Texan boots, contemptuously resting on the table in the conference room behind Jarecki's office, was the hit man. Herbert played the injured party and Bunker the brooding presence. One of Jarecki's associates observed: 'There was a vindictiveness in the air. The Hunts felt like innocent country people who had been monkeyed about by smart

Wall Street Jews, and somehow imputations of bad faith sound more intimidating in a Texas accent.'

The Hunts' anger was based on a common enough motive: fear. 'For a few days they were genuinely frightened that they might have a big credit exposure,' says Jarecki's associate. In that context 'credit exposure' is a euphemism for Mocatta's going broke and taking 10.7 million ounces of Hunt silver into bankruptcy court as part of the firm's assets.

Henry Jarecki was not immune to the atmosphere; his appearance of joviality and insouciance hides a fundamental pessimism, and he, too, was apprehensive about the day when his credit lines ran out. He knew that the men he dealt with at Chase Manhattan understood about hedging, and that all the loans could be paid off eventually. But his debt was growing so large that the day might come very soon when it was referred to more senior men who did not understand the hedging process and who could say to Jarecki: enough is enough. Then the Hunts' fears would be confirmed, and everything that Jarecki had built so spectacularly would collapse in an equally dramatic manner.

In the standard version according to Herbert Hunt, which appeared in *Fortune* magazine: 'On the day silver reached $17.00 an ounce Jarecki rushed into the office and announced "When it hits $22.90 I'm broke – Mocatta is insolvent!" A few minutes later he came back even more alarmed and said: "I've miscalculated. The figure's a little lower.'" (Jarecki does not remember uttering these lines, and suggests that the Hunts arrived at a figure of $22.90 via a mathematical calculation: Mocatta's published reserves were $180 million, which, divided by the $30-million margin for each price rise of $1.00, comes to $6. Add that to $17 and the break point comes at around $23.)

But Jarecki was painfully conscious of the weakness of his negotiating position, and knew that it would remain weak until he was able to demonstrate to the Hunts that there was absolutely no possibility of his bank credit's running out. It was time to use his trump card and call in his minority shareholder, Standard Chartered in London, whose assets then were a well-cushioned £10 billion.

The reaction at Standard Chartered was not at all sanguine. The bank had never been asked to back a single company on the scale that Mocatta might eventually demand: hundreds of millions of dollars if the silver price went on up. But the bankers also knew that Standard Chartered's own good name would be at stake if Mocatta were bankrupted. The bank's deputy group managing director, Michael McWilliam, was dispatched to New York on the first available flight out of Heathrow to measure the risks, to try to reassure Jarecki's bankers, and to show the Hunts that Standard Chartered was still backing Jarecki. One measure of the risk was a panic at Kennedy Airport as soon as McWilliam arrived: the Chicago Board of Trade had just increased their margin, and Jarecki needed an additional credit of $50 million. McWilliam was asked to guarantee that, too, before his limousine left for Wall Street.

Now negotiations between the Hunts and Jarecki began in earnest. Nightly discussions would drag on until ten or eleven p.m. before the Hunts finally left for dinner. In the mornings they would sometimes slip out to buy a clean shirt, but the pressure was rarely relaxed. By this stage, however, Jarecki had had time to think. Observing the Hunts across the table, he thought he had finally understood their motive. They really did want to corner the market. And this new perception gave him a solution to the problem. It being his first priority to save himself, Jarecki decided to appear to help them make their corner. Once he grasped that option, he began to reassert himself.

Jarecki made Bunker and Herbert an offer that was basically simple, though in this case there were complications that took days to untangle. There is a market transaction known as an exchange of futures for physicals, or an EFP, and, in essence, it means that a speculator who holds long futures contracts agrees to take delivery of a specified amount of silver before the contracts have become due for delivery. Once that has been agreed, the futures contracts for that specified amount of silver, both long and short, are cancelled out.

Jarecki proposed to sell the Hunts 23 million ounces of silver – the physicals in the deal – which the Hunts agreed to pay for in cash, some at the time and some at fixed dates in the future. This was an astonishing quantity, the largest single sale in the history of the silver market. By accepting such a large hoard of bullion, the Hunts would make their intentions perfectly clear: they wanted all the bullion they could get. Jarecki knew that this ambition would eventually create chaos in the market, but the deal had irresistible short-term attractions for him. He would get a good price for the 23 million ounces of silver, and, just as important, the exchange would mean that the largest part of his short position on the market would be cancelled (as would 4,600 of the Hunts' long contracts – the equivalent of 23 million ounces). That meant that the margin calls would be drastically reduced and Jarecki would no longer have to worry about his lines of credit at the banks. For their part, the Hunts would be enabled to pay off their $50-million loan early and have their collateral, the 10.7 million ounces of silver, back. The deal was an exercise in mutual self-interest, and, when the Hunts accepted it, with one great bound Henry Jarecki was free; the threat to his beloved Mocatta was removed.

The complication, however, was the silver itself. Mocatta had 23 million ounces available to complete the deal, but by no means all of it in the form of bullion bars. Some of the silver had been leased profitably to industrial companies, such as Du Pont. Millions of ounces were in bags of coins with 725 ounces' weight of silver, which Jarecki had deposited as collateral as banks. The actual bullion content of the vast deal was exactly 12,409,907 ounces, to be delivered in London and Zurich as well as New York, and when the remaining elements of the deal were consummated early in October, the Hunts were still complaining; they said they had been short-changed on the silver in the coin bags. But it was still a very big deal indeed: 23 million ounces of silver at $16.80 an ounce. That was worth $385 million, and Jarecki's position was transformed. One month he was desperately short of cash; the next month it was coming out of his ears.

There was just one surprise: in completing the deal, the Hunts announced that their side of the bargain would be met by a company called IMIC, so *that* secret was thoroughly blown. The papers were finally signed in early October, and when Jarecki announced it to his colleagues on Comex, many of them thought they noticed that he was less vocal about the need to act against the Hunts than he had been in September. The shrewdest dealers only asked whether all the silver bullion would be delivered from the Comex warehouse – if it were, someone would be badly squeezed in December 1979. But Jarecki assured the real professionals that only a small proportion was being delivered in New York.

Henry Jarecki remained convinced that the ultimate goal of the Hunts was a corner, not in December but maybe in March 1980. Fears of a potential squeeze or corner in the silver market were also spreading in Washington, as well they might have been, because the CFTC's commissioners, in their surveillance briefings, had been warned to suspect the worst by their director of markets, John Meilke. On September 28 Meilke said: 'If people are accumulating positions and letting out rumours and taking actions on the floor which raise prices, that would be manipulation.' And that was an accurate description of Waltuch's behaviour. Meilke continued: 'I'm leaning toward position limits, but that would require the declaration of a market emergency.' James Stone and Read Dunn shared Meilke's concern. When the commissioners held another surveillance meeting on October 12, Dunn expressed 'such a helpless feeling at not knowing what is going on. The commission must do something.' Dunn added: 'We are getting on the spot. People are asking me, "What are you guys going to do?"'

Dunn had just returned from Colorado, where he had been a guest at the conference of the Public Securities Association, along with some of the senior commodities traders from Chicago. In Colorado, Dunn had arranged to have breakfast with one of the biggest traders of them all – Warren Leibig, who represented the trade in grain, the commodity that really matters in Chicago (where silver amounts to no more than 10 per cent of the business). Leibig's conversation was a revelation to Dunn, and he described it to me some months later. 'Leibig explained that big grain traders were worried that the chaos in the silver market would slop over into their own. Leibig said that he always believed that no one was bigger than the market, but what was happening in silver was making him wonder. He was also worried that suspicion about the silver market would cause the public to turn away from all commodity markets, or force more federal regulations on them. Leibig told me: "We would rather see the silver market closed than have that happen." It was astonishing. I, a federal regulator, was actually being encouraged to do something by these erstwhile laissez-fairers.'

But how was the CFTC to intervene? If it were to do it boldly, Dunn believed that it could do nothing less than declare a market emergency. 'That is fairly well defined in commodity law,' he says, 'and we looked at the definition most carefully. A national emergency may be declared if it appears that the forces of supply and demand can no longer operate effectively. My interpretation was that it applied to acts of war or the breakdown of the transport system, but not to economic factors.' But even if Dunn and Stone had decided on a bold course of action, they knew that Robert Martin and David Gartner would block it. As far as public action was concerned, the CFTC was impotent.

Martin and Gartner were out of sympathy even with those few proposals Stone and Dunn thought were practicable. For example, Stone had suggested that Bunker and Herbert's silver positions be aggregated for reporting purposes, thus contradicting the brothers' unconvincing assertion that they traded separately; but he could not convert Martin, who foresaw such action as the prelude to another exhausting legal dispute. A second idea sounded more promising: placing position limits in the silver market, not unlike those on soybeans. Since the four largest silver traders controlled 55 per cent of the open interest in the markets – with the Hunts and their allies controlling perhaps 95 per cent of the long side – limits would certainly apply to the Hunts and the Swiss buyers. The idea of how best to get the limits imposed was discussed informally between Stone and Dunn, who now held their discussions in the privacy of the chairman's office, where they could not be shot down by the opposition. Oddly, then, the idea first surfaced in public at an open meeting of the commission on October 16, when it was raised by the unlikely figure of David Gartner, who suggested that the staff prepare another paper on position limits.

Stone was convinced that Gartner's apparently radical proposal was a delaying tactic. If the staff did recommend position limits, and the commissioners agreed, public hearings would necessarily follow, and those would take months. Stone and Dunn, on the other hand, wanted action to be taken quickly, and they had decided that their only option was to persuade the exchanges themselves to take immediate action.

Stone's message – that the exchanges should act – was passed in Chicago to Robert Wilmouth, a banker by trade (he had run the Crocker National Bank in San Francisco), a big, garrulous man. Among his business acquaintances are Bunker and Herbert Hunt, from whom Wilmouth had personally heard about their involvement with the big new buyer called IMIC, even before the CFTC knew of it. But the information had not been volunteered; Wilmouth was told only when he asked. 'They're very reliable, honest businessmen, but they do massage the truth a little bit unless you're very specific in the question you ask,' he says. Not that Wilmouth was blind to the danger presented to his exchange by the Hunts. 'There was the possibility for them to corner the market . . . the potential.'

In October the Hunts received a volley of inquiries about IMIC. Fearing that they were about to denude the warehouses of silver, the CFTC asked on October 10 whether the Hunts had accumulated any large positions in the unregulated cash market for silver. Wilmouth contacted the Hunts, too, because, as Warren Leibig had told Dunn, the Chicago Board of Trade were anxious about their intentions. Like Comex, the Board of Trade had sharply increased the margin requirement for buyers of silver contracts, but this had had no noticeable deterrent effect except on the amateur speculators, who bought a mere handful of contracts. The board even worried that the brothers might be masterminding the Banque Populaire Suisse purchases. When they spoke to Wilmouth, Bunker and Herbert Hunt assuaged his fears by agreeing that they would not buy any more futures contracts in Chicago. However, with the sickening feeling that they had been there before, the Board of Trade next discovered that the Hunt children were entering the market. Houston Hunt,

Bunker's son, who was now all of twenty-one years old, had bought 1,700 contracts in a nearby future, offsetting them with 1,700 short contracts in a more distant month. When the board members heard this on October 18, their patience almost ran out. They seriously discussed the introduction of a rule – known as liquidation-only trading – that would prevent speculators buying any additional long contracts in the market; under the rule, they would be able to sell only what they already owned. The board withdrew from this brink, however; it would have effectively closed their silver market, driving the business – and the dealers' commissions with it – to New York and London.

But Wilmouth was told to have another word with the Hunts, so he telephoned Bunker and Herbert in Dallas and they agreed to fly to Chicago the following Monday, October 22. When the three men met, the Hunts were so emollient that Wilmouth suggested they talk to the CFTC. Wilmouth himself called Read Dunn to say that Bunker and Herbert Hunt had assured him that they had no undisclosed futures positions, either in the United States or in any foreign trading company. Herbert repeated the assurances, and then Bunker came on the line. It is the first instance of Bunker's showing any concern about the impact either the agency or the market might have on his plans for silver, though nothing had yet happened to cause him to doubt his ability to deal with them. Bunker asked Dunn if they could meet to discuss 'areas of mutual interest'. Dunn suggested his office, at three p.m. the following day.

Bunker arrived in Washington a little early, and passed the time with Dunn's colleague, Robert Martin. 'I remember him saying how he was all for free enterprise, and how he did all his own analysis for silver. He was certainly not Machiavellian. Indeed, I got to thinking after he left: if I were a Hunt, I wouldn't have to have all my money in banks, and I sure as hell wouldn't want it in dollar bills. I think I might have arrived at the same position as they did,' recalls Martin.

Bunker's subsequent conversation with Dunn was no less amicable, as is clear from a note taken by a member of the staff. As an example of Bunker's being simultaneously frank and evasive, the note is worth repeating at length.

> Mr Hunt explained that he and his brother, Herbert, had been requested by the Chicago Board of Trade to meet with exchange officials. He said the exchange had questioned him about the Hunts' silver trading. Hunt maintained that he and his brother trade futures independently of one another.
>
> He commented that he thought one of the biggest problems with the silver futures market right now was the high level of margins. Anyone who wanted to

buy silver would have to pay an unusually large amount of money to acquire a single futures contract.

Mr Hunt said that he had long positions in the futures market because he had thought for a long time that the silver market was ready for a substantial upward price movement. This is principally due to the fact that for years the consumption of silver has exceeded production. Over the long term, he expects the gold/silver ratio to decrease to about 5:1. This may not occur in the near future, but in several years it is not unrealistic, in his assessment.

Hunt said he could not understand why anyone would want to be short silver. He said he trades in almost all markets from the long side. He very rarely established a short position except as part of a spread. Hunt and his brother own a substantial quantity of silver that they acquired 4 or 5 years ago. This silver is included in the Chicago Board of Trade and Comex certificated stocks. He said it is located at the First National Bank of Chicago, the Citibank, and Chase Manhattan Bank in New York. He once thought of moving it to Texas, but found out he would have to pay a sales tax if he did so.

Mr Hunt said he did not want to do anything that would be detrimental to the futures market. He said that the futures market had been good to him over the years. Therefore, he and his brother will try to avoid causing any problems. Hunt said that although he and his brother were unwilling to sell the silver bullion they owned because of tax considerations, they would be willing to swap certificated silver stocks for noncertificated silver. He cited, as an example of the steps they were willing to take, the EFPs for silver that they had arranged with Mocatta. Hunt did not think anyone else could have made a deal like that. He said his brother Herbert worked out the details.

The Hunts have also been exchanging vault receipts for silver in New York and Chicago for equal quantities of silver in London and Zurich. They have not shipped any silver out of the United States. He said by making these trades of physical silver they were saving others the cost of shipping silver to the United States. He also indicated, however, he tended to prefer silver located in Europe. He said he was afraid the U.S. government might expropriate silver from individuals as it did in the 1930s, when individual citizens were no longer permitted to own gold.

When asked what the CFTC might expect from IMIC, he said that unless the silver market breaks in price it is not likely that they will add new long positions to acquire additional silver. He said that high interest rates of 16 per cent make him think twice before he will purchase additional silver.

Hunt said the trading decisions of IMIC are made by the board of directors, of which he is a member. Hunt, his brother, and two others meet about once a month to discuss the IMIC investments. They also talk frequently over the phone about IMIC trading.

Hunt said he has only met one of the two Saudi Arabians who are involved in IMIC. He has met Ali Bin Mussalam on a number of occasions. He has not met Mohammed Aboud al-Amoudi, but he believes his brother, Herbert, has met him at least once. These two Saudis travel around the world frequently. They often turn up in New York, Paris, and London.

Hunt said these are the only two Arabs he knows are investing in the silver market. However, he has reason to believe that there are a number of other wealthy individuals who are acquiring silver. He based that statement on conversations with Arab individuals that he has met on his various trips to Europe. He said a number of individuals have asked him about the silver market and have indicated that they are also investing. He said that the Arabs have been purchasing gold for the last 2 or 3 years, and he thinks recently they have moved into silver as well. Arabs, he explained, are afraid of paper assets. They are unwilling to invest in corporations because they don't trust the instrument of the stock certificates. They prefer to invest in real estate, gold and other tangible assets.

Hunt said that he expects to roll forward the long futures positions that he is carrying in his own name. This is how he has been trading in the silver market for the last few years. Normally he rolls his long position forward as that position approaches the spot month. He has held his long position in the March Comex futures, however, for quite a few months. He is attempting to get a long-term capital gain from that position. Consequently, he does not plan on rolling it forward until after the beginning of the year.

Commissioner Dunn thanked Mr Hunt for coming to Washington to visit with the CFTC. He said because of the volatile and rapid price run-up that had occurred in silver over the past two months, the Commission has been concerned with the market. Questions have been raised as to whether silver prices are reflecting legitimate demand for silver or whether someone is forcing them up artificially. He said the Commission had noted that the Hunt positions were large relative to the market, even larger positions than the Hunts normally carry.

Mr Hunt acknowledged that perhaps they are larger. Commissioner Dunn commented that one of the alternatives the Commission was considering to deal with the silver market was the imposition of speculative position limits. Mr Hunt commented that he hoped no limits or artificial restraints would be imposed on the market, particularly not before the first of the year. He said he would incur a substantial tax position if he had to liquidate before the new tax year.

Bunker left the CFTC for National Airport without a reservation for his flight back to Dallas, saying he would take the first flight that came along – a folksiness that often disarmed men so much less rich than himself. It would have been impossible for Dunn to know exactly to what extent Bunker's memory had failed him again: about his trading relationship with Herbert, about his meetings with his Saudi allies, and about his intentions to acquire more silver. Dunn had no evidence to enable him to contradict Bunker, but he had not changed his mind. He remained convinced that the exchanges must do something to control speculation in silver.

Dunn did not have long to wait. Three days later a special meeting of the directors of the Chicago Board of Trade invoked temporary emergency powers and unilaterally imposed position limits. In retrospect, Wilmouth wished they had imposed them right at the start, when the Chicago silver market opened in 1969, but nobody then had thought they would be necessary in a worldwide market. Now the directors ordered that no speculator could hold more than 600 contracts, net long or net short. Thus, if a speculator had 4,000 long contracts, he must now balance the position with 3,400 short contracts. Anyone with more than 600 contracts was ordered to reduce his position – by April Fool's Day, 1980.

The action was dramatic; the reason given was less so. It alluded to the existence of 'a few entities, backed by sufficient reserves, who may threaten fair and orderly trading,' and spoke of 'an unprecedented number of contracts being used as vehicles to acquire bullion.' The real concern was more specific than that. The Board of Trade had acted because it was worried about the essential mechanism of the market, the clearinghouse. Daily margin calls had grown so large that the board thought that one of the clearinghouse members might not be able to meet the strain imposed by a default. Read Dunn understood these fears. 'I was shocked,' he told his colleagues when the Board of Trade's action was reported to them. 'I now realize there are aspects and effects of this position which strike at the foundations of the system.' Dunn was delighted when he heard that Chicago had imposed position limits: 'tremendous precedential value,' he later said.

Bunker Hunt thought that, too – but he was absolutely outraged, and not only because he would have to make substantial adjustments in his silver holdings in Chicago. (His own position was net long, 3,100 contracts.) When he had seen Wilmouth only three days earlier, position limits had not seemed likely. Bunker could hardly believe the news when Wilmouth told him. 'You can't do it,' he spluttered. 'You wouldn't dare. You're the last bastion of free enterprise in the world.'

By the time he telephoned Read Dunn to complain to him, Bunker could hardly contain himself. 'This is like Libya. They're taking my property away,' he wailed. But unlike Libya, the Board of Trade did regard its market as the last bastion of free enterprise in the world, and even at the cost of imposing some limitations on the market, the Board of Trade did not propose to allow anyone, not even Bunker and Herbert Hunt, to destroy its reputation.

The Chicago Board of Trade's placing of position limits was the first of the rule changes that were to turn Bunker Hunt, his relations, and his allies into much aggrieved men. Bunker would fulminate against markets that changed the rules at any available opportunity, because he believed the men running them were conspiring against him; he stated his case crisply to one of the most assiduous students of the Hunt family in the American press, Allen Pusey of the Dallas *Morning News*. 'The fact of the matter is,' said Bunker, 'that the home-town boys who run the markets don't want anybody from out of town to make any money in their markets. If there's any money to be made off the market, they expect to get theirs. And some joker from Dallas, or even St Louis . . . he's not supposed to make any money out of them. I think that's their whole philosophy. I may be wrong about it, but under the guise of regulating, they're manipulating the market.'

Bunker Hunt's basic complaint was that the 'home-town boys' were all on the side of the sellers of silver against the buyers, the bulls like Bunker and his friends. 'The long aren't represented,' Bunker told Pusey. 'You've got the shorts, you've got the suppliers, and you've got the brokerage houses represented, and they're good buddies with the shorts. Then you've got the longs, and they're the terrible ogres who are messing up their playhouse. I think that's their real problem.'

The way the markets were run was Bunker's real problem, too – a problem that had first revealed itself in Chicago, was bound to spread to New York, and was going to get worse.

Chapter 9

November 1979–January 1980: Changing the Rules

The Commodity Exchange Corporation in New York, known more familiarly just as Comex, prides itself on its size: trading takes place under one of the largest unsupported ceilings in the world; it is the biggest metals market in the business, trading gold as well as silver. And since Bunker Hunt was the biggest speculator in the business, it was inevitable that his most significant confrontation would be with Comex in New York.

Bunker was to reserve for Comex his most venomous charges of conspiracy against himself and his friends. Yet the strangest aspect of the behaviour of the men who ran the New York market was the freedom and time they allowed the silver bulls to establish their massive positions. One explanation is that in New York self-interest was defined in a subtly different way than in Chicago. At the Board of Trade, the silver market hardly matters, but at Comex a substantial part of the trading – and thus the incomes of the professionals – comes from silver transactions. The Board of Trade's governing body could contemplate closing the market if the new rules about position limits did not work and the Hunts continued to distort the market; in New York, closure was unthinkable. 'Closure would hurt Chicago, but it would kill Comex,' Read Dunn observed. James Stone and Dunn in Washington had been prodding Comex to introduce position limits, too, but it was not until action was taken in Chicago that the CFTC fully understood the contrasting motivations in the two markets.

What happened at Comex after October 1979 provides evidence with which to judge the charge that the Hunts and their friends in Paris, Geneva, and Jeddah were cheated in the silver market.

The Board of Governors of Comex is responsible for self-regulation in the market, and it is composed of representatives from the three sectors of the market. There are commission houses, like E. F. Hutton and Shearson, for which silver trading is only a small part of their business, jam on the bread; then there are bullion dealers, like Mocatta and Philipp Brothers (the Engelhard subsidiary), for whom the market is a place where they can hedge the value of their bullion, and on which they depend for their lucrative arbitrage business. Last, there are the floor traders, known as the locals or, more picturesquely, as the scalpers, whose income depends heavily on the silver market. One of these traders, Lowell Minz, was chairman of Comex's Board of Governors.

The board makes the decisions, but it is advised by a staff. The staff, which oversees the daily operations of the market, was headed by Comex's president, a lawyer in his mid-thirties named Lee Berendt. Berendt, a self-effacing man, lacked the experience of his opposite number in Chicago, but more than that, he lacked the clout of a Robert Wilmouth.

In an attempt to allay any suspicion that Comex is run by the market for the market, there are also two custodians of the public interest on the board. One of these, in the fall of 1979, was William Simon. He had been secretary of the treasury under President Gerald Ford, and had been thought a great catch by Comex; unfortunately, he found the job arduous and unrewarding, and as the winter approached he became more interested in presidential politics. Simon did not stay long.

The other public member of the board was Dr Andrew Brimmer, who had been a member of the Board of Governors of the Federal Reserve, and was well respected in Washington. Senator William Proxmire, chairman of the Senate Banking Committee, thought Brimmer a suitable candidate for the chairmanship of the Federal Reserve, which would have made him by far the most influential black member of the financial community. But President Carter had not agreed with Proxmire, and Brimmer worked as a financial consultant with a suite of offices in Watergate (the same Washington office building whose name is now synonymous with political skulduggery), and a seat on various boards, including those of United Airlines and Comex.

Early in October 1979 Dr Brimmer observed that the conflicts of interest between the various market participants on the Comex board were becoming more apparent. Some of the commission houses and bullion dealers were growing impatient at the absence of action in the face of the appalling possibility that there would not be enough silver in the Comex warehouse to satisfy the voracious demands for the delivery of silver from the Hunts and the Geneva speculators, who had become known generically as 'foreign investors'. One of the bullion dealers, Philipp Brothers, actually proposed a vigorous counterattack against the speculators, suggesting a meeting of the clearinghouse on October 2, that the speculators no longer be allowed to buy futures contracts on margin. The aim was to remove any threat to the clearinghouse by making silver a cash business, with no credit allowed. No action was taken on the Philipp Brothers proposal, but it was an augury.

On October 3 the board decided that divisions of opinion were undermining its ability to act; the members forecast – with devastating accuracy, as it turned out – that the conflicts of interest would inevitably create suspicion that the board was biased in favour of the shorts. So the board transferred responsibility for regulation of the silver market to a Special Silver Committee, composed of members who had no interest in the silver market; and as chairman it appointed its most disinterested member of all, Dr Andrew Brimmer.

Dr Brimmer's position was clearly crucial, and any uninformed observer taking a guess at his attitude might well conclude that as an American black he would sympathize with the idea of positive federal action to deal with the uncertainties and suspicions in the silver market – such action as the federal government had taken on civil rights. When we met in his office in Watergate, Dr Brimmer quickly disabused me of such a superficial notion. He is a schoolmasterly figure, and lectured me on the virtues of self-regulation in the market. Perhaps it should have been obvious: he would not have taken the job if he had not believed the exchanges should govern themselves. Andrew Brimmer was no Trojan horse. 'I didn't think: what is the philosophy of the markets?' he says. 'I just wanted to make certain that regulatory responsibilities were not pursued to a conclusion which would prevent the working of the marketplace. So I leaned against any suggestion that the market be closed or severely limited.' In doing so, Dr Brimmer faithfully reflected the views of a majority of the board, and invested them with respectability.

Dr Brimmer was much too busy that fall of 1979 to devote his full attention to the problem. 'I couldn't tell you I thought about silver first thing in the morning or last thing at night,' he says. Other jobs intruded on the Special Silver Committee's business. At one meeting, Dr Brimmer left the room so often to make phone calls that Lee Berendt, who had observed only the exits, not the calls, leaned over and asked him solicitously whether he was all right.

The committee's specific concern was that there would not be enough silver in the warehouse in December to meet all demands for delivery. It had a full armoury of weapons to deal with the crisis, quite apart from the higher margins that had been introduced in September. It could impose position limits, or insist that trading be for liquidation only – meaning that speculators could sell only what they already had. The committee's members considered both possibilities and rejected both. Dr Brimmer and his colleagues were persuaded that the intentions of the Hunts, and of the 'foreign investors' under Norton Waltuch's umbrella at Conti Commodity Services, were not dishonourable. After all, on October 25 Conti's chairman, Walter Goldschmidt, had soothed the committee by his assurance that Naji Nahas and the Banque Populaire would take no new positions, and that they would not embarrass Comex by insisting on delivery of their December contracts. Those assurances seemed to remove any reason for precipitate action. Despite pressure from the CFTC, Dr Brimmer's attitude did not change after the Chicago Board of Trade imposed its position limits. That Comex did not intend to do James Stone's job for him is clear enough from this extract from the minutes of a board meeting on October 29: 'Both Mr Minz [the chairman] and Mr Berendt [the president] told the CFTC that Comex, as the world's largest metals futures market, must act in the best interests of all its market participants on the basis of its own independent and professional judgment. . . . Dr Brimmer, in response to questions, stated that the Special Silver Committee had considered imposing position limits, but that a substantial majority of the Committee thought that position limits were inappropriate at that time.'

Dr Brimmer believed that increased margin payments would be strong enough medicine, and during a break in that board meeting, his committee ordered that any speculator with more than 251 contracts must pay margin of $30,000 for each future contract. This was costly for the Hunts, Nahas, and the Banque Populaire group, who would have to borrow to finance the new margin requirements. But the decision to concentrate on margins was a disappointment to Stone and Dunn in Washington, who had wanted Comex to follow the example of the Chicago Board of Trade. 'Our plan at the end of October to have the markets impose position limits was the right one, but Read and I did not have the clout to persuade the Comex board of that,' Stone told me later.

In fact, Dr Brimmer's committee had a meeting with Herbert Hunt on November 6 that made them feel almost sanguine. They reported: 'Mr Hunt advised the Committee that he had never met or spoken to the large foreign interests in the silver market. Mr Hunt expressed his objections to the recent margin increases that had been implemented by the Committee and indicated his willingness to cooperate with the exchange.' The committee was so impressed that it delayed the date on which the new margin payments had to be made to February 4, 1980. Unfortunately, they omitted to ask whether *Bunker* Hunt had met or spoken to 'the large foreign interests'. They were not men of a suspicious nature.

Although Herbert Hunt had satisfied Dr Brimmer and his colleagues, they had failed to appease him, for the next day he was in Washington to complain to Read Dunn about the increased margins, and to outline the belief that was to obsess the Hunt brothers in the coming months: that there was a conspiracy against speculative bulls such as themselves. Dunn reported: 'He understands that certain members of these exchanges hold large short positions. Adoption of speculative limits and the margin requirements proposed would benefit these exchange members to the detriment of non-members like himself.' Not that there was any shortage of silver; Herbert coolly informed Dunn that Engelhard had offered him 40 million ounces of silver at the current price, $16.30 an ounce. But Herbert's main concern was the exchanges. He asked Dunn to organize CFTC hearings into Comex's new rules. He seemed conveniently to have forgotten that only two years earlier he and Bunker had insisted that it was the CFTC that was victimizing them; still, any port in a storm.

Read Dunn remained scrupulously polite, refraining from adding to Herbert Hunt's worries by admitting that he thought Comex had done too little, not too much. Nor was he about to reveal that Comex was complaining to two other CFTC commissioners, Robert Martin and David Gartner, about the pressure that Dunn and Stone were applying to them. Stone and Dunn inferred from these complaints that their pressure was having some effect. When they were rebuffed at the end of October, both thought Comex would adopt position limits in a couple of weeks. But two weeks went by and nothing happened; then another fortnight, and still nothing. 'Read and I had grown tired of waiting from mid-November,' says Stone, but the chairman of the CFTC had to contain his impatience. The commission lacked the power to drag the reluctant exchange into more positive self-regulation unless it could threaten a market emergency, and Stone knew that as long as Martin and Gartner continued to believe that the markets should be allowed to decide what to do, the commission would remain split, two votes to two.

While the CFTC remained inert, Bunker Hunt continued to cut a swath through the silver market. He added 6 million ounces of silver to his stockpile by taking delivery of 1,200 contracts in December. In one of his conversations with Read Dunn (they were taking on the regularity of a business relationship), Bunker announced that he would be taking delivery of even more silver in March. But Bunker's plunder of the silver stock in December was small stuff compared to that of the 'foreign investors'. Dr Brimmer had specifically under-

Bunker (*right*) and Herbert Hunt come to Washington: "Are they not citizens of the United States?"

H. L. Hunt (*right*) with his boys: the sons admired the father rather more than the father admired the sons.

Crown Prince Fahd of Saudia Arabia: a gambler who loves to play, and loses fabulous sums.

Prince Abdullah: a life of opulence in the desert.

Naji Nahas (*left*) and Mahmoud Fustok (*right*): the middlemen confer at Longchamp.

Left: Jerome Smith: the prophet of silver profits in the seventies.
Right: Paul Volcker: never looking the central banker, and never failing to behave like one.

stood from Conti Commodities that they would not take delivery in December, but between them, the Banque Populaire Suisse, Gillian Financial, and Naji Nahas scooped no less than 16,820,000 ounces out of the warehouse in New York. There was no squeeze, however; having hurriedly replenished the Comex stocks, the shorts were able to meet all demands for delivery. A squeeze had now ceased to be a problem – until March 1980, at least. The evidence that Conti's promises were unreliable was more serious. Norton Waltuch himself took delivery of 100 contracts in December.

Comex had had its fill of Waltuch. His antics in the pit, ostentatiously bidding the price as high as it could possibly go, had started in mid-August and were already legend. 'Someday they'll make a movie out of this,' he announced during one day's buying spree. In November, Comex had tried to write him out of the script. Lee Berendt, on behalf of the Special Silver Committee, asked Waltuch's boss, Walter Goldschmidt, to keep him away from the silver pit. Goldschmidt protested; since Waltuch was a member of the exchange, the request was improper. Conti agreed only to ration Waltuch's appearances. Rationing took the form of Waltuch's appearing just before the market closed to remind everyone that he was still a big bull. And he continued to distort the silver price by bidding it up recklessly.

Angered by the behaviour of the 'foreign investors', Dr Brimmer's committee on December 4 reconsidered their opposition to position limits. But that day they had news that persuaded them to delay action once more. The mysterious Naji Nahas had agreed to meet them, within a week, to discuss his holdings. Two weeks later, on December 18, when Nahas finally made his rendezvous, he denied that there was any collusion between himself and the other speculators in Geneva. Dr Brimmer commented: 'I believed him; at the time there was no evidence to demonstrate otherwise.' But he was disturbed by one observation. 'It was clear that Nahas didn't understand the rules of the market. To be frank, he didn't know much about silver, even though he had traded in other commodities.' Position limits were back on the agenda once again.

In the unlikely event that Dr Brimmer had been a student of the Beirut press, his belief in Nahas's denials might have been shaken. It would be unreasonable, of course, to complain that Comex did not subscribe to a well-informed left-wing Lebanese newsletter, written in English, called *An Nahar Arab Report*, but had they done so, Nahas might have been asked about an article in the issue of December 10, which contained an anonymous story headlined SAUDI PRINCE IS MYSTERY SILVER BUYER. The article was the first evidence in

English, as far as I know, of the involvement of the Saudi royal family. It read:

> A love of horses has led to a partnership that has brought together a Saudi Prince and American billionaire in an attempt to capture a sizeable portion of the world silver market. A number of aircraft have been chartered by unnamed Arab buyers to fly up to 1,600 tons of silver bullion from the United States to Switzerland in coming months. *An Nahar* is now able to name the principal Arab buyer.
>
> Bunker Hunt, the Texas billionaire, is well known for his love of horses, especially pure bred Arab horses; he had been buying and breeding Arab stallions for a number of years. Another of his passionate interests over the past 18 months has been to lay his hands on as much silver in production as his means would allow. His conviction was – and still is – that silver is undervalued when judged by its use in industry when compared with the industrial market for gold. Bunker Hunt has been buying silver bullion and shares in silver mines for well over a year and a half.
>
> His activities as an owner and breeder of horses brought Bunker Hunt into contact with another lover of horses who had comparable financial weight. He is Prince Abdullah of Saudi Arabia, the commander of the National Guard and the third most powerful personage in the Kingdom after King Khalid and Crown Prince Fahd.
>
> Discussion with Bunker Hunt over future prospects for precious metals convinced Prince Abdullah of the inevitability of a major increase in the price of silver in 1979 and through into 1980. And silver is something Prince Abdullah knows well – until the late King Faisal modernized Saudi Arabia's finances, silver Maria Theresa thalers were the standard of value in the Kingdom. With inflation eating into paper currencies, the idea of a return to silver coins for Saudi Arabia cannot have been far from Prince Abdullah's mind.
>
> After a review for the potential for increases in the price of silver and the cementing of a friendship which began with their mutual passion for fine horses, the two men decided to establish a common fund with the specific purpose of buying and holding silver, for sale only after the price reached $25.00 an ounce at the end of 1979 or early in 1980. The size of the fund cannot be assessed with accuracy, but an educated guess puts the figures at $500 million for equity financing. Leverage has undoubtedly entered the picture, and, considering that 50 per cent would be a good safety margin, it is possible that $1 billion has been put to work in the silver market for the account of the two men.

In retrospect, the details of *An Nahar*'s report appear remarkably accurate, especially the reference to flying the 1,600 tons of bullion from the United States to Europe, but the most revealing item concerns the intentions of the group: the suggestion that their target price was $25. Bunker Hunt later adjusted that target downward. 'On my side, I wish the market had never gone over $20. That would have been much better,' he told the Dallas *Morning News* the following summer. Coincidentally, that was the price on December 11, the day after *An Nahar*'s report was published. But events were finally beginning to move out of Bunker's control.

The market men might not have noticed *An Nahar*'s report, but they were reading other newspapers. World news moves commodity markets; that is why every dealing room has a Reuter wire-service machine. When news is good, prices tend to move down; and when it is bad, they tend to move up. A crisis in the Middle East, or Eastern Europe, or the minerally strategic parts of southern Africa always causes the price to rise. And in the fall of 1979 the news was already bad; it was to get much worse. On November 4 the staff of the American Embassy in Tehran had been taken hostage. Then, in late November, a group of Saudi dissidents seized the Great Mosque in Mecca, which contains the holy Kaaba and is the most sacred shrine in Islam. The siege that followed gave rise to concern about the internal stability of Saudi Arabia, the source of one quarter of the West's oil. Events in Mecca did not prevent the members of OPEC – the cartel formed by the governments of the oil-producing nations – from increasing the oil price for the second time in six months. That meant more inflation, in itself a boost to the price of silver. At Christmas the sense of external insecurity was confirmed by the Russian invasion of Afghanistan, and President Carter's insistence that economic sanctions should be imposed, internationally, against Iran. In any normal month in the silver market, this sequence of appalling events would have sent the price up, though not necessarily out of control. But December 1979 was not a normal month. In South America an ambitious young man was about to discover the meaning of that old adage 'He who sells what isn't his'n, pays it up or go to prison'. His plight sent the silver price spiralling away again, just as it had done in September.

There is nothing the market enjoys more than gossip about a loser, and in November 1979 a particularly big one was in prospect. Since the rumour was based largely on ignorance, there were not enough facts to spoil a good story, but the full, gory details emerged later. The subject was an undercapitalized, understaffed department of the Ministry of Commerce in Lima, Peru – Minero Perú Comercial (Minpeco, for short). But only a few insiders at a couple of commission houses in New York knew the identity of the ultimate victim of the market's rumours: a fat little man in his early thirties named Ismael Fonseca.

Fonseca had hoped to become a central banker, and had worked for a while at the Banco de la Nación, Peru's state-owned national bank. But by his mid-twenties he had not shown the promise necessary even in a South American central bank, and had been 'released'. Lowering his sights, he had ended up in Minpeco, and in April 1979 Fonseca was sent to New York to 'learn' the futures market from the brokers who did most of the Peruvian business – Merrill Lynch and E. F. Hutton.

His course was in the art of hedging: Minpeco is not in the business of speculation. The Commerce Ministry has a monopoly on the sale of Peruvian minerals, and Minpeco's functions are quite clear: it is the trading and shipping organization responsible for getting ore to refineries and for receiving prevailing world prices for the refined product, whether lead, zinc, copper, or silver. Silver is a by-product from those other base metals, but their volume of production is large enough to make Peru the world's third- or fourth-largest producer of silver (it exchanges positions with Canada). It was natural enough, therefore, that Minpeco should want one of its junior executives to grasp the fundamentals of the silver futures market.

These fundamentals were certainly beyond the executive director of Minpeco, Juan Munir, a pleasant, fifty-one-year-old civil servant whose adroit political manoeuvres had enabled him to survive a succession of military dictatorships unscathed. The implications of the rise in the silver price in the American and London markets escaped Munir, but Fonseca studied them with the passion of a newly made expert. He was still in New York in August, when the price began to move up fast – too fast, he thought. And on his return to Lima, Fonseca conceived a plan that would demonstrate to his superiors that, whatever they had thought at the central bank, he was not a man to be ignored. His New York expertise had made him arrogant, and his contempt was directed at the bosses of Minpeco. 'He always thought he knew best,' said Munir later. Fonseca certainly saw no reason why he should share the credit for the coup he was planning with the Minpeco board.

Fonseca knew in September that Minpeco would have only 3 million ounces of silver that could be guaranteed for delivery later in the year. The conventional action for a man in his position would be a hedge, to lock in the price. He ought to have gone short by 3 million ounces in the December contract to protect Peruvian silver producers against a fall in price. But Fonseca was convinced that the market had experienced a neurotic flurry; at $17.45 he was sure the price was too high. In fact, Fonseca was so convinced that it was too high that instead of entering contracts to sell only 3 million ounces, he added another 10 million for good measure, making his short position in the December contract no less than 13 million ounces, of which only 3 million were hedged. On that unhedged 10 million ounces he hoped to make a killing.

In October the market confirmed his judgment. As the price eased, variation margin payments flowing into the Minpeco account showed a healthy surplus of $6 million. It was good, but not a killing; Fonseca kept the news to himself. He ordered that all telexes about silver hedging be delivered to him personally, keeping Munir in blissful ignorance of Minpeco's activities. Later Munir was to outline his own version of the Eichmann defence. 'I used to make the rounds of the different departments each day, and I'd say to Fonseca: "How's things?" and he'd say: "Fine, nothing special." What was I supposed to do? Read every piece of paper?'

Had he read the telexes late in November, Munir would have seen that as the price rose again, Fonseca's $6-million credit was soon eaten away. As it continued to rise in early December, the brokers began to ask for cash to cover the variation margin on the short position. And that was when the rumours began. The contracts were huge, it was said, and they were not properly hedged. If the price continued to rise, the holder would be forced to cover his short contracts by buying long contracts. He might even default. Whatever happened, the price would continue going up.

One lesson Fonseca had not been taught in New York was how to take a loss. It was, perhaps, not part of the curriculum, since any loss would be put down to Minpeco, which was not in business to make losses. When the silver price rose, Fonseca faced a choice: he could either confess, or he could gamble. There are no prizes for guessing that Fonseca gambled. He called on the Banco de la Nación for loans, not mentioning silver at all, but offering copper, lead, and zinc contracts as collateral. But the value he attached to them was higher than the market value – which seemed odd. When Alvaro Meneses, president of the bank, heard of the requests, he began to suspect that all was not well in the Ministry of Commerce. Meneses asked for a complete report on all Minpeco's positions in commodity markets, and soon discovered that Minpeco was contracted to supply 10 million ounces of silver that it did not possess. Munir then had the galling experience of being informed of his department's vulnerability by a man who did not even work in it.

There was a further insult to add to Minpeco's injuries. Fonseca's teachers had also apparently omitted to tell him about a second vital hedge in futures markets, against fluctuations in the value of foreign currencies. Some of his short positions were in London, which caused Minpeco's losses to rise steadily. As the value of the pound strengthened, Minpeco fell a further $4 million in the red.

Even after he had been found out, Fonseca insisted that the silver price would come down and his gamble would pay off. But Fonseca lacked political muscle; Meneses had the advantage of access to the cabinet of military men whose word was law in Peru. Not being gambling men themselves, they sided with their central banker and ordered Minpeco to cover all its short contracts immediately, whatever the loss.

That decision in a relatively obscure corner of South America had a greater impact on the silver market than more prominent events in Iran, Saudi Arabia, or Afghanistan. As soon as the order arrived from Lima, Merrill Lynch and E. F. Hutton scrambled to buy contracts to offset Minpeco's short position. But rumour had informed the traders what Minpeco's dealers were doing, and there were no bargains around. The average price of the long contracts obtained for Minpeco was $25.50 – $8 an ounce more than the price for which Fonseca had contracted to sell the 10 million ounces he did not have in December. The calculation is easy: his little speculation cost $80 million. Mistakes of this magnitude are not easily forgiven in a country like Peru. Juan Munir was sent to jail, and Ismael Fonseca went into hiding.

The disturbing implications of the Peruvian affair were not confined to Lima. They reverberated in Dallas, Texas, as well. When Fonseca's 10-million-ounce short position was finally covered by expensive long positions on December 28, the price of an ounce of silver was $29.35, another unprecedented level – one at which silver-owning families began to reflect on the advantages of cash over heirlooms. Subsequently, the Hunts' grip on the market began to weaken, because once the idea of selling silver became attractive, stocks in the warehouses were more likely to rise than fall, and the market would be less susceptible to a squeeze or corner. Looking back some months later, Henry Jarecki remembered Theo Hook's saying that the Hunts' plan to control the price would have worked if it hadn't been for that 10-million-ounce Peruvian default in December, and the bad news from the Middle East.

Naji Nahas's grasp of the silver market was not great enough for him to understand how higher prices might shrivel his fortune. Nahas was in Paris shortly after Christmas 1979 and was quite unable to contain himself whenever he met an acquaintance. He had, he boasted, made $1.2 *billion* in less than twelve months. One old Beirut friend remembers asking him: 'Don't you think that's too much of a worry?' Not at all, replied Naji, and added there would be more where that came from. Nahas had no reason to believe that his boast was an idle one. By that Christmas he had personally taken delivery of 8,685,000 ounces of silver, which was worth $255 million at the Comex closing price on December 28; and he had 1,162 long contracts that were worth another $170 million. The total is far short of $1.2 billion, but Nahas had other accounts, such as Litardex, or

Gillian Financial, and the exact sums I have referred to applied only to his American holdings. Nahas almost certainly had silver holdings in London, too. But if he wanted to boast that he was a rich man, he need have said no more than that, in the twenty-four hours between December 27 and 28, the value of his acknowledged personal silver holding had risen by $29,714,750.

In Paris by that time, the silver fever had truly taken hold. 'Silver was the talk of all the salons,' says one Lebanese businessman, of a capital where there are still salons. The conversation, conducted more in Arabic than in French, revealed the classic symptoms of the formation of a bubble. The stories exchanged all had the same theme: a junior bank employee, for example, had started with $5,000, and by pyramiding his silver position was now worth more than a million. When two Arabs met at an airport the talk was of silver instead of the weather. And the hero of the stories was the really big winner, Naji Nahas, who had been in the game from the beginning. Silver had become an obsession, and it made doing business very difficult for those who did not share it. One Arab banker recalls the frustration of appointments during which his opposite number would break off to telephone his broker in New York to ask the latest silver price. It was as much a compulsion as following the score in a Test Match, except that it went on for even longer. It was wonderful, easy money.

In Washington, however, the CFTC had a sinking feeling about 1980. The staff had done some sums over Christmas, and when the commissioners heard the results at a surveillance briefing on December 28, they were appalled. The staff could trace ownership by the Hunts and 'foreign investors' of more than 200 million ounces of silver in bullion and futures contracts. 'It's really scary,' commented John Meilke. Read Dunn added up the silver these buyers had in London and Zurich, and came up with a figure of between 250 and 260 million ounces. 'At this rate,' said Dunn, 'in another two or three years, they'll have all the silver in the world.' (Theo Hook thought Dunn's timing was wrong; he now believed they'd have all the deliverable silver by March.)

The grip the Hunts and 'foreign investors' had on the warehouse stocks was frightening: they had half of the Comex stock and 70 per cent in Chicago. 'Is it a market manipulation or do they want to keep it?' Meilke wondered aloud. The question was too theoretical for David Gartner, who said: 'Irrespective of their intentions, if they're cornering the market, they're cornering the market, and that's manipulation.' For public consumption, the CFTC minuted its concern 'that the futures markets might no longer be capable of supplying the large quantities of physical silver being demanded.' That was a discreet way of saying the silver market would be cornered unless someone did something, quick.

Meeting once more on January 4, 1980, the CFTC did the sums again. The price had now shot up to $37.10, and Dunn commented that when he wrote the figures down 'my pencil gets a-shaking'. These figures showed that the combined holdings of the Hunts and the Saudis, plus their hangers-on, in the futures markets were now valued at $2,227,500,000 in New York and $825 million in Chicago. The figures were so gross that the chairman, James Stone, finally gave up on diplomacy and told his colleagues sharply: 'I genuinely think we're reaching the point where it's going to be embarrassing to the commission when somebody looks back at this sometime, and sees that we let somebody hold three billion dollars of silver in a contract that's just going to end. That just toughens my position: that we've got to do something about the metals markets.'

That was no longer idle talk, because David Gartner, who had vigorously opposed CFTC intervention in the markets throughout the previous four months, had now changed his mind. Gartner had decided that if the exchanges themselves did not curb excessive speculation, he could no longer oppose the declaration of an emergency in the silver market. Stone was delighted: 'We had a majority at last. We knew we could now say to Comex that, although we didn't want to do it, we would declare an emergency if they didn't act themselves.'

Even then, the CFTC was anxious to give Comex a last chance to regulate itself. Stone thought that the New York market would be more susceptible to regulation once the new year had begun. He believed – cynically, perhaps – that Comex had not wanted to act in the old tax year because the traders would lose many of the commission payments from speculators who used the silver market to minimize their liability to the Internal Revenue Service before the end of the tax year. (Stone's notion is impossible to prove, but it became widely accepted in Washington later in the year.)

Read Dunn met Dr Andrew Brimmer on January 4 to inform him of the CFTC's new mood, but his sense of urgency did not appear to affect the chairman of Comex's Special Silver Committee, who seemed, by contrast, paralysed by his responsibilities. The Comex board was scheduled to hold an emergency meeting the day before its officials visited Washington, but on January 7 Dr Brimmer's committee still had no recommendations to make. The Comex board had passed the buck to the committee, which had sat and looked at it for three months before passing it back to the board. Denied an opportunity to put off a decision any longer, the board finally accepted position limits, of 500 contracts in each delivery month, though these were not to become effective until February 18. Now it was Dunn's turn to be cynical: 'The free-enterprisers were afraid we really would take over the exchanges – and proper self-regulation was preferable to that.' What the new rule meant was that the 18,000 contracts held by the Hunts and their friends would have to be reduced to 4,000 – in just six weeks.

At the surveillance meeting that preceded the commissioners' talk with the exchanges on January 8, Read Dunn, who, on the basis of another new figure – that the Hunts and their friends now owned 77 per cent of the world's estimated privately held store of silver – was arguing that the need for action was 'very, very clear', interrupted himself to say that he had just had a note saying that Bunker Hunt was at the front desk. 'We're going to have to pass him on the way to our meeting,' one commissioner complained. Robert Martin added that Herbert Hunt had telephoned him to ask if he could attend the meeting with the exchanges, too. 'Tell 'em No,' barked Stone.

So, passing Bunker Hunt, who was bristling with a sense of injustice (he had been told that Dunn would meet him later), the commissioners went along the corridor to meet the exchange officials. Meilke had yet another updated sum for them. The Hunt and 'foreign investors' group, which both the CFTC and Comex now considered as one, owned 280 million ounces of silver, and that, said Meilke, 'creates a threat of a manipulation or corner on the silver market.' Lee Berendt, Comex's president, explained that Comex had introduced position limits and asked the CFTC to state, on the record, that their action was legitimate. A lawyer, Berendt was conscious that the Hunts might sue Comex for instituting new rules that operated retroactively. He was looking for evidence for Comex's defence, just in case.

When Read Dunn saw Bunker Hunt that same afternoon – because Bunker would not go away – their conversation began as though it were a genial gossip over a beer (or, in Bunker's case, a Dr Pepper). They chewed over President Carter's announcement of a grain embargo against the Russians and the state of cotton farming (a mutual interest) before Bunker finally got down to business.

> He asked whether or not the CFTC had disapproved the emergency action taken by Comex. Mr Hunt was told that the Commission had not. He was also told the CFTC would continue to watch the silver market very closely to determine whether any additional action might prove necessary.
>
> Mr Hunt asked whether the CFTC's objective was to raise, lower, or stabilize silver prices. He was told that none of these was the case. Rather the Commission was trying to ensure the silver futures market continued to be a viable market place

reflecting the forces of supply and demand. Mr Hunt also asked whether the CFTC was considering action to shut down the silver market. He was told that the CFTC had taken no such action to date.

Bunker could not have liked what he heard: the phrases 'additional action' and 'to date' were hardly reassuring. Then Read Dunn started to ask questions: What about Bunker's long holding in the Chicago February future?

Hunt stated that he intended to get out of his long positions in February, and on Comex in March, as best he could. He does not intend taking substantial deliveries unless the spreads get out of line. He said that he wanted to act in a legal and responsible manner. He was concerned, however, that with the higher margins and other restrictions there would be no buyers in the market who could absorb the positions he had to sell.

Bunker Hunt's idea of 'legal and responsible' action was, of course, different from Read Dunn's, or even Comex's. While he was talking to Dunn, Bunker's brokers were exploiting a loophole in the new Comex rules. They sold long March 1980 contracts and bought as many long January 1980 contracts as they could – right up to the new position limit of 500 contracts. Comex suspected that Bunker would be taking delivery of that January silver, and since the Arabs were doing something similar, on an even larger scale, the market once more feared that there would not be enough silver in the warehouses to meet all these demands for delivery.

The Arab speculators were being even less subtle than Bunker. On January 8, seventeen new accounts were opened with two brokers – Conti Commodities and ACLI – each for the maximum limit of 500 contracts for new purchases, and they were all to buy more silver: 42.5 million ounces of it. Some of the names were familiar. Advicorp was there, and its executives Jean Jacques Bally, Pierre Alain Hirschy, and Antoine Asfour; so was Robert Ramsey; even the Banque Populaire, Gillian Financial, and Naji Nahas had new accounts. Mahmoud Fustok's name made its first public appearance. But some were new names, such as Imovest Inter and Coprosol SA. Others were individuals, all with Arab names. If Comex had had contacts in the Lebanese community in Paris, it would soon have discovered that these were, to a man, old chums of the ebullient Naji Nahas. It looked as though everyone but Nahas's uncle was on the list . Only later did ACLI discover that, in fact, Naji's uncle *was* on the list – a man named Antoine Achkar; so was his cousin, Selim Gabriel Nassif, and his secretary. 'We were simply not aware of the web of relationships,' one broker confessed sadly, much later.

By now, the Comex board was frantic; it reacted on January 9 by reducing the number of new positions any speculator could buy to 50, and by increasing margin again, to $75,000 in the spot month and to $40,000 for each contract held by a speculator holding more than 251 contracts. The Arabs in Geneva were finally embarrassed; for the first time the Banque Populaire Suisse group had failed to put up margin money at ACLI, and some of their positions had been liquidated.

Another development was a transaction between Bunker Hunt and Naji Nahas – though it was completed in London, so the CFTC knew nothing of it. Bunker bought 2 million ounces of silver from Najas, who obligingly helped his friend finance the deal by lending Bunker $40 million. With the price of silver still rising, that seemed a trifling sum.

Nonetheless, the squeeze was being applied by Comex now, and it was really ruthless. The bulls, like Bunker, were deeply indignant, but the first people really to be hurt were the shorts. On January 14 the silver price reached yet another new record, $42.50, which meant that margin payments were being demanded of the shorts, and the largest of these was Philipp Brothers, the Engelhard subsidiary. One dealer got Philipp Brothers' account from the clearinghouse by mistake and was horrified to read that their margin call that day was more than $100 million – too much even for so rich a parent as Engelhard.

Philipp Brothers had acquired 40 million ounces of bullion the previous fall from dealers who were delighted to sell scrap at anything over $10 an ounce; and had prudently hedged it by taking short positions in the futures market. With the price rising so fast, their position had become as precarious as Henry Jarecki's had been in September – except that money borrowed to meet the margin calls was now even more expensive. And their solution had to be the same as Jarecki's – an EFP, or exchange of futures for physicals. Engelhard, urgently needing to get rid of as much bullion as possible, offered Bunker and Herbert Hunt a deal. Although the market price was $42.50 on January 14, when the agreement was made, Engelhard offered to sell the Hunts 19 million ounces at a price of $35.00, thus cancelling 3,800 of their short contracts and a similar number of the Hunts' long contracts. Engelhard benefited as Jarecki had done: their net position on the futures market was reduced, so that margin calls ceased to be such a drain on their resources. The Hunts benefited by the acquisition of even more bullion, at a price they still believed was a bargain. Both parties were pleased enough to repeat the operation two days later, Bunker and Herbert agreeing to buy 11 million ounces of silver, thus cancelling 2,200 more contracts in the futures market.

This was testimony to Bunker and Herbert's conviction that the silver price was not going to fall between mid-January and March 31, 1980, when the first deal would be completed, or even before July 1, 1980, completion date for the second transaction. Engelhard was far from certain about the inevitability of higher prices; the package was a billion-dollar deal, and the chairman of Engelhard, Milton Rosenthal, insisted that both Bunker and Herbert Hunt sign the contract. 'That was a *conditio sine qua non* on our part,' Rosenthal said later. A prudent man, Rosenthal also insisted that the brothers deposit 8.5 million ounces of their own silver as an earnest of their good intentions on March 31. This would protect Philipp Brothers as long as the price remained above $26 an ounce.

On January 18, John Meilke, during another CFTC surveillance meeting, reported that the price movements during the week 'had been nothing less than phenomenal' – partly because of Comex's new rules, which had reduced business to a level at which one or two large orders could move the price by a dollar or more. Despite all the EFPs that week (Meilke had counted 33 million ounces changing hands), Bunker Hunt still had 8,580 contracts for delivery in March, and his brother Lamar had now entered the market in a big way. The commissioners still talked of the possibility of a regular old-fashioned squeeze. The previous day the price had risen to $48.70 in New York. 'The real question,' said Read Dunn, 'is how long can this trend continue?'

Bunker gave the appearance of absolute conviction that it could not stop. When the price touched $49 during trading, Abdul Wahab Galadari, whom Bunker had met on the Arabian Gulf in February, telephoned Dallas from Dubai to ask if the price constituted a bubble, and if so, when it was going to burst. 'Not until silver hits eighty-five dollars,' replied Bunker. His optimism had a mathematical basis: at around 1:13, the gold/silver ratio was lower than it had been for a century. No matter what the market was trying to do to him, Bunker exhibited the unflinching certainty of an Old Testament oracle who saw his prophecies being realized. (Galadari lacked the faith, however, and sold out.)

On January 18, 1980, for the first time in the history of the silver market, the price of an ounce of silver topped $50.00. There was a trade at $50.36 on Comex, but the record was set in Chicago, at a price of $52.50. Fifty dollars was a talismanic price, and had it happened naturally, it would have been the confirmation that Bunker's gamble had paid off magnificently. Bunker's fortune would have been nearly as great as if Colonel Qaddafi had not expropriated the Sarir Field. He would have been the richest man in the world for the second time in his life. And the rumours in the market promised even greater riches; the more excitable traders were confidently forecasting that the next step would indeed be to $85.

But not everyone was so certain. When Theo Hook heard the rumours about $85 silver he thought the bubble was full-blown, and had begun to quiver and shake preparatory to its bursting. 'Once they failed to sell half their position at between thirty-five and forty dollars, it seemed obvious to me that they would be victims of their own pure greed,' he says. And Hook was right; Bunker Hunt was about to have another bad accident.

Meeting early on the morning of Monday, January 21, the Comex board decided that the price movements of the previous week, culminating in $50 silver, constituted an emergency in the market, and they declared one formally, delayed the opening of the market, and noted that 'the interest of the large market participants has not materially reduced, and the holders of long positions continue to buy silver for the apparent purpose of taking delivery.' The board concluded that if the speculators were not going to play by the rules, it would change them again and again. It resolved, as it had never done before, that trading should be for liquidation only. The longs could no longer increase their position by buying; 'liquidation only' meant they could only sell; and the only legitimate buyers to whom the longs *could* sell were the hedgers – companies like Mocatta Metals and Engelhard. To ram the message home, the board announced another increase in margins, and, now that it had ceased to hide behind the Special Silver Committee, the board wound the committee up. 'The members were willing to do their duty; they were the regulatory body and they had to take the responsibility,' says Dr Brimmer. The next day, similar rules were imposed by the Board of Trade in Chicago. The Hunts and their friends were locked in.

The CFTC's chairman, James Stone, was gratified but grudging. 'My theory is that for two weeks the talk on the floor was that Comex could not enforce position limits. The Hunts were going ahead; things were not going to change. The importance of the new rules was symbolic; they were the first signal to the world that Comex was going to break the Hunt bubble.'

Bunker Hunt was deeply disturbed by the new rules, and the market on January 21 indicated why. Trading had been allowed to start in the Comex silver pit only after the emergency rules had been announced. When it opened, Theo Hook sold a small package of four contracts at $50.50, and later in the day bought at $39.00. By the day's close the price was $44.00. The next day the price fell by $10.00, because with liquidation-only trading there were no buyers at all.

Throughout January there had been rumours that Bunker and Herbert Hunt were about to sue Comex, and the Hunts were indeed full of wrath. But there was no writ, although its absence did not prevent Bunker's alleging that there had been a conspiracy against him. Was there?

The story of the months between September 1979 and January 1980 reveals two crucial facts. First, that James Stone, at the CFTC, was alive to the potential seriousness of the Hunts' raid on the silver market but was impotent to act until the new year because of the even split among the commissioners. The CFTC was required by law to be market neutral, and it could be nothing else while it was divided. If the CFTC became partisan after the new year, this was surely the result of provocation by the Hunts and their cronies. The second fact is that the Comex governors hid behind Dr Brimmer's Special Silver Committee. Theo Hook observes: 'They just let Brimmer worry about it, and he didn't have a professional's comprehension of the business, and had no apprehension of what Bunker could do to it.' Comex acted only when the CFTC was finally able to bully the board into doing so. These facts reflect badly on both the CFTC and Comex, but they do not add up to a conspiracy. And if there was a counter-conspiracy against the Hunts – and there were elements of one when Stone and Dunn tried independently to persuade Comex to act in October – it was a resounding failure.

But Comex's failure to respond sooner to the crisis in the silver market makes the board vulnerable to serious charges nonetheless. When they finally did act, the market rules were changed retroactively. The fundamental maxim of commodity exchanges is that if the system is to be used properly, the rules have to be adhered to. This maxim does not affect the right of an exchange to change the rules *prospectively*: to state that *in the future* margins will be higher, or position limits imposed. But by changing the rules retroactively, and applying them to trades already made on the market, Comex was susceptible to the charge that the fundamental maxim had been ignored, and that its ruthless actions were designed to save the exchange itself and its regular participants – Bunker's 'home-town boys'.

Comex can argue, of course, that the rules were changed because the market was being manipulated by the Hunts and their friends, who were using the futures market to acquire vast amounts of silver bullion, which was not its purpose. That argument would have been much more effective if action had been taken in September or October, which was just early enough in the game to have allowed Comex to change the rules prospectively.

Bunker's persecution complex blossomed because the emergency rules appeared to suit the people on the opposite side from himself and his allies: the shorts, most especially Philipp Brothers, and Bunker's new hate-figure, Henry Jarecki of Mocatta Metals. And it is true that after liquidation-only trading was announced on January 21, the bullion dealers, as legitimate hedgers, were the only participants with the freedom to buy and sell. Since the longs could only sell, and the hedgers were the only buyers, it was inevitable that the price would fall. The new rules certainly did the shorts no harm, but here, too, the evidence does not really support Bunker's conspiracy theory. As we have seen, Engelhard – Philipp Brothers' parent – had proposed swingeing changes in the margin rules early in October, but these were not acted on, and Henry Jarecki was later to be critical, in private at least, of Comex's tardiness in changing the rules.

The distaste that was felt for Comex's behaviour arose from the fact that its action came so late that it had to be peremptory and brutal – discriminatory against the longs, and partial to the shorts. The board could have done something in September, even if only to throw Norton Waltuch off the floor; in October, position limits could have been introduced. In the fall, however, the floor brokers and many of the commission houses, which knew that 'foreign investors' were taking delivery of silver, did not think that Bunker Hunt would do so as well. They had no conception of the dominance of the position of Bunker and his friends, or of how crazily the market could act. The bullion dealers made less noise than they might have done, because Henry Jarecki had extricated himself from the market in October, and Engelhard was well enough financed to sit out the storm; meanwhile, the small traders were happy making money out of a hyperactive market. 'Only when the price reached thirty-five dollars,' says Theo Hook, 'did most people realize how bad it could get'. By that time it was too late to act with any dignity.

The need for frantic rule changes can be explained either by myopia – the dealers were doing too much business to see what was happening – or by James Stone's more specific allegation that Comex did not want to lose the lucrative year-end business. In each case the motive is instantly recognizable: greed.

Bunker Hunt ought to have understood that motive, but explanations brought him no comfort. When we met in Paris later in 1980, in the spacious lobby of the Hotel Bristol, I said that the one aspect of his plunge into silver that had finally mesmerized the exchanges was the scale of it, especially when the Arab money was included. Bunker Hunt leaned forward, his jacket creasing awkwardly because the middle button was still done up, and poured himself a second cup of tea, stirring two lumps of sugar into the small cup. His companion, the Los Angeles coin dealer Bruce McNall, explained that if you go to Las Vegas you can play for dimes, but it is not so much fun as playing for a few hundred dollars. It is the same with racehorses, added McNall. 'Mr Hunt doesn't buy a dozen, he buys hundreds.'

Bunker Hunt then began a commentary on the rise of all commodity prices. 'My father was once offered a gas deal at a cent a thousand therms, and he said, "Don't bother," because it wouldn't even cover the bookkeeping costs; eighteen months later he sold it for fifteen cents a thousand, and now you can get six or seven dollars a thousand. It's the same with that oil I had in Libya. Now Qaddafi's getting thirty-odd a barrel. We should have been in oil futures in 1973.' He smiled at that, the only time he did so during our conversation. 'My brother Herbert was always bullish in oil. Years ago he said that price would be ten dollars a barrel by 1980, and nobody believed him.'

But, I insisted, what had most frightened the people running the silver markets was just that: the fact that a few people with access to so much oil money could dominate them.

Bunker replied that until 1979 he had not realized there were so many dealers in the market who did not want the price to go up. He named some of them, a familiar litany: Moccata, and the other bullion dealers – Montagu, Sharps Pixley, Handy and Hardman. They wanted the price to come down after it had gone up, Bunker said, hinting darkly that they had allies in Washington, at the CFTC.

I suggested that he simply objected to federal regulation.

'Not to all regulation,' he replied, 'but it must be market neutral, and it wasn't then.'

Bunker's companion made the point more bluntly. The sellers of silver had fixed the market against the buyers, he said.

I repeated that this was because they were afraid that Bunker was going to be the man who broke the bank at Monte Carlo.

Bunker was interested in the analogy, and developed it. 'There is a card game called blackjack, do you play it over here?'

'It's called vingt-et-un.'

'Well, I'm told there are some people who can play so they always win. I don't know how they do it, but when the casino operators find out they're there, they won't let them play anymore. They get thrown out.'

Bunker shrugged his shoulders. In describing the card counters and the 'injustice' they suffer, he clearly indicated that he was a victim of a similar injustice. He was the man who could not lose, so the markets had thrown him out.

Chapter 10

Unconscionable

Reading over what I have written so far, I see that I have given the impression that the designs of Bunker and Herbert on the silver market were all that had happened in the fall and winter of 1979–80. On the contrary, they were events on a crowded scene. The markets were also mesmerized by the gold price, which was rising to unimagined levels as well, past $500 an ounce, then $600, and finally to $875, though that was because of political insecurity rather than a deliberate putsch in the market. I happened to be in the vaults of the Federal Reserve Bank of New York, one of the great gold stores in the world, when the price was near its peak, and few people can have seen as much money as I did then. My expert companion calculated that the gold in the vaults four floors under Liberty Street was worth approximately $225 billion, enough to make even Bunker's eyes glaze over. So the explosion in the gold price tended partly to obscure the aberrant behaviour of the silver price.

President Carter's grain embargo against Russia, in response to the invasion of Afghanistan, drew attention to a different commodity market. Another consequence of that invasion was the boycott by the United States of the Summer Olympics in Moscow in 1980, though that did not apply to the Winter Olympics in Lake Placid, New York (where a prodigious United States hockey team beat the Russians). Governor Ronald Reagan was about to take his first hesitant steps in New Hampshire toward the Republican presidential nomination in July 1980; President Carter had battened down the hatches in the White House, hoping that he might free the hostages in Tehran by concentrating hard. Despite record interest rates, inflation in the United States had also reached the highest level in living memory. But a few people could not take their minds off silver. One of these was Walter Hoving.

Walter Hoving is a patrician. He believes in good manners, which he teaches, and capitalism, which he practises. He dislikes vulgarity, immorality, and socialism. He does not like Bunker Hunt very much, either. Bunker once wrote to Hoving inviting him to a revivalist meeting especially arranged for businessmen. 'It was addressed to "Dear Walter", though I'd never met him in my life,' says Hoving. 'I didn't reply.'

Bunker had written not only because Walter Hoving is an upright Christian gentleman but also because he was then (though he retired at the end of 1980) chairman of Tiffany and Company of Fifth Avenue, New York – a name spoken in the same breath as Cartier of Paris, Asprey of London, and Bulgari of Rome in the jewellery business. Hoving governed the company from a long, narrow office at the top of the store, looking toward Central Park; its walls are panelled, the desk topped with red leather, and the knick-knacks are, like so much else at Tiffany's, tasteful and expensive. Sitting at his desk, Hoving liked to compose advertisements for the company's regular space on page three of the *New York Times*. 'I try to keep them staccato,' he explains. 'The common man, which includes me, gets tired after two paragraphs.' There is no nonsense about the prose, which appears under titles such as 'Is Profit a Dirty Word?' and 'Are the Rich a Menace?' Answers are drawn from life as it is lived by the customers on the floors below.

Early in 1980, Hoving began to toy with a new advertisement, which would be entitled 'Unconscionable'. The lawyers made a few suggestions; for example, they thought it better not to mention names. Hoving's final text (published with unwitting prescience on March 26) read: 'We think it is unconscionable for anyone to have several billion, yes billion, dollars' worth of silver and thus drive up the price so high that others must pay artificially high prices for articles made of silver, from baby spoons to tea sets, as well as photographic film and other products.' The names that the lawyers had erased were those of Bunker and Herbert Hunt, and they, specifically, were the targets of Hoving's wrath. 'What I don't like,' he says, 'is when greed gets too predominant. Men like that, who believe in the free-enterprise system, shouldn't take advantage of it.'

Tiffany's buys bullion in the silver market; it is the raw material for the factory in New Jersey that makes flatware (knives, forks, and spoons) and hollowware (cups, bowls, and trophies, including the extravagant memento awarded to the winners of American football's Cup Final, the Super Bowl. 'There's an awful lot of silver in that, and I wish some of the winners would look after it a little better,' sniffs Hoving.) Higher silver prices began to affect Tiffany's late in the fall of 1979. The company's buyers had a store of silver bought at around $6 an ounce, but when stocks were depleted they had to be replaced with silver bought at $30 an ounce; that cost was reflected in retail prices and in a consequent decline in trade.

Tiffany's was not alone. Handy and Hardman, the New York precious-metals dealer whose annual reviews of the bullion markets are the standard guide, described the winter as 'the most chaotic period in the history of the world silver market.' In Washington, D.C., the industry's lobby, the Silver Users' Association, was telling a tale of woe to anyone who would listen. The association's executive vice-president, Walter Frankland, a man with a mane of hair appropriately coloured silver, had run into Bunker on January 7 at the CFTC. 'I told him that I hoped he realized what he was doing to silver users,' Frankland said. Bunker replied that all he was trying to do was buy a little silver. He had tried it once before, Bunker added, and the time wasn't right; he wasn't sure it was right this time. Fine details of timing were of little interest to Frankland. His tale was of substantial industrial dislocation, especially in the states of the Northeast, from Massachusetts down to Maryland, where silver manufacturers are concentrated. Producers of flatware and hollowware had survived the first wave of price increases in September; it was annoying to have to change price lists so often, but business had held up well – until the end of November. Then a slump set in with disturbing rapidity. 'By the end of December the market had been vacuumed. The industry was in a shambles,' reports Frankland. According to the U.S. Labor Department's statistics, 6,000 jobs in the jewellery, silverware, and plateware industries were lost in four months from November 1979 to February 1980. 'The workers who lost their jobs were not speculators. They were the most innocent of victims,' commented the CFTC's chairman, James Stone.

But the victims of the rise in price were not all Americans. Indeed, the company that suffered the most severe agitation was Ilford, the British-based, Swiss-owned producer of photographic film. Ilford was suddenly placed in such precarious financial straits that its survival and the jobs of 3,500 workers along with it were threatened.

Although the propaganda of the futures market implies that all substantial users of silver hedge against sudden price movements, this is not the case. Photographic companies, like Ilford and Kodak – the largest of them all – do not hedge because their financial controllers believe that to do so is unjustifiable speculation with company funds. Instead, Ilford bought silver when it was required, on the principle that daily purchases would bring costs in line with average silver prices. In general, the company's silver buyers believed that their experience enabled them to buy at slightly less than the average price, but this experience had never absorbed price movements like those which became commonplace after August 1979, and Ilford was less well equipped to deal with unpredictable rises than any of its competitors.

Like so many British manufacturers, Ilford was burdened with ageing equipment and low productivity; the only thing that was increasing was the annual loss. The Swiss owner, the pharmaceutical group Geigy, was anxious to reverse this trend, and had agreed to contribute £10 million to a £28 million modernization programme; the rest was to be raised by Ilford. But the authors of the corporate plan had not contemplated the possibility of a group entering the silver market and driving up the price so fast that the company, which had budgeted £10 million for silver in 1979, was forced to spend twice that sum.

By January 1980 the old equipment and the work force were no longer the arbiters of production costs. Silver, which had traditionally accounted for one-tenth of the selling price of film, now cost one half. With prices at record levels, the company's executives gloomily forecast that Ilford's entire silver budget for 1980 would be spent in a few weeks. Higher costs had to be met by higher prices, and the losses already made in 1979 had to be paid off from money set aside for the modernization programme. To begin with, the market for Ilford's photographic film held up surprisingly well, even though some prices were doubled, but salesmen were uncovering disturbing portents: the X-ray departments of large London hospitals, for instance, were ordering significantly less film, and looking for ways of spending even less.

Had the silver price been less volatile, it is likely that Ilford could have accomplished the transition from a fairly ancient to a truly modern company in a dignified way, but the cost of silver threw its finances into such chaos that the transformation had to be performed ruthlessly. Ilford survived, but a surgical operation that led to the closure of most of its production plants and that cut out two of every three of its employees was precipitated by the silver crisis. Bunker Hunt is not a name that rolls fondly from the lips of Ilford employees.

Ilford's competition in the industry was better able to cope, though not without raising prices, too. The price of Kodak's medical X-ray film rose by 93 per cent, and some colour-printing paper went up almost as much. In Hollywood, film directors who were accustomed to shoot twelve feet for every foot that finally appeared on the screen (the silver screen, of course) were being told by producers to cut the ratio to six to one. In London, the three Express newspapers, which normally spent £150,000 a year on film and printing, found that costs had risen to £350,000. Dentists, who use silver as part of the compound for filling teeth, were forced to charge even more than most normally do. In the electronics industry, finance directors had the unenviable task of having to ask banks to lend them money, at high rates of interest, to buy silver, just as their businesses were going into decline partly because of those same high interest rates. Silver was actually causing the retail price index to rise – not by much, but perceptibly. Though the irony may not have been appreciated by Bunker Hunt, the metal he was buying as a hedge against inflation had now begun to contribute to it. The producer price index rose by 2.8 per cent from December to January, one quarter of this increase being attributed to higher prices of precious metals. The price of finished goods rose 1.6 per cent in that month, and 'much of that acceleration' was because of precious metals, the Bureau of Labor Statistics reported.

One consequence of inflation is that consumer behaviour becomes less predictable. Since World War II, American economists had had no real experience of inflation, and their models had largely ignored it. Curiously, for a man with an obsession about inflation, Bunker Hunt, too, had ignored its impact. The likelihood is, however, that any shrewd economist who had created a model of how people behaved during a period of inflation would have got it wrong: he would have been likely to predict that anyone owning valuable silver objects would hang on to them, knowing that the cost of replacing them was rising steadily each year. The assumption was that people value silver cutlery, teapots, trays, bowls, candlesticks, and baby spoons more than cash. In January 1980 that assumption proved incorrect.

In the side streets between Fifth and Sixth avenues on Forty-sixth Street in New York City, in Hatton Garden in London, and outside thousands of other stores that were offering to buy silver, for cash, by weight, queues formed each day during that January. People held parcels containing silver objects they valued less than the remarkable cash prices they could suddenly obtain for them. Now they could sell silver for much more than they had originally paid for it – if, indeed, they had paid for the objects at all, because many of them were inherited – and could use the money for something they valued more highly: for a mortgage payment on the house, for new kitchen equipment, for anything useful that would certainly cost more next year.

Lovers of fine silver were appalled. Part of America's cultural heritage was being melted down, as beautiful antiques sold for no more than their weight in silver. Hoving recalled his shock when a friend brought him a silver elephant bowl, and on hearing how much it would fetch, went right out to sell it. 'He said he'd spill no tears over it,' said Hoving. One bullion dealer bought a silver tureen so large that it would not fit into the crate in which it was to be consigned to the smelter, so the counterhand put the tureen on the floor and stamped it flat. Bullion dealers could not afford to be sentimental; many of the pieces they took over the counter would, if stored and eventually auctioned, probably have fetched more than the mere price of an ounce of silver. But the dealers had neither the capital nor the storage space to hold on to the pieces for months. The rush to sell silver was one example of the way values can be distorted, not necessarily by greed, but by fear, bred out of inflation.

Yet more silver went on sale because of a second fear – that of theft. Burglars read newspapers, too, and in January 1980 the silver price emerged from the ghetto of the financial pages onto the front page. In wealthy suburbs, patrolmen noticed a trend: robbers would take the silver and ignore everything else. Gangs were alleged to use trucks equipped with small smelters in which they could smelt down stolen silver objects at once. No one was more conscious of silver's increased value than Walter Hoving; in their Rhode Island home, Mrs Hoving carefully packed their silver in two cases and put them in the basement, one marked 'Bills, 1965,' the other, 'Bills, 1966'.

For the most successful of the silver thieves, the rise in the price proved an acute embarrassment. A gang of hijackers in London had known for months that a bullion truck regularly carried silver from the London market to Tilbury, on the Thames estuary, from which it was shipped to clients in East Germany. The gang had planned this robbery so carefully that the slightest variation in the truck's movements caused their scheme to be cancelled. Finally, everything happened as planned; the truck was travelling on the road to Tilbury when it and the accompanying security car were stopped by a man in police uniform and asked to drive into a lay-by where two white-coated men were waiting with clipboards to take down answers in a traffic census. This 'policeman' and the two 'census takers' then produced a revolver and a sawed-off shotgun and, instead of asking questions, bundled the truck driver and the guard into a van, in which they were bound and gagged, and driven away. The bullion truck was taken to a garage in the north London suburb of Enfield, and when the thieves unloaded their loot, they were astonished to discover that there was ten tons of it: 321 ingots of silver, each weighing 1,000 ounces and worth, on the day of the robbery (March 24) no less than £3,418,650. Even allowing for the impact of inflation on crime, this was one of the biggest hauls ever, anywhere.

The heist was so big, and so specialized – because the gang could hardly take a position in the silver futures market either to sell the bullion or to hedge against a fall in value – that the thieves began to wonder what they could possibly do with their newly acquired silver. One told the police later: 'When we read about the value of the silver we realized it was too hot to handle, and we decided to give it back.' But there was a generous reward for the recovery of the silver, and before the gang could pluck up the courage to tell the owners where the haul was, they had been caught.

By the time the silver was recovered at the end of May, it was already worth less than when it had been stolen. But it could not be sold immediately; it was material evidence in the trial, so it was deposited in the vaults of the Bank of England. (One of the gang's lawyers questioned the prosecution's right to offer pictorial evidence of the haul; he proposed that the ingots be brought into court each day. He was overruled.) The gang was not found guilty until February 1981, and when they were finally sentenced to a total of thirty-seven years, the silver no longer belonged to the East German purchasers, Intrak, but to a Lloyds insurance syndicate, headed by one of London's most substantial insurance brokers, Willis, Faber and Dumas.

The East Germans had quickly claimed insurance on the value of the silver when it was stolen, and the Lloyd's brokers had no reason not to pay it. A cheque went to East Germany for the sum of £3,418,650. But when the insurance brokers were eventually able to reclaim the silver from the Bank of England vaults and sell it in the London bullion market, it was worth £1,250,000 less than they had paid out in March 1980. Among the big losers in the silver market, the men at Lloyd's were the most philosophical. 'If none of the ingots had been recovered, we wouldn't have got any money back at all,' commented one of the hardened insurance investigators. And, like most other professionals in financial markets, what Lloyd's brokers lose on the swings, they expect to gain on the roundabouts.

Moreover, ten tons of silver was small stuff compared to the millions of ounces being released from the hoard of privately owned silver, accumulated over a century and more by generations of Europeans and Americans. The people who first realized the size of this hoard were the managers of the smelters that were refining 'scrap' silver. The pressure on the refineries was described in a letter Henry Jarecki of Mocatta Metals sent later in 1980 to Read Dunn of the CFTC:

> In September 1979, space was still relatively available, even though refining charges were up a bit from the usual 3–5 cents an ounce. Throughout the Fall,

> space became more and more scarce, and refining charges rose steadily. By January some refiners said refining capacity was unavailable. Johnson Matthey (Canada) was not accepting new orders for three months, and Norddeutsche Affinerie would not commit itself but said it had to 'make a reassessment of its overall silver position'.
>
> During February 1980 alone we had to ask refiners for quotes over 40 times. A study of the responses we got to those telexes shows that over eleven refiners mentioned how heavily booked they were. Johnson Matthey Chemical in London, for example, cited 'the current world situation in silver' as the reason they could not accept new material for three months. Compagnie des Métaux Précieux in Paris said it could accept no new material for four months; Kennecott in the U.S. said that it could accept no new material until 1981. The British Lead Company in the U.K., Electrolytic Refining and Smelting Company in Australia, Noranda in Canada, Broken Hill in Australia, Comptoir Lyon in France, Penoles in Mexico, Boliden in Sweden, and Société Générale de Métallurgique in Belgium all reported that their plants were at full capacity and that they would not accept new material.
>
> The refining space shortage was also reflected in the refining charges. In September 1979, we were quoted 7.5 cents (approximately ½ per cent of value). By October the rate had escalated to 16 cents an ounce. In November that rate had inflated to 31 cents an ounce and in December the quoted rate was 41 cents an ounce. The rate rose rapidly until it reached its peak on February 14, 1980 when we were quoted $4.34 an ounce (11.7 per cent of value).

Not only were there lines outside the metal dealers, but miners in the Western states realized that, with silver fetching so much, it was now worth resurrecting old silver mines that had gone out of production when the price was $2 an ounce but that could be profitable now the price was more than ten times higher. Nor was this surge of prospecting confined to miners with an interest in old seams. Large mining companies began to invest in silver again; the prospect was promising enough, for example, to confirm the good sense of companies as large as Occidental Petroleum, and its wily old chairman, Armand Hammer, in its decision to take a half share in a Colorado exploration company called Candelaria.

The astounding rise in price also promoted industrial users themselves to buy less silver. Statistics compiled later in 1980 were to show that demand for silver fell by one-third in the first three months of the year, which contradicted Jerome Smith's confident forecast, made in 1972, that higher prices would not affect demand for silver. Research into the use of substitutes for silver was conducted with uncommon vigour. The bullion trade has always been amused by regular announcements from the photographic industry about dramatic discoveries that would reduce silver usage: with the silver price at $6 an ounce, the trade had sufficient reason to doubt the industry's determination to reduce consumption. But with the price above $20, such research became critical. Slower films, using less silver, were produced; lasers were used to make plates for picture magazines; and there was great interest in a new process for developing X-rays that left the silver in the developing tank rather than on the plate.

The laws of supply and demand were proving far more influential than Walter Frankland's lobby in Washington. The Silver Users' Association pulled every string it knew. At the CFTC, Frankland had suggested position limits and liquidation-only trading at a time when the commissioners were still trying to persuade the exchanges to regulate themselves. At the Treasury Department, Frankland proposed that Secretary G. William Miller authorize the sale of 40 million ounces of silver that the department had stockpiled and for which it had no foreseeable use. Sell 40 million ounces, Frankland pleaded, and the price will stabilize, perhaps even fall. But Secretary Miller was more concerned with the gold price, and believed there would be strenuous opposition in Congress to any sale from the silver stockpile.

(Miller was not wrong. A small but vociferous lobby in the House of Representatives had already opposed sales from a separate silver stockpile administered by the General Services Administration. The lobby was led by three men who had received campaign contributions from the Hunts: Larry P. McDonald of Georgia – who also had membership in the National Council of the John Birch Society in common with Bunker; Steven Symms of Idaho, who had speculated in the silver market himself; and the brazen Richard Kelly of Florida, who was soon to be deposed because of his own spectacular role in the Abscam affair, when he was shown on videotape stuffing $25,000 into his pockets. Coincidence that lobby might have been, but it is nevertheless a fact that the major sufferers from any sale from the stockpile would have been Bunker and Herbert Hunt.)

In desperation, Frankland even visited the Justice Department in January to inquire into the possibility of an indictment of the Hunts under the Sherman Anti-Trust Act. But he got nowhere there, either. Frankland's problem was perhaps that the concern of the Silver Users' Association was so evidently motivated by self-interest; they *always* thought the price was too high. Frankland was never regarded in the regulatory agencies or on Capitol Hill as the most convincing witness against the Hunts. And by the time he visited the Justice Department, the market place had become a more influential arbiter of the silver price than the Users' Association.

By January 1980 the professionals were saying that silver was coming out of the woodwork. The effect of the glut was to undermine the position of the Hunts and the 'foreign investors' in the futures market, because a gap grew between the cash price for silver and the spot price in the commodity market. Moreover, the market had, to use the technical phrase, gone into backwardation – which meant that the spot price was higher than the price quoted for future months. The cash price more accurately reflected the law of supply and demand, while the spot price had risen feverishly, ignoring that same law. By mid-January, the cash price was $10 an ounce lower than the spot price on the market, and shrewd dealers realized that the two prices – cash and spot – would have to meet again. They were sure that it was the spot price that would be coming down, and not the cash price going up.

Market professionals naturally liked to dwell on how the newly refined silver that had 'come out of the woodwork' affected the market, because it drew attention away from the rule changes the exchange had newly introduced, which were already the subject of legal actions in Chicago and New York, initiated by small investors who had been caught out by the emergency actions. But there is no doubt that the massive meltdown had an effect on the price. And, as Jarecki pointed out at the close of his letter to Read Dunn: 'the deliveries from the refineries actually exceeded the expectations of those who did not know how much was being refined.' First estimates put the figure at 20 million ounces of silver; later that figure was revised until it reached the unconvincing total of 50 million ounces. Even if the total was only half that, it shows that there was an awful lot of silver in the woodwork.

There were still silver bugs, of course, who persuaded themselves that the January 15 spot price of $50 was not an aberration. Among those who saw it as a perfectly reasonable reflection of market forces were Bunker and Herbert Hunt, who believed that it was all a matter of the gold/silver ratio's moving in the right direction. Herbert had already outlined his belief in $50 silver when he met Read Dunn in November 1979. Dunn had found the assertion quite remarkable. 'You mean the general price level has to adjust to fifty-dollar silver?' he asked Herbert.

'Sure,' Herbert replied.

'My God, what do little guys like me do?'

'Buy silver,' Herbert insisted.

'I can't; it's not permitted,' replied the upright commissioner of the CFTC.

'Well, just don't keep it in paper,' advised Herbert.

But the effect of $50 silver had been precisely the reverse of Herbert's confident forecast, because a great deal of paper currency had been exchanged for silver. Still, the Hunts' conviction that the price would go on rising was never seriously shaken. The fact that in January 1980 they sold *no* silver contracts in the futures market, when they could have counted their profits in billions if they had done so, seemed to confirm that. But as the market began to settle early in February, the Hunts perhaps began to wonder whether it had not all happened a little too quickly.

There were others, too, whose confidence had not been dented by the fall in the market after the rule changes of January 21, and among them were the authors of Jerome Smith's newsletter, *World Market Perspective.* The issue dated February 21, 1980, reflected Smith's own persuasive bullishness. It noted that there had been a period of correction in the price, but said that the period was drawing to a close. 'A rise in the London silver fixing to the $40 level will satisfy us that a new rally is underway. A move up to $42 will, we believe, lead fairly quickly to a test of the previous high at the $50 level. Looking a bit further ahead, we believe that a successful breakout above the $50 level will lead to a further rapid advance of a major proportions.' Up to Bunker's $85 perhaps?

As a precaution, Jerome Smith's newsletter advised readers what to do if the correction period was not over. 'We would expect any further price decline to stop above the $28 level and we would buy aggressively if silver were to become available at $32 an ounce or less.' Because he usually echoed their own opinions, Bunker and Herbert Hunt always thought that Jerome Smith knew what he was talking about. Here, it seemed, was proof.

Chapter 11

A Borrowing Spree

As the silver price fell in late January and early February 1980, the bulls became less frisky. For the first time since they had begun to play in the market six months before, they were being asked to make variation margin payments. Instead of collecting money daily from the clearinghouse and using it to buy bullion or to increase their holdings in futures contracts, the longs started paying money to the clearinghouse, to be collected by the shorts. This unscripted development created embarrassment not just for Bunker, Herbert, and Lamar Hunt (who had begun buying very heavily in January), and for the Saudis, but for the banks that had lent them the money to help finance their great speculation. The loans had been generous – though with the silver price going up, the risk had appeared minimal. With the price going down, the first sour notes could be heard.

One of the sourest stories about these days was told me much later by a bullion dealer in New York City. It concerned Mahmoud Fustok, the Saudi 'Maharajah' who had been Prince Abdullah's representative in the silver market. Fustok had established long lines of credit with the Swiss Bank Corporation in Zurich, and as the silver price fell this credit was swallowed up by margin calls. The bank was concerned enough about the deficit in the Saudi account to send one of its most senior executives, Walter Frey, to Jeddah, where Fustok was then to be found, to insist that Fustok provide the additional funds to cover the margin payments. Otherwise, Frey threatened, the Saudi silver positions would be sold out. Fustok, unaccustomed to being spoken to like that, curtly informed Frey that if the Swiss Bank Corporation did any such thing, he, Fustok, would arrange for Frey to find himself in a Jeddah jail that very evening.

Since Fustok had such easy access to Prince Abdullah and his National Guard, this was not an idle threat. Saudi commercial law is rather different from the gentlemanly procedures in American and European courts; it is ill-defined and abrupt, and Western businessmen sometimes find it difficult to leave the kingdom if they have offended any Saudi colleagues. Frey took Fustok's threat so seriously that he fled to Jeddah airport and took the first available flight out of the country. (The story I heard lacked a last chapter; the storyteller did not know whether Frey had in fact sold out any of the Saudi silver positions; the normal rules of banking do not account for customers like Mahmoud Fustok. But not long afterward Walter Frey resigned from the Swiss Bank Corporation and, it was said, retired to a sanatorium for a few months.)

Anger over the outcome of the Saudi speculation was not confined to the Arabian bulls in the silver market. Westernized Saudis, including the best known of them all, Oil Minister Ahmed Zaki Yamani, were indignant at the ease with which their fellow countrymen had been able to obtain credit to speculate in futures markets. Yamani's reaction was significant because he perfectly represents the educated Saudi technocrats who have been embraced by the royal family to provide the necessary expertise to run the newly rich kingdom. So firmly held were the fears of the technocrats that these were, most unusually, spelled out in print in Saudi Arabia, even before the markets changed the rules. In a January 16 article in the Arabic newspaper *Al Riyadh* that was published later in English in the weekly magazine *Saudi Business*, Farouk Akhdar, director of the new Saudi industrial ports at Jubail and Yanbu, warned of the dangers inherent in speculation in gold and silver.

> The classic explanation for speculating in precious metals is that Arabs no longer have confidence in currencies like the U.S. dollar, the British pound sterling, or the French franc and so on. This may be true to some extent. But the aim of the buyers is really speculation in the hope of enhancing their wealth by buying and selling, just as it was in Saudi Arabia when speculation in land holdings was at its peak. Some made money when they sold at the right time. Many others suffered considerable losses. . . . When this happens in precious metals we will learn that the whole operation was an attempt to defraud the Arabs of their wealth and return to the industrial economies what we earned by selling our oil.

Exactly as Yamani and Akhdar had feared, the passionate conviction that they had been monstrously conned flourished among the less highly educated, but richer and more powerful, princes of the royal family. But since their original speculation had been made so secretly, they could hardly complain publicly. Their humiliation had to be suffered more or less in private, and it was only just beginning.

Bunker Hunt managed to put a remarkably good face on things after the markets changed the rules. Though a man with a distaste for public appearances, he was quoted by reporters with uncommon regularity after January 21, and his message – always the same – was relayed to a larger audience than usual, for he allowed himself to be interviewed by the lustrous and expensive television artiste Barbara Walters. (Bunker and Barbara had a friend in common, Seymour Weintraub. Weintraub had invested heavily in the silver market as well as in Bunker's horses.) Given the opportunity to advertise the virtue of silver, Bunker took it wholeheartedly. 'Invest in silver if you want a good investment on a long-term basis. . . . With silver you can't go wrong. I think prices are going up,' he said predictably, though he did add a cautionary note: 'It is too risky to buy on credit.' That remark should have astounded his bankers and brokers.

Bunker Hunt was at his most winsome for Barbara Walters. Had Bunker cornered the silver market? she asked. 'No, I don't think so. I'll take the question as a compliment.' How much silver did he own? 'I don't really keep track. I don't count my money. It's bad luck, and bad taste, maybe.' He doubted whether he spent more than $1,000 a month on himself (he was referring to cash transactions only); confessed that he had been accused of being 'a little bit overly soft-hearted'; conceded that 'on the personal side I'm cautious, but businesswise, I'm the least conservative person you could meet'; and announced that, although money can't buy happiness, 'I don't have to try to be happy. I guess I was born that way.'

But Bunker Hunt did not have much to be happy about in the silver market, and there was a revealing symptom of inner fretfulness shortly after the rules were changed. This concerned a deal with his acquaintance in Dubai, the bullion merchant Haji Ashraf, not one of those who consider Bunker to be 'a little bit overly soft-hearted.'

Ashraf, a small, wiry man who speaks English in the singsong accent of Pakistan, from which he emigrated to Dubai in 1967, is a man who makes meticulous calculations. He knows, for example, that he has sent 163 million ounces of Indian silver to Europe and the United States since his arrival in the Arabian Gulf. Ashraf has a retentive memory and can give you the silver price on any particular day; with barely a reference to his well-thumbed notebook, he remembers the last few days of January 1980 with painful clarity. Ashraf, who was staying in his London house that January, had 465,000 ounces of silver bullion, which was hedged by a short position on Comex. His bullion was in London, something Bunker Hunt found particularly desirable because of his unwavering conviction that one day soon the United States government might take his silver away from him. And Bunker, for his part, had a long position in the futures market that the market had now ordered him to reduce, against which Ashraf could offset his short position by an EFP – exchange of futures for physicals.

A bullion deal between the two seemed desirable, and their dealers in London and San Francisco discussed it eagerly. Ashraf made one condition, however. Knowing how keen Bunker was to own silver bullion in Europe, he asked that Bunker pay a premium of $3.00 an ounce for the convenience; instead of $38.50 an ounce on March 31, when the silver was to be delivered, Ashraf wanted $41.50. Bunker's dealer in San Francisco demurred at first, but twenty-four hours after negotiations opened, he accepted. Both Ashraf and his dealer were quite sure that he had done so with Bunker Hunt's knowledge.

Two days passed and Ashraf was eager to confirm the trade, but when his dealer telephoned San Francisco he learned that there had been a hitch: the $3.00 premium had suddenly become unacceptable. Ashraf complained personally to Bunker Hunt. 'Mr Hunt spoke to me and said that his dealer had been drunk when the deal was made. "He's a drunk, and that deal was no deal," Mr Hunt told me. The deal went through at $38.50 without the premium and I am short by $1,395,000, and Mr Stephen, I'm still waiting for it,' said Haji Ashraf sadly. Ashraf's London dealer was familiar with the social habits of his opposite number in San Francisco, and he comments: 'I know when he's drunk, and I'm sure he was sober when Ashraf's deal was made.' But Bunker Hunt was not to be moved.

Perhaps Bunker suddenly realized he could no longer afford to pay premiums. Since November 1979 he and Herbert had been spending money as though it were going out of fashion, and not only in the silver market. After an expensive junket in the stock market, each had portfolios that contained substantial holdings in shares such as Penn Central, Global Marine, and the First National Bank of Chicago. Bunker had bought half a million dollars' worth of shares in Columbia Pictures Industries. (This purchase was later to cause the president of Columbia, Francis T. Vincent, to accuse Bunker of participating in an illegal manoeuvre to take over the company, an attempt led by MGM's head, Kirk Kerkorian, and including Bunker's old chums Seymour Weintraub and Gordon McLendon. 'It was an effort to take control of Columbia which failed because of the silver collapse, which adversely affected Hunt to the point of having to sell his shares,' Vincent told *Variety* in October 1980.)

There were rumours that Bunker and Herbert were also buying heavily in one of the Seven Sisters of the oil industry, Texaco, though it was thought that the full cost – at least $10 billion for control – might be beyond even the Hunts. These purchases seemed to complement heavy buying by the family's Placid Oil Company in Louisiana Land and Exploration Company, and Gulf Resources and Chemical Corporation, because Texaco also has substantial concessions in

Louisiana. An article about these rumours in *New York* magazine was accompanied by a drawing of two cowboys lassoing Louisiana.

But the most interesting new shareholding, and the one most relevant to our story, was in a New York broker, the Bache Group. By March 18, 1980, Bunker had acquired 288,350 shares, and Herbert, 288,250 shares. Those holdings indicate a new strand in the tale, one that draws the Hunts into special relationships with some of the largest financial institutions in the United States and Switzerland.

Bache had been the second-largest brokerage house on Wall Street in the late 1960s, and its executives had optimistically anticipated the day when it would overtake Merrill Lynch. The company's speciality was share dealings for small customers through a large network of branches – unsophisticated business by the most superior Wall Street standards, which judged Bache a successful but 'schlocky' firm. As Wall Street standards became more exacting in the 1970s, and brokerage houses expanded into investment banking, insurance broking, and commodities, Bache had a problem staying in the first division. If total capital is the arbiter of success, Bache was down in fifth place in the Wall Street brokerage league by 1977; two years later it was in eighth place. Financial journalist Chris Welles wrote damningly in *Institutional Investor* in 1980: 'Without the benefit of interest income, Bache would have shown a pre-tax operating loss for each of the past four years, a far worse showing than other major firms.'

Bache had made acquisitions designed to broaden its experience and its business. A Chicago investment bank, Halsey Stuart, was bought, but many of its best customers drifted away. In the mid-1970s another takeover added a small brokerage company, Shields, and the group became known in the market as Bache Halsey Stuart Shields. But the mergers, instead of creating a stronger unit, sapped the vigour of the firm so badly that by 1979 Bache's chairman, Harry Jacobs – then fifty-eight years old, and having spent thirty-three of them with the company – feared that Bache itself was vulnerable to a takeover bid. If that were to happen, Jacobs knew that not only would the company's independence be threatened but his own job would be at stake, too.

And there was a bid. In the summer of 1979 three Canadian entrepreneurs, the Belzberg brothers from Vancouver, began to buy Bache stock. They said it was an investment, but it was, judged by Bache's profit record, a peculiar one; and when they owned 10.3 per cent of the shares it had become a sizeable enough 'investment' to make Jacobs look for ways of repelling the invasion of territory that he had come to regard as his own, especially after surviving decades of bitter office infighting. Jacobs changed Bache's rules so that an enemy would have to gain 75 per cent of the stock before winning control. This tactic was of dubious legality, but there was a possibility of a second defensive strategy. Bunker and Herbert had just become clients of Bache in a wholly typical manner: all of a sudden they were the biggest clients of all. Perhaps they would help.

The Hunts' prodigious position at Bache was established in September 1979 when George Lamborn, senior managing director of Shearson Loeb Rhoades, had in effect told Bunker and Herbert that Shearson did not want their business. Eliot Smith, Bache's executive vice-president in charge of commodities, had enthusiastically taken over the 2,600 silver contracts the Hunts had at Shearson, together with Scott McFarland, the San Francisco broker who specialized in the Hunt accounts. The addition of the Hunts' silver holdings from Shearson brought the brothers' account at Bache to more than 4,000 contracts – 20 million ounces of silver. As a sweetener for Bunker and Herbert, Bache – unlike Shearson, where Lamborn had insisted on the extra insurance of a margin of $25,000 for each contract – wanted only minimum margin. Since this was only $7,500 at the time, the decision conveniently freed more millions of the brothers' assets for speculation. And as an incentive to McFarland, he was guaranteed half of the the firm's proceeds from the Hunts' business.

It appears to have been a particularly unbusinesslike decision, for George Lamborn calculates that Bache made no more than $15,000 net profit from Bunker and Herbert's vast holdings in futures contracts. (Lamborn's reasoning, based on his own experience of the business, is that the broker's commission of $35 a contract on 4,000 contracts gives potential earnings of $140,000; but half of that went to McFarland; another $24,000 went to floor brokers; and as it costs $16,000 to clear 4,000 trades, this leaves $30,000. And the profit would be halved after taxes.) Lamborn judges that at that time Bache could not have been primarily interested in the business as a means of maximizing profits. And in October 1979, when Comex raised margins again, Bache was happy to lend its new customers money to pay: Bunker Hunt got $30 million, and Herbert Hunt, $7 million.

For the Hunts were being immensely obliging. In October 1979 Jacobs had approached them and asked if they would purchase any Bache shares that came onto the market. Acting as if one good turn deserved another, the Hunts agreed to establish a joint account to buy Bache stock, provided it was available at the right price. Between October 23 and 29, the brothers bought 50,000 shares, half a million dollars' worth. They had acquired a further 526,000 shares by March 18, 1980. (A purchase of 100,000 shares made on January 16 gave them a joint holding of more than 5 per cent of the common stock of

Bache. The rules of the Securities and Exchange Commission require that a holding of that size be reported publicly. somehow, the report was overlooked.)

On February 16 the joint account was separated, thus allowing Bunker and Herbert to argue that each had a separate, unreportable, position of less than 5 per cent of Bache stock. But purchases between then and March 18 followed the earlier pattern, with Bunker and Herbert buying similar packages of stock on the same days, at the same prices. By March 18, the date of their last purchase, they owned 576,000 shares, valued at more than $6 million. It was 6.5 per cent of the total stock – a useful weapon with which to confront the Belzberg brothers.

It must be made clear that from Harry Jacobs down, Bache denies the allegation, but I have nonetheless come across no single dealer on Wall Street who does not believe that the Hunts' shareholding was the reason why Bache was behaving with such generosity in February 1980, when the silver price was falling and both Bunker and Herbert Hunt were paying heavy margin calls. Bunker borrowed a mere $4.6 million from Bache in January, but in the following month he was lent a rather more substantial sum – $186.8 million. Herbert borrowed, too, and by the end of February the brothers' total indebtedness to Bache was $233 million. The loans were considerably larger than the stockholders' equity of $147 million, but they were collateralized by 17.4 million ounces of silver bullion. With silver above $30 an ounce in February, the collateral was worth almost four times that equity – as long as the price stayed at that level.

Bache had, in turn, borrowed the money it lent to the Hunts from ten banks, offering the same silver bullion as collateral. The banks included such distinguished names in the business as Bankers Trust, Irving Trust, and Barclays Bank; but the largest of all the lenders to Bache, and, therefore, indirectly to the Hunts, was the First National Bank of Chicago. Its contribution was $75 million. This loan was later to be the subject of one of the most acutely embarrassing experiences ever suffered by a lending banker appearing before a congressional committee. The victim was Richard L. Thomas, president of the First National Bank of Chicago, and the forum was open hearings of the Senate Banking Committee. The inquisitor was Senator Donald Stewart of Alabama, and their exchange went as follows:

MR THOMAS: We made loans beginning in the late fall of 1979 to a subsidiary of Bache Halsey Stuart Shields: Bache Metals. We had had a relationship with the parent for 35 years, with the metals subsidiary for five years. These loans were secured ultimately by only silver, and we had a $75 million facility for the usage of Bache and/or its subsidiary which was guaranteed by the parent, and this facility was drawn upon and was fully outstanding by the end of February.

SENATOR STEWART: Now were you aware of the fact that this $75 million made its way perhaps back to the Hunts in connection with their either taking positions in the market or margin calls?

MR THOMAS: We were not aware of that until March 26, I believe it was. We were advised that these were hedged positions in silver owned by Bache and/or customers, and we were not advised that the Hunt brothers were involved in any way in these transactions.

SENATOR STEWART: Did you later find out, though, that they were?

MR THOMAS: Yes, we did.

SENATOR STEWART: And were they hedged positions?

MR THOMAS: They were not. The loans were advanced on the basis that they were hedged positions, however. And I will have to state that there was certainly a misunderstanding as to the terms of that particular loan.

The inference from Thomas's testimony is that the First National of Chicago assumed the $75-million loan was intended for Bache customers in the commodity business, who would automatically hedge any long positions by taking offsetting short positions – that was how the market ought to operate. But Bunker never bothered to hedge – why should he insure against a fall in the silver price, when he was so sure it was going to rise, especially after he had taken such pains to see that it did so? Thomas's explanation for the First National's exposure to the risk was that its loan officers never asked who was receiving the loan, and that Bache did not volunteer the identities of the borrowers. But even if the loan officers at the bank (and, in a gruesome detail, they were all named at the Senate hearing: 'Robert Yohanon, Mr Putko, and Ray Groselak') had asked the right question, had learned that the loan was primarily intended to cover Bunker Hunt's margin calls, and had then dutifully referred the loan to the most senior executives of the bank, it is possible tht the loan would have been made, anyway; because Bunker, Herbert, and their younger brother, Lamar, had a special relationship with the First National Bank of Chicago, too.

Bunker and Herbert Hunt, like their father, H.L., understood the importance of being able to establish large credits with banks that could be called upon when needed. They, like H.L., had always banked with the First National Bank in Dallas, which understood a gamble in the oil industry and was happy to finance one. But in other industrial sectors the First National in Dallas was more conservative – in commodities, for example. So Bunker and Herbert began to use the First National of Chicago. They were good customers, and the bank was glad of their business.

The First National of Chicago is a substantial institution, the ninth-largest bank in the United States, and judged by the soaring black tower that houses its headquarters, it is also a prosperous institution. But like Bache at that time, the First National was not without problems. To begin with, the internal politics of the bank were rough; its casualties who had fled were to be found in senior positions in other banks throughout the nation. The man who had emerged on top, as the chairman, was a small, tough banker of Lebanese descent named Robert Abboud.

Abboud had progressed rapidly through the international department of First National, for a while running its offices in Beirut, where he began to develop extensive contacts in Arabia. He rose all the way to the top of the management hierarchy, and, once there, behaved as though he intended to stay, but he was an uncommon, intriguing, and atypical figure in the banking business: an Arabist, and a Democrat. Robert Abboud achieved a kind of national prominence shortly after the election of Jimmy Carter in 1976, when the First National gave substantial loans to the Georgia bank owned by Bert Lance, President Carter's lamented and lamentable director of the Office of Management and Budget. As the Carter administration took root in Washington, Abboud became one of its favourite bankers. His access to the White House was easy, and it became particularly useful when he wished to perform some favours for his Arab friends, especially those in the Saudi royal family. Abboud had established a relationship with no less a figure than Crown Prince Fahd; he also had been helpful in advising the kingdom's inexperienced banking industry. One of the Saudi bankers whom Abboud knew well was Khalid bin Mahfouz, and one of the businessmen of his acquaintance was Gaith Pharaon. (Bin Mahfouz and Pharaon used their banking interests in the United States to buy into Bert Lance's National Bank of Georgia, which conveniently relieved the First National of the embarrassment of its own loan, which was paid off.)

During the Carter administration the lending policies of the First National of Chicago began to reflect, perhaps unconsciously, the expectations of the president and his advisers, and in the spring and early summer of 1979 their expectation was that bank interest rates would not rise. In Chicago, the First National echoed this assumption by lending money at fixed interest rates. These were attractive to customers and increased the volume of business, but they were prudent only so long as interest rates did not, in fact, go up.

It was unfortunate for the bank, and for its chairman, that Paul Volcker should have succeeded G. William Miller as chairman of the Board of Governors of the Federal Reserve System in August 1979. Miller (who then became secretary of the treasury) had agreed with President Carter that interest rates ought not to rise; Volcker, on the other hand, was concerned by the rapid increase in borrowing from the banks and thought it dangerously inflationary. He insisted that interest rates rise to staunch the flow of money into the American economy. So they did.

As interest rates rose, the First National began to look less secure than banks that had been less generous with fixed-interest-rate loans; and the peril hidden in the balance sheet began to affect Abboud's position as chairman. Anxious for business that would return quick profits to the bank, Abboud began to invest in the risky short-term Eurodollar market; and to find investors who would buy shares in First National, and support the stock-market value of the bank, Abboud went to his old friends in Saudi Arabia. One of the names listed in the register of shareholders was Ali bin Mussalam, a director of IMIC, the spectacular new corporate player in the silver market in which Bunker and Herbert owned half of the shares.

When Paul Volcker introduced the first stage of his anti-inflationary policy on October 6, 1979, the Federal Reserve requested that American banks avoid loans for speculation, especially for commodities – a direct response to the rise in the price of silver and gold. The request was contained in a letter sent to all banks, and when it arrived in Chicago, all senior lending officers at the First National were duly informed. Richard Thomas recalled for the Senate Banking Committee: 'It was certainly the intention of the Bank from that time forward not to engage in loans for speculative purposes.' But those good intentions did not necessarily apply to all the bank's customers. In February 1980 Lamar Hunt borrowed $50 million to meet margin calls on his silver position. The purpose of that loan, Thomas explained, was not to finance speculation but 'to avoid precipitous liquidation of the position'. Another $35 million was borrowed by Bunker Hunt, and $15 million by Herbert Hunt; if not all that $50 million went to pay margin calls, most of it certainly did.

Of course, none of these loans was at fixed interest rates, either. They were very profitable for the bank. The First National needed profits, and the Hunts were willing to bear the high interest rates; they had always been willing to pay for money when they really needed it. As Richard Thomas explained to the Senate committee, the brothers had been 'very productive customers for us over the years.' Moreover, not only were the loans collateralized by silver bullion; the Hunts had also put up as security potentially valuable oil and gas concessions in the Beaufort Sea, north of Canada and Alaska. By the end of February 1980, directly and indirectly, the First National Bank of Chicago had lent the Hunts $175 million, most of it during that one month. Still, it looked good on the balance sheet.

Another bank was willing to lend even more generously. That was the Swiss Bank Corporation in Zurich. The largest bank in a country where there's one on every street corner, the Swiss Bank Corporation had expanded swiftly after World War II. The pace of its growth and of other Swiss banks, too, has been attributed by its detractors to the holdings of gold and jewellery deposited by East European Jews and not reclaimed after the war because so many of the bank's clients were victims of the Holocaust. But this is a very imperfect explanation. The Swiss banks grew because so many non-Swiss wanted the security of a Swiss bank account. Moreover, although Swiss bankers deliberately project an image of secrecy and caution, behind this facade they are as assertive, as willing to take risks, and as ruthless as any in the world. Unlike most American and West European bankers, many Swiss are enchanted by speculation, especially in precious metals. The Swiss Bank Corporation, among a myriad activities, is one of the world's leading distributors of South African gold. In Dubai, I was shown the 3¾-ounce gold bars that are slipped into specially designed small pockets in an undershirt before being smuggled into India; all bore the imprint of the Swiss Bank Corporation.

When the silver market became exciting, the Swiss Bank Corporation was part of the action; as we have seen with the disquieting experience of Walter Frey in Jeddah, the bank was a conduit for a chunk of the Saudi Arabian money that poured into the silver futures market. And their generosity was not confined to the Arabs. For the first five months of IMIC's raid on the silver market, its source of finance was the Swiss Bank Corporation, which loaned the infant company $150 million. Early in 1980, however, this loan, plus another $70 million lent personally to Bunker and Herbert Hunt, was taken over by a second group of banks, most of them in Europe – the Schroder Bank and Bank Leu in Zurich, and the Banque Arabe Internationale d'Investissements and the Saudi Finance Corporation in Paris. (The only American banks lending to IMIC were Citibank in New York and the First National in Dallas, which had grudgingly stumped up $15 million.) But the transfer of IMIC's loan did not terminate the Swiss Bank Corporation's interest in the silver market, for in February, Bunker and Herbert Hunt told the bank's New York office that they would like to draw on the $200-million line of credit they had already established. Each of the brothers borrowed $100 million from the obliging Swiss, and the loan was secured by 18.6 million ounces of silver. Showing some prudence, the bank asked that it be shipped to Zurich. But not enough aircraft could be chartered to fly it across the Atlantic, and it stayed in New York.

Bache, the First National of Chicago, and the Swiss Bank Corporation were the Hunts' largest creditors, and two of them (for the Swiss were never in real danger) had one thing in common: the lenders needed the borrowers as much as the borrowers needed them. What had begun as a case of greed had been transformed into an exercise in survival. But besides this trio, the Hunts were old customers of Citibank in New York, which had come up with $50 million for them and $40 million for IMIC. The New York branch of Crédit Lyonnais provided the brothers with $30 million. Even the First National in Dallas, despite its known distaste for commodities speculation, managed $20 million for the Hunts, on top of the loan to IMIC. Any sum, however small, was useful, and Bunker, who had already borrowed $8 million from the J. Henry Schroder Bank and Trust Company in New York, managed to squeeze another million dollars out of it in February.

Nor was Bache the only broker to lend money. ACLI International (a brokerage firm whose major shareholder is Adrian C. Israel, better known as Ace Israel, the owner of the People's Drug chain in Washington, D.C.) had extended loans of $147 million. Merrill Lynch had lent Herbert $102 million, and although this is not exactly peanuts, it was considerably less than the Merrill Lynch loan to IMIC to meet margin payments, which amounted to $287 million. Even E. F. Hutton, which had intended to behave circumspectly toward the Hunts after September 1979, were owed $100 million by them in March 1980.

This detailed study of Bunker's and Herbert's finances is available by courtesy of a small organization with a long title: the Subcommittee on Commerce, Consumer and Monetary Affairs of the House of Representatives' Government Operations Committee. The staff subpoenaed this information, and it is unusually valuable, because without the details it reveals of the size and pattern of Bunker's and Herbert's borrowing early in 1980, the totals would scarcely be credible. Before adding them up, it is worth reflecting that they were loans made to two American citizens from Dallas, acting independently of their companies. Ignoring IMIC for the moment, Bunker and Herbert borrowed no less than $1,074,000,000, most of it in just two months. Of that total, $654 million was credited to Bunker and $420 million to Herbert. The collateral was land, oil concessions, bags of coins, and, most of all, silver bullion: 70 million ounces of it. Add the brothers' share of IMIC's indebtedness of $498 million, and we finally have to stop counting in millions, for the brothers were in debt to the tune of more than $1.3 *billion*. This borrowing spree was without precedent in the history of banking.

The implications for the banking system of these astonishing loans were later analyzed by the Federal Reserve Board. Its estimate of the amount loaned to the Hunts was slightly more modest than that revealed on Capitol Hill; the Federal Reserve's statisticians calculated that total bank credit to the Hunt interests peaked at 'about' $1 billion. But the concern of the Federal Reserve system was domestic bank credit – loans made in the United States during a period in which the central bank had requested that loans not be made for speculation. During February and March alone, the domestic bank credit involved was $800 million. 'By contrast,' stated the Federal Reserve's interim report on the financial aspects of the silver-market situation, 'total business loans and total bank loans rose by $6.2 billion and $9.3 billion on a nonseasonally adjusted basis, respectively, during this two-month period.'

That dry analysis can be stated rather more dramatically, even on a nonseasonally adjusted basis. What it means is that of every extra $100 lent in the United States during those two months, $8.60 went to Bunker and Herbert; of each extra $100 lent to business, no less than $12.90 went to the Hunts. Clearly, it was not just the First National of Chicago that considered the Hunts as very productive customers.

Meanwhile, Bunker, forgetful as ever, was still dispensing advice about silver. 'You need to hold it,' he told Barbara Walters, 'because if the price comes down, you're in serious trouble. You could lose your shirt if you did it on credit.'

Chapter 12

Silver Bonds

By the middle of March 1980, Bunker Hunt was in danger of being taken to the cleaners. But he is a resourceful man, and his worst enemy would never accuse him of being a quitter. The professionals in the silver market had been wondering for months how Bunker proposed to get out – how he and his chums would liquidate their futures positions and take their profits. This was how market men expected manipulators to behave. But Bunker's terms of reference were quite unlike theirs. When I asked him about his motive, Bunker insisted that he was interested in silver as an investment. For a man who had speculated on such a scale, it was hardly a complete explanation, but his behaviour in the silver market, in the end, never actually contradicted it. Bunker and his allies had effectively squeezed the market by buying huge long positions and taking delivery of so many millions of ounces of silver; the increase in the value of their silver allowed them to borrow more money from the banks – a process known as leverage – and with more money they bought more silver. All the classic conditions of a squeeze existed; but Bunker Hunt did not stop there, and the longer he dominated the silver market, the more the professionals suspected his objective was to corner it. If Bunker, his family, and his friends cornered the market, accidentally or not, they would control the price for long enough to make a great deal of money. But contemplating a corner had its pitfalls: one of the agencies of the federal government might be able to prove that they had intended a corner, and that was illegal; almost as unpleasant was the prospect that a cornered market might be closed by the Commodity Futures Trading Commission, and then there would be no forum in which Bunker could achieve his ultimate objective. For logically it seems that he must have aimed to establish control over the price of silver, and to transform a short-term market coup into a money tree that would go on producing profit for years – just like an oil field. Bunker's tactics never suggested that he wanted to 'get out' in the traditional market use of the term.

Naturally, Bunker Hunt had pondered on what he would do with silver. Four years earlier, the Hunts had tinkered with the idea of barter: exchanging silver for sugar with the Philippines. But that had never been tried, because in 1976 international bankers did not regard silver as a proper substitute for hard cash. In the ensuing four years, however, the reputation of money had suffered; it was not 'hard' anymore. Traditional markets in stocks and bonds were based on capital investment and interest in cash, and they were beginning to suffer the consequences of a growing scepticism about paper money. The uncertainties of the previous four years had created a vogue for the minerals that had replaced cash as hard assets: gold, silver, platinum, strategic metals such as cobalt, and oil (before the great glut of 1981). Henry Jarecki often speculated that Bunker Hunt eventually intended to barter silver for oil – an attractive solution that would marry Bunker's two great preoccupations. There is, however, no evidence that Bunker considered the oil option.

But he certainly did consider another ambitious scheme, its attraction being that it was a step toward a goal Bunker Hunt devoutly desired. As soon as he had grasped the concept, Bunker became an enthusiastic proponent of the notion that currency should be backed by precious metals – gold and silver – just as it had been in the nineteenth century. The advantage of the remonetization of gold and silver, as the concept is known, is that governments cannot casually print money to pay for deficits in their spending unless they have sufficient gold or silver to do so. Since precious metals are in limited supply, remonetization acts as a brake on government spending, and it is an effective way of attacking inflation. Consequently, remonetization is a concept much admired by the conservative rich.

On the face of it, there was not much Bunker Hunt could do about remonetization, since control of the currency is quintessentially the business of government rather than of the private citizen. But he was not entirely powerless. There was a way of using silver as a substitute for money that would invest silver with some of the properties of money, and that was by issuing bonds backed by silver, which could be redeemed in silver instead of cash. Silver-backed bonds could be Bunker's revenge on the 'Crime of '73,' when silver had been eradicated as a guarantee of the dollar's value.

Tracing the development of the silver-bond scheme introduces a subplot of Byzantine complexity. I shall make it as simple as I can, but these are deep waters, my friends. The story begins in 1976. Bunker and Herbert Hunt had a protégé, a flamboyant Texan in his mid-thirties by the name of Michael Boswell. Having studied finance and law at Southern Methodist University, Boswell went to work at Great

Western United, the sugar-refining conglomerate that the Hunts had bought in 1975, where he acted, spoke, and dressed like a young man in a hurry. Indeed, working for Bunker and Herbert Hunt was attractive because they expanded their companies so quickly, that there were always opportunities for loyal young executives.

In 1977 the brothers shifted their attention away from the silver futures market to the actual source of bullion and tried to buy from the Sunshine Mining Company the largest single silver mine in the United States, its Sunshine mine, near Coeur d'Alene, Idaho. But the price they offered for the shares was too low; Great Western obtained only 28 per cent of the shares, though that was enough to make the Hunts the largest single shareholder, and they used that power to install Michael Boswell as president of Sunshine Mining.

Sunshine had profitable subsidiaries making fencing materials and electronic equipment, but Boswell was sure the company's most fruitful course was to concentrate on silver. Surveying Sunshine's silver properties, he decided that output could be expanded if new shafts were sunk to bring more ore to the surface. But the developments would cost millions of dollars and the money would have to be borrowed.

As an enthusiastic convert to Bunker Hunt's belief in silver as a means of exchange, like money, Boswell was convinced that the best security he could offer was the new silver he was proposing to mine. While he was at Great Western, Boswell had been involved in the silver-for-Philippine-sugar barter plan. Later, according to a February 1980 report in Jerome Smith's newsletter, *World Market Perspective*, Boswell offered silver as collateral for a loan from an Arab country. 'The idea was for Great Western to pay the Arabs a low interest rate while giving them a share of the profits if the silver price rose. Regarded as "premature" at the time, the plan foundered.' But the idea was discussed once more when Bunker and Herbert put Boswell in charge of Sunshine. 'We know,' reported Smith's newsletter, 'that Herbert Hunt contributed at one time to Boswell's by now fervent desire to see silver used as more than just an industrial metal.' And if Herbert was keen, Bunker was sure to know about it.

When, early in 1979, Bunker and Herbert mounted a bid for the remaining shares in Sunshine, they might reasonably have expected the support of their protégé. But after two years at the top, Boswell was relishing his independence, and he frustrated the efforts of his employers to buy the outstanding shares, telling stockholders that the Hunts' offer of $15 a share was not good enough. Bitter words were exchanged, particularly when it became clear that the shareholders sided with Boswell. Finally, in a rare concession of defeat, the brothers agreed to sell their own minority holding to Sunshine at $18.77 a share. The sale left Boswell in control, and by late 1979 he was intent on transforming the company according to his own design. So that Sunshine could concentrate on silver production, the manufacturing divisions were sold. Then, in December, Boswell recouped the money spent buying the Hunt shareholding by selling those shares, at $21.25 each, to a Luxembourg-based company known as the Arab Investors Group. On paper, the transaction seemed unexceptionable: the sale price showed a profit to Sunshine, and the Arabs, whose stated objective was a long-term investment in silver, were happy to be sleeping partners, allowing Boswell – who had become chairman – to get on with his reorganization unhindered.

But nothing in this subplot is that simple. There was a hindrance, in the form of a voluble New York investment analyst, Andrew Racz (pronounced 'Rats'). Hungarian-born and British-educated, Racz, who had never learned about reserve at Cambridge University, loudly protested that Boswell had given insufficient attention to a rival bid from an American company he represented, and he proceeded to draw a web of conspiracy covering the Arabs, the Hunts, and Sunshine. He suggested that they were jointly attempting to form a silver cartel that would shake the financial system of the United States.

Racz's evidence was entirely circumstantial, and sometimes contradictory. For example, he had taped a conversation with Michael Boswell in November 1979 in which Boswell explained how he had undermined the Hunt takeover of Sunshine: 'I told [Bunker Hunt] that if he got into a fight, I would force him to disclose to the SEC his activities in silver, his transactions and his positions, which I used to monitor while working for him,' Boswell said. This did not sound like a sound basis for a cartel, but internal contradictions in his case did not prevent Andrew Racz sending a succession of impetuous letters, in his wildly declamatory style ('I accuse!!!' he would write), to various congressmen, demanding an investigation based on his interview, and the presence of the Arab minority shareholders. It is true, nevertheless, that there were coincidences surrounding the Arab investment in Sunshine that did not occur even to Andrew Racz. One of the Arabs in the Arab Investors Group, for instance, was Joseph el Khoury, a Lebanese banker resident in Paris, who happens to be an old friend of Naji Nahas's. But coincidences do not support the burden of Racz's charges, which were that Bunker and Herbert never really lost control of Sunshine Mining, that Boswell remained their creature, and that Sunshine was part of a wider conspiracy to control the silver market. If all that was in fact true, Racz did not prove it. The silver story is full of red herrings, and I believe this to be one of them.

Racz's allegations did muddy the waters, making it more difficult to see what was happening. Out of the confusion, the silver-backed bonds re-emerged. Boswell had mentioned them in his interview with Racz in November 1979; as Racz reported, 'He discussed the possibility of raising money through silver-backed bonds and inquired as to who in America was qualified to carry out such a transaction.'

The man Boswell was looking for was an executive vice-president at Drexel Burnham Lambert in New York named Chris Anderson, a craggy, youthful, and unconventional figure among Wall Street investment bankers, who had been analyzing the effect of inflation on the bond market. Bonds are Anderson's business, and he understood that the fear generated among investors by inflation was changing the character of the bond market. As mistrust of money grew, investors either wanted a great deal more interest on their money than government or private borrowers had ever thought it would be necessary to pay, or they wanted a return in something other than money. 'When money is no longer a store of value, the investor wants someplace to hide,' says Anderson.

In 1979 Anderson was trying to contrive a bond that would enable an investor to purchase a refuge against inflation. He toyed with the idea of a bond whose return would be related to the retail price index, but when he ran the idea up the flagpole, nobody saluted. Next he turned to commodities and discovered that one of his clients, Sam Wyly (a Texan from Dallas, coincidentally), and his company, Earth Resources, wanted to raise money to develop a silver mine. Prodded by Wyly, Anderson produced the outline of a silver-backed bond. It would return an annual interest rate in cash, like other bonds, but the return would be lower than the prevailing market rate, and the principal could be redeemed in silver when the bond was due for repayment. The assumption was that the value of silver would rise even faster than the rate of inflation, thus compensating the investor for the relatively low annual cash payment of interest. But when the plan was put to the board of Earth Resources it caused dreadful internal dissension, and Anderson's bold project was stifled.

Not for long; Wyly, frustrated, wanted someone to benefit from the idea, and thought of Michael Boswell. Simultaneously, in mid-December 1979, Anderson heard about Boswell; within forty-eight hours they were breakfasting together, and it took them less than a week to agree to market a silver-backed bond the following April.

Anderson deliberately announced the Sunshine silver-backed

bond in a bland, matter-of-fact press release. Because the concept was original, it had to be reviewed by the SEC, so Drexel Burnham's lawyers cautiously refused to let Anderson announce what rate of interest the bonds would pay, and since the silver market was so volatile in January, when the preliminary announcement was made, there was no indication of the number of ounces of silver a $1,000 bond would be worth when it was redeemed. Despite these omissions, the response astonished Anderson. Sunshine had proposed raising $50 million to develop silver properties in Idaho, and in the first week after the announcement there were indications of interest from banks, financial institutions, and individuals with a total of no less than $1 billion to invest; in the second week, investors with a further $700 million added their names to the list of potential buyers. Nor was the clamour confined to the United States; prominent banks in West Germany and Switzerland were on the list. The idea had all the features of a resounding winner for Sunshine Mining; and this was hardly surprising, because, when the missing figures were supplied, it was apparent that the cash raised by Sunshine would allow the mine to raise silver production by 23 million ounces, while silver committed to the bondholders when their investments were redeemed amounted to only 1.5 million ounces. Meanwhile, Sunshine would be paying an interest rate of 8½ per cent – significantly less than any other company borrowing in the bond market in 1980. It was altogether an enchanting way of raising money.

By February 1980, Bunker Hunt was aware of the remarkable response to Sunshine's silver-backed bonds. Sam Wyly, who knew Bunker as well as Boswell, made sure he heard about the bonds, in case he had missed the announcement in the newspapers. As for Anderson himself, he is a conventional enough banker to feel bound by the discretion imposed on the relationship between himself and a client, but when I asked whether he had tried to contact Bunker and Herbert Hunt in February 1980 about issuing silver bonds, he replied: 'Of course I did. Anyone who was interested in silver at the time would.' But Anderson will not say more than that he met Bunker Hunt in Dallas that February.

To describe the outcome of those discussions I shall have to do something that I have so far tried, quite rigorously, to avoid doing: that is, to speculate. First, then, a list of what we know:

We know that as the silver price went down, Bunker and Herbert Hunt were borrowing immense sums from banks at high rates of interest – twice as much as the 8½ per cent Sunshine would be paying bondholders; and in February the interest rate was still rising. We know that Bunker was anxious to stabilize the price of silver: once it stopped falling, the daily margin calls would cease, and so would the drain on the Hunts' lines of bank credit and their cash reserves.

We know that Bunker Hunt relished the idea of expanding his silver interest into mine production. This is clear not just from his interest in Sunshine but from his acquisition of a 20 per cent interest in the St Cloud silver exploration project in Sierra County, New Mexico, from Goldfields Corporation on February 14, 1980.

So we may safely conclude that a silver-backed bond would have stimulated Bunker's curiosity. Indeed, everything we know suggests that Bunker Hunt and Chris Anderson *ought* to have formed an immediate alliance and, under the eminently respectable auspices of Drexel Burnham Lambert, announced that the Hunts and their Saudi allies would also issue silver-backed bonds. But they evidently did not, so we must wonder why it was that Bunker did not seize the opportunity when it was offered.

Perhaps it was the scale of Sunshine's bond offering. It was originally $50 million, and although this was briefly raised to $100 million – opportunistically, Anderson thought – when the silver price was at unprecedented levels, even the larger of those two sums was not big enough to animate Bunker. He was, perhaps, not in the mood to think of sums counted in less than billions of dollars, but it is unlikely that Drexel Burnham would have underwritten a billion-dollar issue, based on such an untried concept.

My final speculation is about what might have been. The Sunshine Mining Company's silver-backed bond was issued in April 1980 after the collapse of the silver price. Because of the uncertainty of the market, Sunshine's issue was scaled down to $30 million, but Drexel Burnham found the bonds easy to sell, and another issue was planned immediately. Had Bunker been willing to start modestly himself – with, say, a $100-million issue – and had his bonds sold as well as Sunshine's, he, too, could have come back for more, and more, every couple of months or so. Bunker and his friends might well have raised $2 billion in eighteen months, and there need have been no problem about explaining how the money would be spent. All Bunker had to say was that he proposed to buy as many silver-mine shares as were available on the market. He could have afforded to make shareholders – including Sunshine's – offers they could not refuse, and by controlling a significant share of the output of silver, Bunker could have achieved the ultimate objective and have established effective control over the price of silver. (There might have been anti-trust problems with the Justice Department, but any legal action would take years to come to judgment; and although Bunker could not have planned for it, the anti-trust laws were to be interpreted much less rigorously after President Ronald Reagan's inauguration, nine months later.)

So why did Bunker fail to announce his bond issue in February, while he still had the power in the silver market? Possibly he felt no sense of urgency and remained confident of the outcome of his speculation. Maybe he choked on the thought of paying commissions to Drexel Burnham. Perhaps the problem was that he wanted to raise too much too quickly; that would have been greed, and entirely in character.

By mid-March, Anderson already had intimations that Bunker had waited too long to launch a substantial issue of silver bonds successfully. The evidence was sketchy, but it did suggest that Bunker's game was turning sour. One day in the middle of March 1980, the preliminary orders for Sunshine's silver bonds, which had been made by the Dresdner Bank in Frankfurt, evaporated. The next day, all the orders from Switzerland dried up. 'We knew something was happening,' Anderson says, 'but we didn't know what.' It was Anderson's turn to speculate. If the European banks were no longer interested in silver bonds, their enthusiasm for silver itself must have begun to wane, and there must have been some sound reason for that. Perhaps it was something to do with Bunker himself; Anderson just did not know. He was soon to find out.

Chapter 13

Jetstar to Jeddah

Chris Anderson was one of the few people who felt any sense of foreboding in mid-March 1980. Various banks had lent the Hunts large sums of money, but they did not know that other banks had lent heavily, too; they had no indication of the magnitude of all the debts. It was the same thing among the brokerage houses; each knew how many silver contracts it was holding for Bunker and Herbert, but no one, except the brothers themselves and their faithful accountants in Dallas, knew what the complete jigsaw picture looked like. In Washington, the Commodity Futures Trading Commission, which was supposed to have the best idea of the picture because it had access to all the confidential reports the Hunts were obliged to file daily, was positively sanguine about the brothers' prospects.

At a surveillance meeting on the morning of March 14, the commissioners were informed by the staff that, despite a steady fall in the silver price, 'they [the Hunts] can handle short-term losses, because they bought at low prices'. The Hunts were rather more concerned than the federal regulators, and they would have been even more worried had they known what was happening eight blocks down Twenty-first Street, toward the Potomac, at the Federal Reserve Board. For, later that day, backed by an announcement from President Jimmy Carter himself, the Federal Reserve ordered a swingeing attack on inflation in the American economy. For a start, interest rates were up once again, making the Hunts' loans even more expensive to finance, but there was worse than that.

Among the weapons was a special credit restraint programme directed at the banks, and one item stated: 'Special restraint should be applied to financing of speculative holdings of commodities or precious metals.' The chairman of the Federal Reserve's governors, Paul Volcker, was aware that similar advice issued the previous October had had virtually no effect on loans to speculators. This time the banks were left in no doubt: 'restraint' was 'special', and although this section of the anti-inflation policy was voluntary, banks were clearly not expected to interpret the items as they wished. Central bankers have a phrase to describe the authority they use to back up voluntary policies: 'moral suasion'. The Federal Reserve expects banks to do their duty, and the banks rarely ignore a really serious request from Washington, because federal officials can, if provoked, make life awkward for them. Consequently, no bankers wished to incur the wrath of Paul Volcker, and after March 14, 1980, American banks and branches of foreign banks in the United States stopped lending money for speculation in silver and gold. Just like that. Morally, they had been suaded.

Whether Volcker did or did not realize the effect this 'special restraint' would have on Bunker and Herbert Hunt is uncertain. Volcker's assistant at that time, Gerald Corrigan, thinks not; on the other hand, one of Volcker's friends is quite certain he did. There is no doubt, however, that Bunker and Herbert themselves grasped the policy's full meaning immediately: they could expect *no more* credit from banks and brokers in the United States. The silver price was still falling, and the Federal Reserve's anti-inflation programme gave it another nudge downward. The brothers still had margin calls to meet, and so had IMIC. To raise more cash they would simply have to go abroad; and that was a role for Bunker.

But before Bunker Hunt left Dallas, soon after the Federal Reserve's March 14 package was revealed, there was one more special relationship the brothers were able to tap for funds: the Placid Oil Company. Formally, neither brother had any control over Placid. H. L. Hunt's first family's oil company is owned by trusts set up in 1935 by the old man for the sons and daughters of Lyda Bunker Hunt. Tax laws prevented the trusts' being controlled directly by the beneficiaries (though Bill Bledsoe recalled Bunker's buying land and informing his own trustees later that they had bought it for him), so neither Bunker nor Herbert was on the board of Placid, though their elder sister, Margaret Hunt Hill, and their younger brother, Lamar, were both vice-presidents.

Margaret is a tough lady who learned the oil business as a young girl by literally following in her father's footsteps, and she has never been very tolerant of Bunker's wilder flights of fancy. (In this respect she is more her father's child than Bunker is.) Margaret is reported by students of the family's politics to have been openly critical of Bunker's manoeuvres in the silver market. But when her three brothers, in desperate straits, came to Placid for help, Margaret was not so hard-hearted as to turn them down. There had been advance warning that the brothers might call on Placid for some money, when on February 23 they mortgaged oil and gas properties valued at $250 million in Custer County, Oklahoma, to Placid; now, in mid-March, they borrowed $50 million from the family firm – the first of two substantial loans. They were not substantial enough.

Any other American trying to raise large foreign loans would usually start in the City of London, but Bunker's refusal to pay damages into a British court after losing the Libyan case against British Petroleum meant that he was formally bankrupt in Britain. This was hardly a suitable background for a man coming to ask for a few hundred million dollars. His request for more cash had to be limited to Paris, Zurich, and Frankfurt, and it turned out to be an unhappy business, probably unique in his experience; he discovered that he was no longer welcome in the bankers' parlours. There was no money to be had anywhere, not even at the most exorbitant rates of interest. News of the Federal Reserve's credit restrictions had been absorbed quickly in the head offices of banks in Zurich, Geneva, and Berne, where the message was clear and understood. The Swiss Federal Banking Commission added weight to Volcker's request to American banks by announcing that it, too, was discouraging loans for speculation in silver and gold. Institutions like the Swiss Bank Corporation, which had unhesitatingly lent $200 million to the Hunts only two weeks earlier, now issued policy instructions that enough was enough. (Despite this edict, one of Bunker Hunt's old friends at that bank managed to extend Hunt's credit by means of a complex forward commitment in the foreign exchange market. Since this particular Swiss banker was also speculating in precious metals, he had a personal incentive for helping Bunker out; but his breach of the bank's policy was of no help to either of them, and when the Swiss Bank Corporation found out what he had done, he was fired.)

A week in Europe raised hardly any money at all, and the silver price continued to fall. On March 17 the Hunts' cash began to run out; for the first time a margin call from Bache was not met by an immediate telexed transfer of funds, and by March 19 Bunker and Herbert were forced to meet Bache's margin call with bullion instead of cash. On receiving this information during a business trip to Europe, Bache's chairman, Harry Jacobs, was disturbed enough to fly back to New York. By the time he returned, the bullion had dried up, too, and he agreed that, apparently as one last favour to two major shareholders in the company, Bache itself would meet the clearinghouse's margin calls on the Hunts' account, for the time being.

The Hunts were not the only clients in the silver market who could not raise the cash for margin calls. At Conti Commodities and ACLI International the 'foreign investors' accounts (which hid the identity of the Saudi speculators) and the small sect clustered around Naji

Nahas were also failing to meet the demands of the clearinghouse. ACLI sought out Naji Nahas to ask for money, but the closest they got to him was his cousin, Selim Gabriel Nassif. Though Nahas and Mahmoud Fustok had apparently found the search for cash as fruitless as Bunker, Nassif told the worried executives at ACLI that they had nothing to fear; Nahas, Bunker Hunt, and Mahmoud Fustok were just about to fly to Jeddah in a Jetstar. 'It will all be fixed,' reported Nassif calmly. 'They're going to come back with a pile of money.'

The Lockheed Jetstar is built for speed and comfort, though the cabin is necessarily cramped for a man the size of Bunker Hunt, who fits more comfortably into an open space, like a racetrack. The small, sleek aircraft has a range of 3,200 miles and a cruising speed of 560 miles an hour, and it takes only six hours to fly from Paris to Jeddah on the Red Sea. The Jetstar is functional, but it is not cheap. Still, by March 22, a Saturday, Bunker was willing to sacrifice economy to speed; the Saudis were absolutely the last special relationship he could call on.

Jeddah is a puritanical city, and no one visits it for fun (the Saudis do not even bother to include 'holiday' among the reasons for going there that a visitor must tick off on his entry visa). The port is a place for transacting business, but it is convenient. In March 1980, before the opening of a new airport twenty miles out of town – the Saudis needed the space to build the biggest airport in the world – the old terminal was only ten minutes' drive from the new hotels and royal palaces, which had totally changed the Jeddah skyline in the previous five years. But Bunker was even less inclined than usual to look at the few sights; he had no time to waste. He needed money, urgently, before Monday, because Bache's generosity was sure to run out soon, and in a week's time the Hunts would owe even larger sums to Engelhard, since March 31 was the date Bunker and Herbert were due to pay for 19 million ounces of silver that they had been contracted to buy in the exchange of futures for physicals made in January.

The visit did not start auspiciously, since Bunker had not had the time or the foresight, as the case may be, to obtain an entry visa. The Saudi bureaucracy normally moves slowly, but Bunker was an important enough visitor to rouse the immigration officials to almost immediate action. Nor did Bunker have to hang around in his hotel room, as most Western businessmen do, waiting for the telephone call that never seems to come. Mahmoud Fustok had access; a couple of phone calls, and the usual frustrations of doing business with the royal princes disappeared. Bunker himself would have had no trouble seeing the front man for the princes, Khalid bin Mahfouz, who popped up regularly in Houston; or in meeting Mohammed Aboud al-Amoudi, one of his co-directors in IMIC, the International Metals Investment Company, in Hamilton, Bermuda.

Bunker had to convince his Saudi allies that the price drop was a mere temporary aberration. There was no need to tell them that he had already borrowed as much as the American and Swiss banks would lend. His case was that if the princes would provide a few hundred million dollars more, that would be seed money to ensure a rich harvest in a few months' time. And that last investment would be even more in their interest than in the Hunts'. The Saudis' average buying price was around $25 an ounce, some $10 higher than the average price the Hunts had paid.

What Bunker did not know – for he would hardly have gone to Jeddah if he had known – was that the Saudi princes had by now become demoralized. The silver markets in New York and Chicago had proved more complicated than Bunker had ever hinted they might be; the rules of the game had been changed unilaterally by the markets; and the new financial policies of the Federal Reserve were exacerbating the difficulties. The princes thought that the whole business seemed to have turned into a conspiracy against *them*. With the Arab accounts showing losses for the first time since the great speculation began, the Saudi players felt frustrated – humiliated, even. The royal princes, proud men, had decided to nurse their bruises in private. They declined to play any more in such treacherous markets.

This flat message was communicated to Bunker Hunt, Mahmoud Fustok, and Naji Nahas by one of the children of Prince Abdullah, Prince Faisal Ibn Abdullah, and by the bankers bin Mahfouz and al-Amoudi. It was a rude awakening. The bottomless pit had a floor after all, and the trio had reached it; there was no more money to be had. The three visitors from the West climbed into the Jetstar and flew back to Paris.

But Bunker Hunt, as we have seen, was not a quitter. On his return to Paris he sought the privacy of Nahas's apartment in the sixteenth arrondissement, and of a small office in a bank in the Place Vendôme in which Khalid bin Mahfouz had an interest. The Banque Arabe Internationale d'Investissement also had a commodity dealing room, where Bunker could keep an eye on the silver price. Meeting with his collaborators, Bunker decided on one last venture to raise money, hoping that it would turn the silver price around, stop the devastating margin calls, and restore the confidence of those bankers and brokers who had turned off the tap. The idea was not new; Chris Anderson of Drexel Burnham Lambert had already discussed it with Bunker, who now decided to turn to a source of funds that, being a private person, he had always ignored before. Bunker prepared to announce an issue of silver-backed bonds to the general public.

The announcement had to be prepared at great speed because Bunker was engaged in a race to turn the silver price around before Bache decided to stop meeting his margin calls – which would certainly cause the price to plunge still further. And it was a race that Bunker appeared to have lost on the evening of March 25, when Herbert Hunt, who was minding the store in Dallas, received Bache's call informing him that the fall in the silver price during the previous five days' trading had led to margin calls of $135 million, which Bache had paid. Herbert was told they would do so no longer. Herbert knew, too, that there were even bigger debts at Merrill Lynch (which managed the IMIC account the Hunts had established with the Saudis), and there were further demands from brokers with smaller parcels of the Hunts' business. Bunker's companions on the flight to Jeddah were also in trouble, on a scale that paled only beside Bunker's and Herbert's debts, for the Levantine merchants and their Saudi associates owed their brokers, Conti and ACLI, some $70 million.

Herbert Hunt coolly informed Bache on March 25 that the Hunts could not pay, and on the telephone to Bunker, in Paris, Herbert received his final instructions. Agreed, there was nothing they could do about the silver that had been collateralized. That would certainly be sold by their brokers to pay their debts. But there was still a mass of silver that had not been used to secure loans. Bunker, whose faith in silver never wavered, decided to cling to what they could. The banks and the brokers would have to bankrupt them before getting their hands on the unsecured family silver. For without it, the proposed silver bonds would be meaningless – indeed, if the bonds were to be backed by silver the Hunts did not own, it would be fraud, and Bunker had never had to resort to that. The silver bonds were the Hunts' last throw; Bunker informed Herbert that the announcement would be made the next day.

Late in the afternoon of March 26 a letter was hand-delivered to the offices of the Associated Press news agency on the Rue du Faubourg Saint-Honoré in Paris, just down the street from the Elysée Palace, the residence of the president of France, and from the Hotel Bristol, Bunker's customary residence when he was in town. The letter was from a little-known public-relations company, Homsy Delafosse et Associés, and it read (in French): 'Dear Sir: You will find enclosed a communiqué about an agreement reached between a group of holders of silver for the issue of bonds. Given the importance of the communiqué, we hope that it will be of interest to you, and we ask that you distribute the news as soon as possible.' It was signed Pierre Homsy.

The announcement was taken to the room occupied by the AP-Dow Jones Financial Service, where the only man on the desk, David Pearson, was not merely interested by the enclosed communiqué; he was amazed. He read (in English rather than French):

> Mr NELSON BUNKER HUNT announced today that agreement in principle had been reached by a group of silver owners to join in the marketing of silver backed bonds.
>
> The group is composed of:
> H.R.H. PRINCE FAISAL BEN ABDULLAH AL SAOUD OF SAUDI ARABIA
> Mr MAHMOUD FUSTOCK OF SAUDI ARABIA
> Mr NAJI NAHAS OF BRASIL
> SHEIKH MOHAMED AL AMOUDI OF SAUDI ARABIA
> Mr NELSON BUNKER HUNT OF DALLAS, TEXAS
>
> Together these persons and their associates own in excess of two hundred million ounces of physical silver purchased for investment. Under the agreement in principle, a substantial portion of the silver would be dedicated to the backing of international interest bearing silver backed bonds distributed through financial institutions in denominations small enough to attract a wide range of investors.

The announcement was signed Nelson Bunker Hunt and dated March 26, 1980.

The silver price in New York on the previous day, March 25, had been $20.20 an ounce, and Dave Pearson's quick calculation showed that Bunker's bonds could amount to a remarkable $4-billion offering. It was clearly a significant story, and Pearson wanted to talk to his bureau chief about it before he put anything on the wire. Jack Aboaf, a small, cheerful, and very experienced reporter, was out on a job, at the Organization for Economic Cooperation and Development, but he called into the office shortly after the announcement arrived. When Pearson read it to him, Aboaf's suspicions were aroused immediately. He thought it could be a hoax, and he told Pearson to send it as a service message to New York to have them check it. Within an hour the announcement went over the AP-Dow Jones wire, datelined Paris, and timed 18.56 – just before two o'clock in the afternoon in New York.

Before the message got on the wire, Pierre Homsy was spreading the news in Paris. The financial editor of the *International Herald Tribune*, Carl Gewirtz, had been busy when Homsy telephoned and said that he represented Nelson Bunker Hunt, who proposed to market silver bonds. Gewirtz, who had never heard of Homsy, also thought it was a hoax, and growled into the telephone: 'Oh, yes, and you're speaking to the king of England.' Eventually, a reluctant Homsy agreed to send the announcement by telex to Gewirtz's office, but even then Gewirtz remained as suspicious as Aboaf had been. 'The only information we had, apart from the names, was that it did involve Hunt, that it could be for four billion dollars, and that nobody had ever announced a bond issue of that size except, conceivably, the United States Treasury,' Gewirtz recalls. There was nothing in the announcement to satisfy the curiosity of an experienced financial journalist: nothing to suggest what rate of interest the bonds would pay, or which banks and brokerage houses would sell the bonds. Gewirtz decided that he would have to call Homsy back and ask to speak to Bunker Hunt himself.

'You wouldn't know what he sounded like, anyway,' replied Homsy to this request, though he added that a *Wall Street Journal* reporter in New York named Julie Salomon had telephoned Mr Hunt in Paris as soon as she saw the story on the wire, and that she was satisfied that it was genuine. Still suspicious, Gewirtz telephoned the *Journal* in New York. Only then, after he had finally been convinced of its authenticity, did he write his own story. It appeared on the front page of the *Herald Tribune* the following morning, March 27, under the headline SILVER OWNERS SAID TO EYE $4-BILLION BOND OFFERING. But the second paragraph reported ominously: 'Bankers who said they had heard of the efforts by Mr Hunt to raise cash in Europe were sceptical, saying that such a mammoth offering could not be done.'

The same conclusion had been reached in New York as soon as Bunker's Paris announcement had been ripped off the tape machines and the news yelled through the noisy dealing rooms in the brokerage houses and the bullion merchants. At ACLI, which had done substantial business with the Arabs and the Hunts, Jerome Katz, the company president, looked gloomily at the AP-Dow Jones message and said abruptly: 'The jig is up.' The silver market thought so, too. Already weakened by some heavy selling by Bache, the price slumped in the last few minutes of trading, to $15.80 – down $4.40 on the day. Bunker's last throw was a loser.

At Bache, the senior executives had not even waited for the news from Paris. Earlier on the morning of March 26, fearing the implications for the silver price when knowledge of the Hunts' default on their margin payments became public, Bache had asked the board of Comex to close the market. The board refused, fearing in its turn that, once it had closed, there would be so little confidence in the market that it would not reopen for another decade. So Bache took the case to Washington. As Bunker's announcement was being made in Paris, Bache spoke to the chairman of the Federal Reserve and to the Commodity Futures Trading Commission. The CFTC was asked to close the market, and Volcker, to press the commission to do so. Bache, faced with impending bankruptcy, had panicked.

After the debacle, Harry Jacobs of Bache declared that his company had acted 'responsibly and prudently', a statement that left his colleagues on Wall Street breathless. To begin with, few of them thought it prudent to borrow $233 million from banks against silver that was not hedged. By hedging the 18.6 million ounces of silver that secured the loan, Bache would have protected its value against a precipitous fall in price. Having failed to hedge, Bache was totally unprotected once the silver price fell below $9.85 an ounce, because at that price the banks could demand that the money be repaid immediately. Of course, the Bache managers had shared the Hunts' conviction that silver could not possibly slump so badly, but they had short memories. Silver had stood at $9.85 only eight months earlier. Sharing the conviction of the most ardent silver bugs in history is a gamble; it is not responsible.

The $233-million loan had been arranged in order to pay for margin calls in the Hunts' vast futures position of 4,070 contracts – no less than 20.35 million ounces of silver. The loan needed to be that large because every time the price of silver fell by $1 the Hunts had to meet a further margin call of $20 million. And when the loan money ran out, Bache accepted more unhedged silver as further collateral for paying margin calls; and when *that* ran out, Bache paid the Hunts' margin calls for them. This was not just good customer relations; Bache had to pay the margin calls or it would have been in default with the exchange. If Bache did not pay the Hunts' margin debts, all Bache's positions in the market would have been liquidated, and that would have been the prelude to bankruptcy.

Bache's problem was twofold. First, as the silver price fell, so did the value of the collateral it held. Second, selling the collateralized silver might speed the decline of the silver price, pushing it, perhaps, below the critical level. In the expressive phrase of Deputy Treasury Secretary Robert Carswell, 'Bache was on the high wire without a net.' Bache in fact asked that a net be provided by Comex and the CFTC; that was the purpose of its decision on March 26, when the silver price was $15.80, to send no less a man than Bache's president, a well-groomed and immensely smooth figure named Virgin Sherrill, to ask that the silver market be closed. Once it had been closed, all silver contracts, including the Hunts' 4,070 at Bache, would be settled at prices comfortably higher than $9.85, and the threat of bankruptcy would be lifted.

The drawback to this solution was that it was designed entirely to help Bache and the Hunts, and there were innumerable brokers in the futures market who not only wanted the market open but found the idea of helping the Hunts quite obnoxious, especially as it would have been done at the expense of colleagues who had sold silver short at less than $15.80. But their opposition to Bache did not spring only from a belief that the company had been irresponsible and imprudent, because its sins were not confined to lending against unhedged silver. There was, for example, the complex matter of Bache's London subsidiary. This story was bullied out of Bache by George Lamborn, of the rival broker Shearson Loeb Rhoades. Lamborn was a persistent scourge of Bache, because he believed its mismanagement threatened the existence of the markets in which he and thousands of others made their living.

Lamborn understood that Bache's London branch Bache, Halsy, Stuart Ltd, was a nonguaranteed subsidiary of the parent company with a capital of £200,000; this meant that if it were to go bankrupt, its creditors would have no claim on the resources of Bache in New York, only on the £200,000 capital in London. But Bache's London branch had conducted business, presumably for the Hunts, on a scale that made the capitalization look dangerously insufficient, and the five London dealers from whom Bache bought silver had insisted that, if they were to trade with Bache in London, the contracts would have to be guaranteed by the parent company in New York. Anxious to get the business done, Bache agreed; any London losses would be met in New York.

On March 26, when Bache began to sell out the Hunts' silver to meet margin calls, the London transactions showed a loss of $26 million; naturally, London dealers insisted on payment from Bache in New York, and, responsibly, Bache paid out the money. It sounds like a perfectly honourable transaction, but it contravened the rules of the Securities and Exchange Commission and of the New York Stock Exchange, both of which had been led to believe that Bache's London debts were not guaranteed by the New York parent company. On discovering that in this case they were, Lamborn – who was worried that chaos in Comex would spill over into the Sugar Exchange, of which he was caretaker/chairman – interrogated his opposite number from Bache for three days, until the poor man finally conceded that the London branch's debts were guaranteed by Bache in New York. In retrospect, the episode sounds somewhat trivial, but it was nothing of the sort. The $26-million debt should have been deducted from Bache's capital in New York, and because the company was thus less well capitalized than its balance sheet suggested, its condition was even more serious than most observers understood.

But Bache was not the only commodities broker causing severe anxiety in the marketplace. ACLI International, the parent company of ACLI International Commodity Services, had lent $140 million to the Hunts, and the commodities subsidiary was owed millions of dollars of unpaid margin on accounts held by Naji Nahas, his friends, and the shadowy men behind the Banque Populaire Suisse accounts. At Conti Commodity Services the deficits on the various Nahas and Saudi accounts amounted to $50 million. The debts on the IMIC account at Merrill Lynch were the largest of all, $287 million, which was collateralized with gold, Treasury bills, and 14.6 million ounces of silver; and Merrill Lynch could not get Herbert Hunt to return telephone calls, which was worrying. Its exposure was the largest in the market, but Merrill Lynch's fears were concealed most effectively. Just by looking at the scale of the company's trading for the Hunts, other dealers knew that Wall Street's largest brokerage house must be in trouble, but the shrewd judgment of an executive in the London office two months earlier had spared Merrill Lynch from the humiliating prospect of serious defaults by Arab customers. Having failed to meet margin calls from Merrill Lynch in London, the Arabs said that if the firm insisted on such unsympathetic behaviour they would take their business off to Conti. At no time, during the panic or after it, did Merrill Lynch allow its appearances of composure to falter; that decision in London helped the company maintain it.

The brokerage houses and the bullion dealers in New York were in a terrible quandary: split between those whose own troubles were so bad that they were willing to sacrifice the silver market to save themselves, and those who believed they themselves would be sacrificed if the market were to be closed. On March 26, Comex, reacting to the fall in the silver price, dropped its margin requirements from $75,000 for each contract to $25,000, which released $80 million to Bache to pay the mounting margin calls as the silver price slumped. But Bache still wanted the market closed the following day. If the market remained open, Bache feared a further dreadful fall in the silver price. A majority of the Comex board, however, sensed a different kind of disaster. 'Close the market and we'd have been naked,' says one of the big bullion dealers, aware that if there were no silver markets in New York and Chicago, there would be nowhere else in the world, not even London, that could absorb the volume of their hedging business.

But the fallout from Bache's panic was not confined to the markets.

Within hours of hearing from Bache at lunchtime on March 26, Paul Volcker called a meeting of the men who would be involved if a Wall Street brokerage house were to collapse. These were the chairmen of the Commodity Futures Trading Commission and of the Securities and Exchange Commission, of course, as well as the comptroller of the currency and a representative from the Treasury Department. Their discussion immediately induced in the Treasury man, Deputy Secretary Robert Carswell, a sinking feeling; he had a frightened sense of what he later described as 'dereliction'. As the maelstrom grew he grasped for the first time that, despite all the talk about Big Government in Washington, authority was in fact hopelessly dispersed. The United States government is not organized to handle a complex, fast-breaking financial crisis.

The worst thing was that none of the participants knew what was happening. They did not know how deeply involved the Hunts had been in the silver market, or what the repercussions of their default might be, or whether the threat to Bache might spread to other brokerage houses. And what made it all the more frustrating was that the man whose job it was to know the largest part of the story seemed to be so unhelpful. James Stone, the youthful chairman of the Commodity Futures Trading Commission, had never before met Paul Volcker or Robert Carswell, and their first impression of him was poor. Neither appreciated just how little Stone knew or what peculiar constraints he worked under.

Those who slept at all on Wednesday night did so fitfully, because they knew that the crisis had only just begun, and what was really frightening was that, lacking any experience of this kind of breakdown, they had no idea how it might work out.

Chapter 14

Silver Thursday

There was no shortage of news on March 27, 1980. Within three days of the Shah of Iran's flight from Panama to Egypt, the Iranian parliament suspended its debate on the release of the hostages in the American Embassy. There was no comfort to be had anywhere for President Jimmy Carter, with political commentators mulling over his defeat by Senator Edward Kennedy in the New York and Connecticut primaries two days earlier. The early news bulletins reported the loss of 123 lives when an oil platform in the North Sea collapsed and sank. So there was plenty to discuss, but in the financial community the conversation was only about silver, the Hunts, and whether their failure would cause a panic during the day's trading.

Before most of the traders and brokers had woken up that morning, Carl Gewirtz in Paris – who had been told the previous evening by Pierre Homsy, Bunker Hunt's public-relations man, that Mr Hunt would give a press conference that day, Thursday – was trying to find out where it would be. By the morning, however, Homsy had become evasive. He no longer knew whether there would be a press conference or not, and he would not give Gewirtz Bunker's telephone number. Gewirtz was persistent, however, and by lunchtime he had a number, and got through to Bunker.

'That was a fine story this morning,' Hunt told Gewirtz, who then asked the question to which all the market men thought they already knew the answer: was the silver game really finished? 'I won't comment on that. I'll let events work out for themselves,' Bunker replied. But his plans suggested that he understood that the silver-backed bonds would not save him; he was about to leave Paris, and he never mentioned the bonds again. In New York, Chris Anderson at Drexel Burnham Lambert believed he had analyzed the fatal flaw in Bunker's bond announcement. Anderson's faith in silver-backed bonds was proof against shocks in the market, and he thought that if the announcement had been more skilful, it would have had the desired effect. 'The success of a bond issue depends on how you are going to use the proceeds,' Anderson says. 'If Hunt had said: "Gentlemen, I'm going to put all my silver in bonds so that my friends and I can double up our silver holdings," the price would have been up five dollars, not down.'

Before Bunker left Paris, there was still one little deception to perform. Pierre Homsy had told Gewirtz that Bunker was *going* to Saudi Arabia to raise money, not that he had already been and returned empty-handed. Homsy's version appeared in the *International Herald Tribune* the following morning, but what Bunker actually did was fly to London, on his way back to Dallas. His active role in the great silver gamble was finished.

While Bunker was telling Gewirtz, with uncharacteristic passivity, that he would let events work out for themselves, Herbert Hunt was still conducting a last offensive in New York. Telephoning the CFTC at eight a.m. from the offices of Comex, Herbert told the commission's staff that conditions in the silver market were now so bad that the Hunts could not, and would not, pay their debts by selling the silver that was not already hocked. Herbert advised the CFTC to close the market and force all holders of futures contracts to settle at the previous day's price of $15.80, because there was no more money coming from him, or Bunker, or Lamar. The attraction of that solution to the Hunts was not difficult to analyze; the silver they retained would be worth about $2.5 billion; they could pay off their debts and still clear a profit of around $1 billion. The winnings would not be as great as they had hoped for, but they would do. Then Herbert outlined the alternative – what would happen if the market were not closed. 'All the Hunt family will be washed out. We will go broke,' he said. Since the family was so rich, it was an awesome prospect.

No sooner had the conversation ended than a lawyer representing Bache telephoned the CFTC, from a pay telephone at Comex, to reinforce Herbert's advice: that the CFTC should declare a market emergency and dictate a price for the liquidation, or sale, of all contracts. It was only at this stage that the CFTC learned that Bache's problem was not confined to the Hunts' failure to meet margin calls: there was the $233-million loan that had financed their speculation as well. As a registered commodities dealer, Bache had to be able to demonstrate, daily if necessary, that it had sufficient capital to meet all its obligations. What the attorney was spelling out to the CFTC that morning was that, if the price plummeted again, Bache might not be able to do that.

The commissioners met to consider all this advice at nine-thirty a.m. 'It was a typical emergency meeting,' said one. 'We had nine people on nine phones, and no two people knew the same thing.' They did, however, piece together the information that the Hunts had not only refused to meet their margin call at Bache; they had silver accounts of varying sizes at eight brokers, and their debts, so far, added up to eight hundred million dollars. Moreover, Herbert Hunt had said, in effect, that the problem was the CFTC's, not his.

'What about oil wells as collateral?' one commissioner asked.

'The Hunts say they have collateralized everything,' replied a staff man.

'We just don't know,' said Chairman Stone.

Nor did the CFTC seem anxious to learn how this precarious financial condition had come about. One staff member mentioned a conversation with a Bache employee, who had suggested the possibility of a corner on the market – hinting at an illegal manipulation. But the staff man had cut him off; that was the business of the CFTC's enforcement division; the rest of the staff were not supposed even to speculate about the possibility. As for the requests from Herbert Hunt and Bache, the commissioners eventually judged that these had been founded on pure self-interest, and the CFTC ruled that the market would remain open.

There was only one more thing to do at that morning's meeting, and that was to agree that the CFTC should not reveal confidential information about market positions to the Treasury, the Federal Reserve, or the Securities and Exchange Commission. It was a startling decision, and the reasoning behind it was curious. 'They've exhibited great ignorance about the markets. We know the significance of the number of contracts in jeopardy, but I don't think they do,' said one commissioner. It was as though the problem would go away if its dimensions were kept in the dark.

When the silver market opened, the crisis deepened. The Hunt default at Bache was common knowledge by now, and the silver price slumped. Theo Hook remembers that the atmosphere in his dealing room was 'maniacal', with one contract being sold for as little as \$10.40 an ounce. By lunchtime on Thursday the price was \$10.80, so an ounce of silver was worth \$5.00 less than the evening before. And the fever this uncontrolled fall had created had washed over into the stock market. Bache had begun the day by selling some of the Hunts' futures contracts in the silver market, but with the price falling so fast, that was a dangerously unprofitable venture. So, to shore up its ailing finances, Bache turned to the stock market, where prices had not fallen so sharply, and began to dump the stocks the Hunts had deposited as security. Shares in the First National Bank of Chicago, the oil giant Texaco, and the Penn Central holding company flooded onto the market, and the index of share values on the New York Stock Exchange began to dive. An hour before trading closed, it was down thirty-two points, and the velocity of the fall seemed to be increasing. The one Hunt shareholding Bache had not sold was the 576,600 shares Bunker and Herbert held in Bache and Company.

The only good news in New York that afternoon was that, in the last hour of trading, the share index suddenly went into reverse. Large institutions, in a bold move to salvage the value of their own holdings, waded in with massive orders to buy. At the end of the day the index was down only two points. The experience had, however, been nerve-racking enough to earn the day the title of 'Silver Thursday' – Bunker's memorial day. It is the kind of title Wall Street reserves for the blackest days in its history, and the last day so designated was Black Thursday in October 1929, the augury of the Great Depression. It had been a damned close-run thing in the market, and the crisis was not over yet.

The bullion dealers were still deeply worried that Bache might yet be able to use the catastrophic fall in the silver price to persuade the CFTC to close the market. That, Henry Jarecki announced, would be a 'pseudo-solution', and he came up with an alternative. On Silver Thursday, Jarecki recalled a similar threat to the London silver market in 1913 when the Indian Specie Bank had tried to corner the market, and Chunilal Saraya had shot himself when the bank collapsed; Mocatta and Goldsmid in London had formed a consortium to buy up the Indian bank's silver and stabilize the market, and had made a profit, too. Now Jarecki decided that he would form a consortium to buy the Hunts' silver, and make a profit, again.

Even at so late a stage in the game, Jarecki still did not know how much silver the Hunts owned. At first, he thought he would have to buy 80 million ounces, and he started telephoning Europe, the Middle East, and the Far East to raise the cash. His proposal was that the consortium should offer the Hunts $8 an ounce, and there were eight or so institutions that found the idea attractive, including his minority shareholder, Standard Chartered Bank, which had also been involved in the 1913 consortium. Apparently, the prospective buyers were not discouraged when they discovered that Jarecki had made a mistake: they would have to take anything from 100 to 150 million ounces to buy out the Hunts. 'In strong hands,' Jarecki explains, 'it would have been an extremely profitable transaction.' The Hunts seemed to share this view because throughout Silver Thursday there was no response to the tentative and indirect approaches Jarecki made to them. History was not to be given the opportunity to repeat itself.

As midnight approached on Silver Thursday, the debate about the closure of the market was still unresolved. Jarecki, George Lamborn, and James Stone, plus a dozen or so more brokers and lawyers, discussed the issue during a conference call on the telephone that began at eleven-thirty p.m. and finished at two in the morning. Jarecki argued at length that the market should be opened that morning, and Lamborn interrupted occasionally with a single piece of advice: 'Make Bache liquidate the goddam Hunt position, but don't close the market.' Lamborn was not sure that a panic might not ensue if the market remained open. He did believe, however, that if the market opened, the problem would be shifted away from the brokers to the people with whom he believed responsibility properly lay – the bankers who had financed the speculation in the first place. Stone himself was uncertain; the length of the conversation indicates that closure was still an option.

Stone was concerned that at least three brokers – Bache, ACLI, and Conti – and perhaps Merrill Lynch and Paine Webber, another brokerage house that had done business for the Hunts, were in such trouble that if one or more of them were to go bankrupt, the clearing-house, whose members are contracted to meet the debts of defaulters, would either refuse to do so, because the sums were so large, or be unable to do so, for the same reason. 'Had any substantial clearing member failed to pay his assessment during the silver crisis, there is no reason for confidence that the others would have made good,' Chairman Stone wrote later. The failure of the clearinghouse would have destroyed the exchange overnight.

Nor was Bache the only company advising closure. New York bankers who thought it prudent to close the silver market had been telephoning the Treasury, and Carswell passed on their advice to James Stone without a recommendation. 'I was less than clear that closure was the right thing to do,' Carswell recalls.

The other recipient of much free advice was Paul Volcker, and he was no more certain of the course that ought to be followed than was Carswell, though he was one of the few people who understood the appalling dilemma closure would present to the administration. One of Volcker's difficulties was his sketchy knowledge of the intricate workings of commodity markets, and in some desperation he telephoned the former governer of the Federal Reserve, Dr Andrew Brimmer, who was on the board of Comex and certainly knew more than Volcker did. The two men spoke at midnight on Silver Thursday, and Volcker outlined his concern: if the silver market were closed the following day, every broker and bank that had lent money either to meet margin calls or to finance silver purchases would demand that it be repaid immediately; they would be irresponsible if they did not. And the only way the debtors could repay the money would be to borrow all over again; loans for margin calls would then be the largest single item of bank credit on Friday. But only two weeks earlier Volcker had explicitly ordered banks *not* to lend money for speculation of any kind, and that included margin calls. This policy of vigorous credit restraint, Volcker was certain, was the correct one. Nonetheless, if the market was closed and the policy applied, the bankruptcies it generated would be too awful to contemplate – partly because Volcker would be able to identify his own responsibility for them so clearly. Dr Brimmer strongly recommended that the silver market remain open. Volcker replied that he would wait and see what happened in London the following morning.

The London Metal Exchange sets the tone for trading in New York and Chicago later in the day. Because of the five-hour time difference, the result of the London silver fixing at midday – when the leading London bullion dealers meet at the offices of Samuel Montagu in the City to decide their price for silver – is known on the East Coast of the United States shortly after seven a.m. Early on the morning of Friday, March 28, Robert Carswell was waiting for the news at his desk in the gloomy bulk of the Treasury building, hard by the White House. So were Volcker and Stone, in their own offices.

When it came through, they learned that the London silver dealers were more optimistic than the New York and Chicago markets had been on Silver Thursday. Silver had traded on the London Exchange in a price range of $11.00 and $15.00 an ounce, and the bullion dealers had fixed their price at $13.99; that was down $2.00, but it was sufficiently higher than the New York closing price the previous day to convince both Volcker and Carswell that the case for closing the American silver markets had been greatly weakened.

The commissioners of the CFTC thought so, too, when they met a couple of hours later. Comforted by the news from London, the commissioners decided that the instability of a single broker – Bache – did not constitute a market emergency, and once more voted unanimously against closure. Stone reported Volcker's concern that many Arab customers, as well as the Hunts, were not meeting their margin calls, but the commissioners had not yet established any link between the Hunts and their Arab friends. They acted on the principle they had adhered to all along: where ignorance is bliss, 'tis folly to be wise.

On learning that its advice had been spurned again, Bache frantically dumped the remaining 3,316 silver futures contracts owned by Bunker and Herbert (the others had been liquidated the previous day) to raise the money to pay back what they had borrowed on behalf of the Hunts. It was a gamble; it could have been the last straw for the silver market; but it was not; and by the end of trading on Friday, silver was up, settling at $12 an ounce. Bache was able to pay off the $233-million loan, and the worst of its crisis seemed to be over.

(But Bache's relief was short-lived. Over the weekend a book-keeping error was discovered which revealed that there was still a loss of $50 million on the Hunt business. So the bookkeepers, having failed to spot the potential loss, were given the responsibility of putting it right, and they impudently juggled the accounts of various Bache subsidiaries to save the company from a breach of the New York Stock Exchange regulations. This juggling act caused Bache one last indignity: a lawsuit was initiated by Irving J. Louis, the aggrieved president of one of the subsidiaries, Bache Metals, who claimed to have lost $734,000 in shared profits when the bookkeepers switched profits out of the metal company into another subsidiary. And despite the juggling, there was still a substantial loss. These, you might have thought, were desperate days for Bache's chairman, Harry Jacobs; yet he is apparently one of those participants who have most successfully erased the memories of March 1980. His urbanity restored, Jacobs coolly confessed that there was one lesson to be learned from the affair. 'One thing we're looking at is whether Bache should have more stringent guidelines for the extension of credit,' he told *Fortune* magazine. Another thing Bache looked at was executive remuneration: some months later Jacobs was rewarded with a larger bonus than anyone on Wall Street, with the sole exception of the rather more discreet bosses at Merrill Lynch.)

The relaxed opinion on Wall Street after the event was that a Bache bankruptcy would have been no disaster, for there would have been a bid from another company, keen to acquire the extra business. But the financial system in commodity markets, as in all others, is like a genetic chain; beginning with the client, this chain spirals upward to the brokers and the bullion dealers, reaching the clearinghouse and the banks, and ending with the federal regulators and the Federal Reserve. Each link in the chain is affected by whatever happens to another link, and if any of them displays aberrant behaviour, the effect will be felt throughout the chain. Like the genetic functions of the body, the efficient operation of the financial system is taken for granted, until something goes wrong. Anyone in the financial world who had forgotten this truth was rudely reminded of it on Silver Thursday.

At the Federal Reserve Board, Paul Volcker's assistant, Gerald Corrigan, remembers sharing James Stone's fears about the stability of the clearinghouse. 'I did feel that if there had been a sizeable default, it could have gotten very nasty indeed.' But Bache survived – just. ACLI and Conti were both able to call on their immensely wealthy owners for more cash. Ace Israel poured $47 million into his commodities subsidiary; at Conti the infusion of cash was even greater. Michel Fribourg, chairman of Continental Grain, one of the two largest privately owned companies in the United States (the rival is Cargill) needed only to pick up the telephone and make a couple of calls to raise the $91 million that bolstered Conti's capital. The clearinghouse was going to be all right.

The flow of information from the CFTC had improved, too, because Robert Carswell, who, like Paul Volcker, was outraged by the commission's obstructionist attitude, had called a meeting of the heads of federal agencies at the Treasury on Silver Thursday and used all the authority of his office to force a bitterly humiliated James Stone to tell everyone else what the CFTC knew. Only then did the others discover the scale on which the Hunts had borrowed. The figure was $800 million and rising; on learning that, the comptroller of the currency, a small, crisp fifty-year-old New Yorker named John Heimann, became very worried indeed.

Heimann urgently wanted to know where the Hunts had got $800 million from, and ordered his staff to telephone twenty-five banks that might have lent to the Hunts. The comptroller's staff soon discovered that the money had indeed come from the banks, but that no one bank had a consolidated statement of all the Hunt loans, because Bunker and Herbert had refused to allow them to see one. The Hunt business had been too good for the banks to insist, and the absence of a consolidated statement caused Heimann to worry that the Hunts had used the same collateral to secure different loans; they would not have been the first gamblers to do so.

The comptroller's list of lenders to the Hunts showed that one bank had been especially generous: The First National of Chicago. Hearing this, Heimann ordered the staff to find out how the loans were secured; by silver, the bank replied, in depositories in New York and Chicago. Next, Heimann ordered bank inspectors to visit the vaults immediately to check that the silver was really there. It was the sort of day when no banker could be taken at his word.

Heimann felt only slightly less concerned when the inspectors reported that it was there, for if the price of silver fell below $7 an ounce – and that was still a possibility – the value of the collateral would be less than the sum of the loans. Although the Hunts had also provided the First of Chicago with oil concessions in the Canadian Arctic and the North Sea as further collateral, that did not relieve

Heimann of the dismal case of the Chicago bank. The only good news was that this collateral had not been used to secure loans from other banks because Heimann already had quite enough to worry about. He was simultaneously grappling with the problem of the First Pennsylvania Bank of Philadelphia, whose fragile financial portfolio was not unlike the First of Chicago's; and if the scheme to save the First Pennsy did not work, Heimann and his friend Paul Volcker would be left to mop up after the largest bank failure in the history of the United States. If the First of Chicago were to become as bad a case as the First Pennsy, money could move out of both with quite remarkable velocity when the financial community got the message, and Heimann was concerned that two bailouts would be beyond the resources of even the lender of last resort.

Heimann was especially aware of the deeply unsettling effects of Paul Volcker's anti-inflation policies, introduced two weeks earlier on March 14. The prime interest rate charged by commercial banks had risen to 20 per cent, a level that would have been inconceivable only a decade earlier. Such high interest rates had moved the banks into uncharted territory, and no one, certainly not Heimann or Volcker, knew what the immediate effect on the financial system might be. A few banks had already seriously misjudged the pattern of interest rates, and, among them, the First Pennsylvania was the classic case. The bank had invested $1.2 billion in fixed-interest loans at 8 per cent, and suddenly found itself paying interest rates that were more than twice as high to support the fixed-interest portfolio. The bank was losing money hand over fist, and the large institutional investors that had cash in fixed-term deposits began to withdraw the money when the term was up, instead of keeping the money in the bank as is their normal practice when they are confident of its management. Heimann could look down the list of deposits at the First Pennsy and, assuming that all were withdrawn when their term was up, forecast the date of the bank's bankruptcy with disturbing precision.

Most of the money deposited with the First Pennsy came from the Eurodollar market, a huge pool of funds invested in short-term notes with American and European banks. This new market in money has only two gears, forward and reverse; and when the Eurodollar market goes in reverse, the effect on a single bank can be devastating. Heimann feared that the First Pennsy was about to be devastated, and he knew that the sophisticated money men would be asking: who's next? With the failure of the Hunts' silver ploy, and the severe embarrassment of Bache in New York, the answer was obvious: the First Chicago was next.

The stewardship of Robert Abboud, chairman of the First National Bank of Chicago, had created a portfolio not unlike the First Pennsy's. It was not quite so violently out of line with the trend of interest rates, but the portfolio was showing losses. And those financiers who ask who is next do not wait to see if their answer is correct – they cut and run at the first sign of real trouble. Runs on a bank are no longer triggered by individual customers' lining up outside the doors to withdraw their life savings, as they were in the 1930s. (The Federal Deposit Insurance Corporation – the FDIC – guarantees the accounts of depositers with less than $100,000 in the bank, so the public does not panic anymore.) Now a run is created by the institutional money managers who look at the bank's balance sheet and say: 'I'm not going to risk a row with my board if there's trouble at the First of Chicago.' The money managers just withdraw their money when short-term loans come due, and it ebbs out of the bank like the tide on a shallow beach. And there was one money manager of consequence who was threatening to do just that. A mutual fund with a balance of half a billion dollars at the First of Chicago doubted the wisdom of keeping it there when the notes were due for repayment in April. The rumour was moving through the money market, and other depositors were wondering whether they should not follow the mutual fund's lead.

That was the scale of the threat to the First of Chicago, the ninth-largest bank in the United States, and Heimann decided that the only way he could prevent the rot spreading was to make sure that he successfully bailed out the First Pennsy, no matter how undeserving its management. The message he urgently wanted to transmit to the money men was that the United States government was not willing to let free-market forces operate in the banking system. Acting instinctively, the free market could destroy the thirty-fifth largest bank in the United States, and then move on to consume the ninth largest; if that were to happen, the credibility of the whole banking system would suffer, and depositors would begin to look for other places to keep their money. The comptroller, backed by the central bank, did not intend to let that happen. Money would be lent to the First Pennsy to save it from bankruptcy. By implication, the First of Chicago, if it found itself in dire straits, would be lent money, too. Bunker and Herbert might despise federal government intervention in free markets, but their excursion into silver had driven their friends in Chicago into possible dependency on it.

At the comptroller's office in L'Enfant Plaza on Friday, March 28, a delegation from the First National Bank of Chicago arrived to explain its problems to John Heimann. They sat in one room, while nervous executives from the First Pennsylvania Bank sat in another, and Heimann shuttled down between the two. By the end of Friday morning he thought he at least knew all the relevant facts, and provided these did not leak out and scare the financial community, Heimann thought he could manage the survival of both institutions.

(Heimann's concern about the two banks was an episode in the silver affair that was shrouded in discreet silence. He knew that public speculation about the danger would intensify the problem, and the similarity between the First Pennsy and the First of Chicago was never openly spoken about. Nor, obviously, was the possibility of the withdrawal of $500 million by a single customer of the First of Chicago, especially after the mutual fund's managers were persuaded in April to relent. But the threat to both banks was not lifted for another agonizing month, until the bailout of the First Pennsy, financed by both the Federal Government and the commercial banks, was announced at the end of April.)

After forty-eight frightening and largely sleepless hours, the crisis was beginning to appear manageable. At least the facts were known, although the consequences of what had occurred were still unclear. At lunchtime on March 28, after spending two days and most of Thursday night on the telephone, Gerald Corrigan at the Federal Reserve began to feel more comfortable: the clearinghouse had weathered the storm, banks were at least properly collateralized, and the silver price was up, not down again. Corrigan had the relieved feeling, as he puts it, that 'the parameters were properly defined'.

'And then,' says Corrigan, 'along came Engelhard.' A call from Engelhard's bankers, Salomon Brothers in New York, first alerted the Federal Reserve to this new dimension to the crisis. The problem was familiar enough: the Hunts did not have the cash to pay $665 million for 19 million ounces they were contracted to take delivery of on March 31, the following Monday. Volcker was informed on Friday afternoon that the tough-minded management at Engelhard wanted that money, all of it, by Monday morning. The inference was that the Hunts would be bankrupted at the beginning of the following week unless they found the cash to pay off Engelhard. And if the Hunts did default, the gossip in the silver market that Friday afternoon, when news of the latest crisis spread, was that silver would open at $6 on Monday, and the panic would begin all over again – except that it would be much worse.

It was a melancholy prospect for Volcker; if one creditor – Engelhard – sued, others were likely to follow, and the litigation would be endless, involving banks as well as brokerage houses. Volcker was not worried about the Hunts; it was unlikely that they would be penniless when the affair was finally unravelled. But their fate had become inextricably linked with that of the financial system of the United States, which was itself linked with that of the City of London, Paris, Frankfurt, and Zurich. In Europe, too, bankers waited anxiously for the latest news from New York and Washington. Looking back, only twenty-four hours after Silver Thursday, Swiss brokers – especially those of the Banque Populaire Suisse and the Swiss Bank Corporation – had decided that the international banking system was experiencing the most severe strain since the collapse of the Herstatt Bank of Cologne in 1974, which led to an international rescue operation. They were afraid that they might have to repeat that operation, on a larger scale, but what made the suspense difficult to bear was that they did not know. No one knew.

The question Volcker now had to ponder was whether it might not soon be necessary to sanction a bailout of the Hunts to protect the whole financial system. The complex relationship of borrowing and lending that fuelled the nation's economy was already suffering strain from the combination of record rates of both interest and inflation. Soon there would be the added stress of unemployment. Volcker could not ignore all that when he wondered about a bailout. Such a decision would be politically unpopular, and there would be no help from the White House. President Jimmy Carter and his chief domestic policy adviser, Stuart Eizenstat, were not interested in bailing out the Hunts. 'The president expressed that view in quite pungent terms,' Eizenstat recalls. The reaction was not fundamentally different elsewhere in the administration. 'Nobody wanted the Hunts bailed out; they're the least favourite characters anyone could dream of,' says Robert Carswell. But the personalities of Bunker and Herbert Hunt were not the issue. Bankers had begun to describe the problem as 'systemic', and a decision would have to be taken about the best way to deal with the monumental debts of the Hunt brothers.

Coincidentally, most of the participants in the drama had the same fixed engagement in their diaries for the weekend. The Reserve City Bankers' Association was to hold its annual meeting at the Florida coastal resort of Boca Raton. Overnight bags were packed by Paul Volcker and John Heimann. The treasury secretary, G. William Miller, who had kept a low profile so far, would be there on Sunday. The chief executives of all the biggest banks – Chase Manhattan, Morgan Guaranty, Citibank, Bank of America, and the First National banks of both Chicago and Dallas – were on their way, too. Later in the weekend they were to be joined by the top men from Engelhard, and by Bunker, Herbert, and Lamar Hunt.

There was no idle chat by the swimming pool that weekend.

Chapter 15

Boca Raton

The events that caused an agreeable spring weekend to be ruined could be traced right back to the previous summer. The rise in the silver price then had caused the amount of scrap arriving at the refineries to mount so fast that, after August 1979, Engelhard's own refinery in New Jersey had been working day and night throughout the autumn and winter to melt the scrap silver down into bullion bars. Consequently, the company had a uniquely large stock of bullion, even for the largest bullion dealer in the world. Prudence dictated that this stock of silver should be hedged to protect Engelhard from a fall in the silver price. And as the price rose, the margin calls on this short position became horrendous, even for Engelhard, whose resources are backed by the vast wealth of Harry Oppenheimer, the South African who controls, through his family's ownership of a substantial proportion of its shares, the Anglo-American Corporation, which, through direct stock ownership and trusts, controlled 27.6 per cent of Engelhard.

To relieve itself of the cost of those margin calls – running to more than $100 million on some days – Engelhard had undertaken an exchange of futures for physicals with Bunker and Herbert Hunt in January 1980. The Hunts had agreed to buy two small mountains of silver: the first was 19 million ounces, payment for which was due on March 31, 1980; the second, involving 11 million ounces, was not due for payment until the early summer. The price agreed for this hoard of silver was $35 an ounce, so, on Monday, March 31, the Hunts owed Engelhard $665 million. This was the biggest deal in the history of the silver market, easily beating Henry Jarecki's record, set with his 23-million-ounce deal in October 1979.

Engelhard had tried hard enough in January to guarantee payment, asking first for a bank draft, but, when the Hunts said they were unable to provide one, accepting 8.5 million ounces of silver as security instead. Their pocket calculators told the Engelhard executives that the Hunts' 8.5 million ounces would make the deal safe as long as the price stayed above $26 an ounce. They were content with that; although they expected the price to fall, they felt confident that they had been sufficiently prudent.

Yet, on March 28, when Volcker learned of the problem, the silver Bunker and Herbert were contracted to buy from Engelhard the following Monday was worth no more than $228 million, and the silver deposited as collateral, only $102 million. The difference between the value of the silver and the price the Hunts had contracted to pay was $335 million. Two days earlier, Herbert and Lamar Hunt, accompanied by their lawyers, had arrived at Engelhard's headquarters at the top of a skyscraper on Sixth Avenue in midtown Manhattan, and informed Milton Rosenthal – the company's chairman, president, and chief executive officer – of their cash-flow problem. They explained that, although they did not wish to default, they had no liquid assets with which to complete the deal. Herbert added that they would be back in Dallas on Saturday and invited Rosenthal to fly down and see if there were any Hunt assets that might be acceptable instead. Of course, Engelhard would retain all the silver, including the 8.5 million ounces' collateral, but Rosenthal wanted the difference to be paid in cash. Still, the Hunts had been polite. The decent thing to do, he thought, would be to go to Dallas.

Late on Friday, once Volcker knew about the problem, Rosenthal telephoned him to ask for an interpretation of the special credit restraint programme, which had banned loans for speculation. Rosenthal wanted to know whether the Federal Reserve would object if the Hunts could be persuaded to borrow the money they owed Engelhard, and could find the banks to lend it to them. Volcker replied the following morning; if the loan could be raised, he would have no objections, he said. It was a liberal interpretation of his own rules, but Volcker saw that the consequences of a Hunt default might be worse even than Silver Thursday; there was suddenly a spectre of a truly Black Monday.

Engelhard's private jet, flying to Dallas that Saturday, carried a highly priced cargo. Milton Rosenthal, his silver hair beautifully barbered, his suit discreet and very expensive, had received salary, director's fees, bonuses, and stock options totalling $2,007,726 in 1979. The vice-chairman and executive vice-president of Engelhard, a stocky, black-haired forty-two-year-old named David Tendler, who was also head of the hugely profitable commodities trading division, Philipp Brothers, had done even better: his total remuneration in 1979 had been $2,202,938. They were flanked by aides and lawyers who, if not quite in the same league, never had to ask where the next hot meal was coming from. But their total wealth would have seemed inconsequential to the Hunts. Despite the brother's present difficulties, they were still infinitely richer than mere salaried men.

No matter how great the value of their assets, Engelhard's lawyers were prepared to start legal action against the Hunts if they continued to assert that they had no cash. But this prospect depressed the business executives. Although a default by the Hunts would not ruin the company, it would involve hundreds of millions of dollars – the accountants had calculated that four months' earnings could disappear down the drain. It would look bad on the balance sheet; there would be awkward questions from the shareholders; it would not do their bonuses any good, either. Yet the crisis atmosphere seemed not to have communicated itself to Herbert or Lamar Hunt. When they met Rosenthal and his colleagues in the brothers' offices in Dallas, one observer noted: 'They were so alert and polite, it was almost as though nothing had happened.'

The Hunts rattled through a list of their assets: oil and gas concessions, office properties and land, even Bunker's racehorses. The Engelhard delegation was momentarily cheered by the thought that if the man who built the company into such a force, Charles Engelhard, had still been alive, he would certainly have plumped for the horses; he had loved them as much as Bunker did. Charlie Engelhard was a bold, rumbustious spirit, who, it has been said, provided Ian Fleming with the non-villainous characteristics for Goldfinger. On his death, the firm's buccaneering spirit died, too. His successors were of a more bureaucratic frame of mind, and they still preferred cash to any of the jewels in the Hunt empire.

By Sunday, Bunker had limped into Dallas from Europe. After his extensive travels of the past fortnight, which had taken him from Texas to Jeddah and back, by way of most of the commercial capitals of Western Europe, Bunker was exhausted. He played only a bit part in the negotiations, though he had the best line. On March 30 he guaranteed himself a place in future books of quotations when he allowed that 'a billion dollars isn't what it used to be'.

Since Engelhard continued to insist on cash, the Hunts eventually agreed that they would try to raise it, and they could have chosen no better day in the calendar for doing so. The Federal Reserve City Bankers Association was meeting that weekend in the resort of Boca Raton in Florida, and all the luminaries of the banking business were present. That meant all the Hunts' American bankers were, without exception, under one roof: Richard Thomas of the First National of Chicago, Elvis Mason of the First National of Dallas, William Spencer of Citibank, and W. T. Mundt of the Swiss Bank Corporation. Besides these, there were the chairmen or presidents of the

Chase Manhattan, Morgan Guaranty, Manufacturers Hanover, and the Bank of America. Such eminent men could certainly commit their organizations to a loan that would satisfy Engelhard.

If the bankers wanted advice, that was available, too. William Miller, secretary of the treasury, was due to speak at the formal dinner on Sunday evening; John Heimann was present; and on Sunday, Paul Volcker arrived. Volcker had had a particularly harrowing week, and not only because of the silver market; he was piloting legislation associated with his anti-inflation programme through Congress as well, and – to finish off a bad week – an Argentinean bank had collapsed on Friday night, which might add to the turmoil in New York on Monday. Volcker went to Florida hoping for a decent night's sleep. He was not so lucky.

The Hunts had telephoned William Spencer of Citibank and established that the bankers would discuss their cash problem on Sunday evening after Secretary Miller's speech. Boarding the aircraft once more, they flew to Florida and arrived in time to meet the bankers, at ten p.m. The Hunts and Engelhard were seated in separate rooms, and Volcker wearily told the bankers that he would like to be kept informed. Meanwhile, the CFTC was contacted yet again to ask whether the commissioners would consider closing the silver market if the negotiations broke down.

What followed was a kind of poker game: Engelhard wanted cash; the Hunts did not have it; the bankers did. Those were the hands, and the bankers' first response was to say no: the loan would not be prudent. As they were all in the same place, they had been able to draw up a fairly complete list of the Hunts' debts, and looking at it, they said there were too many loose ends to justify a loan. That, at least, was the diplomatic way of refusing; a few simply felt that it would be wrong to provide a safety net to protect the Hunts from the outcome of their speculative excesses.

Volcker, meanwhile, had left the dinner and returned to his room, where Gerald Corrigan was manning the telephone, as he had done since his arrival on Saturday. (I asked Corrigan who paid the phone bill. 'Most of the calls were incoming,' he replied dryly.) Volcker talked with a number of the bankers, and continued to do so after Corrigan went to bed at one a.m. The curious matter of Paul Volcker's pyjamas occurred after Corrigan left. In the following months, one of the strongest images retained in the collective memory of the whole silver debacle was of Paul Volcker in his pyjamas at Boca Raton, allegedly bailing out the richest family in America. The story infuriated Volcker, mainly because of the suggestion that he had bailed out the Hunts, but also because of the notion that so august a central banker should have been wandering about in his pyjamas. Both allegations seemed to undermine his authority; and central bankers really care about their authority because without it their power of moral suasion is reduced. (The pyjama story stuck, nonetheless, and my own theory about it is that Volcker, who does not much like the black tie he had been wearing at dinner, changed out of his shirt and jacket in the small hours of the morning and was spotted in one of the loudly checked sports shirts he wears for fishing.)

However he was dressed, Volcker did not protest when the bankers reported their refusal to lend more money to the Hunts. At four a.m. on Monday morning, the bankers told Engelhard's executives to concentrate on the Hunts' assets instead. It was a crucial moment in the game. If Engelhard had continued to insist on cash, the stakes would have become uncomfortably high: a breakdown would have caused chaos in the markets later that morning, and neither Volcker nor the bankers wanted that. One independent observer in Boca Raton that night believes that if Engelhard had stayed stubborn, the bankers would reluctantly have had to agree to the loan. But Milton Rosenthal and his companions were tired, and perhaps too gentlemanly to force their opponents' hands. Rosenthal finally agreed to accept second-best.

The only properties that interested Rosenthal and Tendler when they studied the list of Hunt assets were the oil concessions in the Beaufort Sea. Engelhard had sought a toehold in the oil business – it was one of the few resource industries in which the company was not already engaged. They chose those. Then the technical experts began to haggle about the exact number and location of the concessions that would be transferred to Engelhard ownership, and by five a.m. the bankers, tired of the arguments, told the Hunts that it was time they settled with good grace. Finally, Engelhard accepted 20 per cent of the Beaufort Sea concessions belonging to Bunker, Herbert, and Lamar Hunt.

The deal was not the one Rosenthal had actively sought, but he made the best of it. 'The Beaufort Sea has the potential of being the largest single oil-producing area outside Saudi Arabia,' he announced. Pressed, he had to concede that the value of the concessions might be anything between $1.00 and $17 billion, adding sagely that the truth probably lay 'somewhere between the two'. His rationalization when he spoke to Engelhard's shareholders on May 7, 1980, was that 'barter is an old and ancient practice'. In spite of the risk inherent in the Beaufort Sea acquisition – it might prove insufficiently productive or too expensive to develop – Engelhard employees who had not been in Boca Raton were exultant. 'We had those anti-Semitic bastards by the goolies, and we squeezed them dry,' said one to a friend in Congress. Milton Rosenthal was too dignified a man to put it that way, although he might secretly have found the sentiment unexceptionable.

The best compensation was also the most immediate. One Engelhard executive recalls the drama of the weekend. 'Can you image what it is like to be involved in a situation like 1929? We foresaw the financial world coming to an end. When we left New York for Dallas forty-eight hours earlier, the talk in the market, despite the recovery on Friday, was that silver would open on Monday at six dollars an ounce if our difficulty was not resolved.' When they finally returned to New York at noon on Monday, Rosenthal and his colleagues learned that the market had opened only 20 cents lower than on Friday. With the news of the settlement at Boca Raton, the price rose to $14.20.

Catastrophe had been averted, and it was time to pick up the pieces. James Stone tried. At the first surveillance meeting of the Commodity Futures Trading Commission after the crisis, Stone, as chairman, announced that he thought a speculator who could not meet margin calls should not be allowed to hold positions in other commodities. Bunker had speculative positions in Treasury bills, oil, soybeans, Swiss francs, deutschmarks, French francs, sugar, cocoa, gold, feeder cattle, pork bellies, and hogs. Stone moved that the Hunts be excluded from commodity markets, and waited for one of his colleagues to second the motion. None did. Read Dunn, once Stone's only ally on the CFTC, said sternly: 'I am not willing to sit here and make law on the spur of the moment.'

Stone was insistent. 'We're not talking,' he said, 'about Mrs Jones in Peoria missing a two-hundred-dollar margin call. These people can disrupt the market.' Still no response. Stone asked: 'Are there ripple effects which are going to affect the economic fabric of the whole United States?' Since no one else did, Stone replied rhetorically: 'My answer is yes.' But Stone was an isolated figure now, and the CFTC, behaving according to form, did nothing. But that was only a momentary relief for Bunker and Herbert Hunt. After the settlement with Engelhard at Boca Raton, they still owed $1.2 billion. Possibly more.

For others who had played the game, the losses had been smaller but even more devastating. A Lebanese friend of Maurice Zilber's, Bunker's French racehorse trainer, saw him in the street in Paris early in April. Zilber did not stop, but as he walked by, he muttered: '*Nous sommes foutus*.' Whether Bunker and Herbert Hunt were to suffer the same fate was still uncertain.

Chapter 16

The Billion-Dollar Loan

There was one plausible solution to the problem of debts, and that was the silver. Of course, Bunker and Herbert Hunt had seen their hoard reduced after their doom-laden week in the market when Bache sold off all the silver and futures contracts held as collateral; that enforced sale diminished the Hunts' silver mountain by nearly 40 million ounces. But that was not the half, or even the quarter, of it. At the beginning of April the Hunts still had more silver than any individuals had ever owned anywhere, at any time. Exactly how much is not entirely clear, despite the volume of information that later poured out of the confidential files of the Commodity Futures Trading Commission. From this information we know that on April 2, 1980, the Hunts owned 158 million ounces of silver; we do not know how much was subsequently sold off to repay loans. By the end of April, however, the brothers owned 63 million ounces of silver; we have their bankers' word for that. But that 63 million ounces did not include the silver belonging to IMIC, which still owned 34 million ounces. Details of the internal politics of the Bermuda company that brought the Texans and the Saudis into partnership have remained an uncommonly well kept secret, but at least we know that Bunker and Herbert Hunt were responsible for IMIC's debts to Merrill Lynch in the United States, and the inference to be drawn is that the brothers would also have owned IMIC's silver in the United States. If that was the case, the Hunts would have possessed 97 million ounces; and even if only half of the IMIC's bullion belonged to Bunker and Herbert, they would still have had 80 million ounces of silver. When the price recovered to $14 an ounce from its lowest depth on Silver Thursday, the value of this silver would have been $1.1 billion. Coincidentally, this sum was exactly the same as the Hunt debts to the banks and brokerage houses at home and abroad. And there was a margin for error: the total value of all their holdings in precious metals and coins came to $1.3 billion. If this story were to end symmetrically, the debts would have been cancelled by selling the silver.

This tidy solution occurred to a number of congressmen, too. An exchange between Paul Volcker and Elliott Levitas of Georgia at a hearing on April 30 outlined the possibilities.

> LEVITAS: Mr Volcker, if the Hunts were to sell the silver which they now own, do you have any sense that it would provide sufficient funds to honour their present commitments without a loan being made to them?
>
> VOLCKER: It depends on the price of silver, of course.
>
> LEVITAS: It is about $14.00.
>
> VOLCKER: I think it would, at the present price of silver. To the best of my knowledge the loans are margined, in effect.
>
> LEVITAS: At the present price. According to your information that a liquidation by the Hunts would not be adequate to meet their present commitments . . .
>
> VOLCKER: I think they would be [adequate], at the present price. But I just don't know. That is an impression I have.
>
> LEVITAS: That is an impression I have too. If that is the case, the U.S. banks involved – and I emphasize U.S. banks – and the U.S. brokerage houses that are involved would not be at risk.
>
> VOLCKER: There are risks depending upon the silver price.

The simple, tidy – if risky – solution did not appeal to Bunker and Herbert Hunt. Bunker's faith in silver as an investment was still not shaken. He had persuaded himself that he was the victim of an unscrupulous market, the bias of the CFTC, and the policies of the Federal Reserve. He believed the silver price was too low and made it clear that he would not voluntarily divest himself of his silver. But the Federal Reserve, Congress, and the banks did not have to pander to Bunker's desire to hold on to his silver. Why, then, were the brothers not forced to sell their silver to pay the debt and let the punishment fit the crime?

The reasons are illuminating, because it becomes clear that in a free society it is difficult to force a very rich man to sell something he is determined to keep. If Bunker had worked on an oil rig instead of owning oil fields, and had fallen into debt after speculating unwisely in commodity markets, the banks would not have hesitated to repossess his car or sell his house. They could have done so without a second thought because the sale of one house would not affect the price of property. But the rich are dealt with more gingerly. The sale of 80 million or more ounces of silver might well send the price plummeting again, especially if such a sale were involuntary and the market knew that the owner had no choice. That would reduce the value of the collateral backing the original Hunt loans – something the banks thought most undesirable. Moreover, the bankers feared that, faced by the prospect of an enforced sale of their silver, Bunker and Herbert might stubbornly choose another option available only to the very rich: they could threaten to default on the loans. The creditors would be able to collect eventually, for there were quite enough assets to cover debts of more than a billion dollars; but the prospect of wrangling with a battery of Hunt lawyers, and squabbling over who should have a lien on what, was hardly agreeable. For the bankers, a more gradual course was infinitely more attractive, and, best of all, removed the risk. So Bunker and Herbert Hunt were allowed to keep their silver.

Now there was only one alternative, and that was to lend to them all over again so that the loans could be paid off over a longer period of time. When the bankers returned from Boca Raton to New York, Chicago, Dallas, and San Francisco, they had decided in principle that there would have to be another loan. The Hunts would not increase their indebtedness, of course; the idea was that their creditors would be paid off from the proceeds of a new loan, raised by a consortium of banks, which would take over the existing loans from the banks and brokerage houses that had financed the great silver speculation; the principle is familiar to anyone with a mortgage because it meant 'rescheduling' the loan. The Hunts were just taking out a second mortgage, except that the principal involved would purchase a few city blocks rather than a humble home.

The new lenders did not want to have anything to do with the silver market; that was still risky. So the banks looked around for solid, guaranteed assets, and their gaze fixed on the Placid Oil Company. Their proposal was this: they would reschedule the loan if Placid would put up all the assets of the family firm as collateral. The banks would lend to Placid, which would, in turn, lend to Bunker, Herbert, and Lamar Hunt. It would then be Placid's responsibility, not the banks', to ensure that the brothers repaid the loan. The brothers mortgaged their possessions to Placid instead of to the banks; the bankers felt safer that way.

The principle was quickly agreed – necessarily so, for the brokerage houses were desperate for money to replace their lost capital. Citibank started the rescue operation as soon as its chairman returned from Boca Raton, and by April 8 an interim loan of $300 million had been made to Placid. This was the first tranche of what became the largest single bank loan to three private citizens in the history of the American banking industry; indeed, it was the biggest ever, anywhere. And, inevitably, such a loan had to be referred to the nation's bank manager, Paul Volcker.

Central bankers often seem to be Olympian and somewhat enigmatic figures. Always appearing to know what is best, they tell us that we are spending too much, that we must understand there are virtues in unemployment, and that we generally ought to shape up and tighten our belts. The image that accompanies this stereotype of a central banker is of a dapper, pinstriped man. Paul Volcker is not the physical type. He stands six feet seven inches tall, and he is a slouching, sprawling man with a penchant for suits off the peg and cheap cigars. (His taste is actually for expensive cigars, but he smokes so many that they have to be cheap.) One of his colleagues, Thomas Timlen of the New York Federal Reserve Bank, recalls: 'In formal meetings with the governors of various central banks, his legs would be spread across the coffee table, and cigar ash would be falling over his belt and trousers.' Other bankers seemed to find this engagingly eccentric, possibly because they recognized Volcker, nevertheless, as one of their own. Volcker himself says: 'I don't necessarily fit the traditional image of central bankers, but I do share with them a belief that the central banker's role is as the defender of stability and continuity.'

Volcker's training for the role was remarkably complete. After graduating from Princeton, receiving an M.A. from Harvard, and attending the London School of Economics for a while, he worked for the Federal Reserve in New York, and for Chase Manhattan, before going to Washington for the first of two interludes in government. During the second of these, Volcker was under-secretary for monetary affairs at the Treasury Department and was personally involved in the episodes in the early 1970s that led to the end of fixed exchange rates and two devaluations of the dollar. The Treasury was a prelude to his appointment as president of the Federal Reserve Bank of New York, and when Volcker returned to Washington again, at the age of fifty-one, in August 1979, to run the whole system, one of his predecessors, Arthur Burns, said of him: 'He has lived through a great deal of economic history first hand, so I think he's had a unique education. I'd say that among the central bankers of the world, he's had more experience than any other.'

Volcker saw that inflation was undermining the nation's financial continuity and stability, and his policies as chairman were designed to halt the erosion of the value of money. This approach ought to have appealed to Bunker Hunt, preoccupied as he also was by inflation. But while Volcker wanted to enlist the whole of American society in the struggle, Bunker felt the battle was already lost, and was trying to ensure his personal survival. Volcker's policies led to high interest rates, to stop consumers spending so much money, but those interest rates meant Bunker and Herbert Hunt also had to pay more to *borrow* money. It would have been surprising if Bunker had not felt Volcker's doctrines were an assault on his freedom. The two men never met; it is difficult to imagine what they could have said to each other if they had.

To Volcker, the evidence against Bunker was damning. Inflation was not the sole factor threatening stability and continuity; Bunker, his brothers, and their Saudi friends were undermining it, too. In the circumstances, a stern central banker might well wish to see the transgressors punished, as an example to others. But Volcker could not be sure what the consequences would be if a punitive course were followed. If the loan were withheld, it was possible that the Hunt silver could be sold at high enough prices to pay off the loans. It was possible also that the most vulnerable brokerage houses and banks could survive a default by the Hunts. It was possible, but it was a gamble; and it was stability and continuity that were at risk.

After the loan was announced, whether Paul Volcker was questioned on Capitol Hill or by inquisitive reporters, he always insisted that he had not 'instigated' it, or 'initiated' it, or 'guided' it, or 'organized' it, or 'sponsored' it, or even 'shepherded' it. Any more denials and he would have had to reach for Roget's *Thesaurus*. Strictly speaking, Volcker was quite correct. As at Boca Raton, he asked the banks to do nothing more than keep him informed. He pointed out with some regularity that the United States is a free country and the agreement was made between two private parties. That was strictly true, too. But Volcker could have stopped the banks' lending to the Hunts. The special credit restraint programme was only voluntary, 'but I think,' Volcker told Congressman Levitas, 'I have sufficient "moral authority" to have stopped it if I thought it violated speculative precepts.' Because Volcker had that power of moral suasion, Elvis Mason, chairman of the First National in Dallas, one of the two banks organizing the loan, telephoned him on April 5 to ask for guidance. If Volcker had said then that he disapproved of the loan – and there were grounds for doing so, because the new loan was rescheduling old loans made for strictly speculative purposes – most of the banks in the consortium would have retreated from the project. But Volcker decided that possible opprobrium on Capitol Hill was less important than the risk of real financial instability. Volcker did not say 'No' to Mason; he said, 'Yes, but . . .'

Since it was speculation in commodity markets by Bunker, Herbert, and Lamar Hunt that had been 'destabilizing', Volcker insisted it must be a condition of the loan that the brothers stop speculating in commodity markets entirely for the whole term of the loan – which was for ten years, until 1990. A further stipulation was that the main instrument of their speculation, the silver itself, must be sold 'in an orderly manner'. Both Volcker and Heimann kept a wary eye on the loan negotiations throughout April to make sure that the conditions were met (though the banks were delighted to be able to include them), and that interest was to lead to accusations that Volcker had somehow bailed out the Hunts.

This attitude was most clearly expressed by Congressman Benjamin Rosenthal, a lean and stern New York lawyer who was chairman of the House Subcommittee on Commerce, Consumer and Monetary Affairs. At a hearing on April 30 Rosenthal had a tart exchange with Volcker that concisely expressed their conflcting attitudes to the Hunt loan:

ROSENTHAL: Could it be described that you are shepherding this loan along?

VOLCKER: No.

ROSENTHAL: You seem to be helping it move along. You spoke to the banks.

VOLCKER: If you interpret 'helping it move it along' as making as clear as I could possibly make it that any loan of this sort had to contain safeguards against renewed speculation, that is not exactly my definition of 'shepherding'. Maybe it is yours.

ROSENTHAL: If the Hunts don't get this loan, what will happen?

VOLCKER: If the Hunts don't get this loan I think some of the creditors will feel that they are in a somewhat less secure and stable position than they would otherwise be in, and that this could have some repercussions for the market generally and, from my point of view, we will be less protected on the speculative side than otherwise.

ROSENTHAL: Do you think the banks are acting more favourably towards the Hunts because of your presence or involvement, your interest, your concern?

VOLCKER: Quite the contrary. But in saying that, I think the banks themselves were sensitive to this speculative point. They were aware of the loan restraint programme. I think they were aware of the public policy issues involved, but I certainly don't make life any easier for them.

ROSENTHAL: But does any other private individual in this country have your interest to the extent that the Hunts do?

VOLCKER: The Hunts have my interest? I'm not sure that would be a general interpretation.

ROSENTHAL: Do you want them to get the loan?

VOLCKER: I have no objection to the loan, provided that these conditions are met. I think the loan is not inconsistent with the public interest.

ROSENTHAL: Do you want them to get the loan?

VOLCKER: Do I want them to get the loan? I don't want them to get the loan on any terms other than what I suggested with respect to the speculation. Look, you are suggesting something. It is not my function to 'want' or 'unwant' in some sense. I don't want or unwant any borrower to get a loan or not get a loan. If we have loan restraint, after going through this experience, I certainly do not want the Hunts to resume speculation in silver or other commodity markets.

ROSENTHAL: If they don't get this loan, they are not resuming speculation, you can bet on that.

VOLCKER: I don't know. They are not tied down. If the price of silver goes up, they will be in a good cash position. They can do what they want as things now stand.

Volcker, then, did not approve of the loan and he did not disapprove of it. As the lender of last resort, he simply decided not to use his powers of moral suasion to prevent the private banking system bailing out Bunker, Herbert, and Lamar Hunt, but he did insist conditions, and when they were written in, he approved them.

So, on May 1, 1980, a letter was sent on behalf of thirteen banks to the Placid Oil Company confirming a loan of $1.1 billion. The list of lenders was impressive, containing the names of virtually every big bank in the United States and Canada. The First in Dallas and Morgan Guaranty were the leaders of the loan; then came Citibank and Chase Manhattan, the Bank of America and Manufacturers Hanover, Continental Illinois, Chemical Bank, and Bankers Trust, the Canadian Imperial Bank of Commerce and the Royal Bank of Canada, the First National of Chicago, and, finally, Republic National of Dallas. The two Dallas banks contributed least; Citibank was the largest participant, with a loan of $200 million, followed by Chase Manhattan.

The Federal Reserve did its best to identify all the recipients of this munificence, and a surprising number of them were foreign banks. The figures were very approximate, but this is the Federal Reserve's list:

To United States banks that lent directly to the Hunts, such as First National of Chicago and First National in Dallas
$135 million

To U.S. branches of foreign banks that had lent indirectly through brokers such as ACLI
$150 million

To branches of foreign banks that lent directly to the Hunts, such as the Swiss Bank Corporation
$175 million

To foreign banks, mainly in Switzerland and France
$100 million

To Placid Oil Company to pay off its direct loans to the brothers
$110

To brokers to meet miscellaneous obligations
$50 million

To Merrill Lynch to pay off IMIC's debts
$260 million

That comes to $980 million, and the shortfall, the Federal Reserve explained, was 'in part a cushion' to meet any debts that had not surfaced so far. That total does not include the silver and the futures contracts that had been sold by Bache, ACLI, E. F. Hutton, and Merrill Lynch to meet other debts. Include these liquidations, and the sum rises to $1,375 billion; put the cost of the transfer of assets to

Engelhard at $450 million, and the total indebtedness arising from the Hunts' venture into the silver market amounts to a grand total of more than *one and three-quarter billion dollars* – $1.825 billion, to be exact. Perhaps the most astonishing thing about these debts is not their size, but that the Hunt family could pay them. It was inconvenient, of course, but the restructured loan could be collateralized without any insuperable problems.

The collateral put up by Placid to secure the $1.1 billion loan from the thirteen banks included one of the richest properties in the North Sea, the L/10-11 field off Holland, which supplies gas to Northern Europe. Schedule 3 of the loan lists another 114 oil and gas properties in North America – in Louisiana, Texas, Mississippi, Alabama, Arkansas, Colorado, Montana, Oklahoma, Alberta, British Columbia, and Saskatchewan – all collateralized, along with the refineries and pipelines. The loan was not only the largest of its kind; it was also one of the most generously secured. The banks conservatively estimated the value of Placid's security as being more than $3 billion. Herbert Hunt, speaking to *Fortune* magazine, put the value at between $8 and $9 billion.

By deliberately refusing to deal directly with Bunker, Herbert, and Lamar Hunt, the banks had forced Placid to make a second loan agreement with the brothers themselves. A partnership was formed, reflecting the wealth and influence of each (Bunker had a 59 per cent interest, Herbert 40 per cent, and Lamar 1 per cent), its purpose 'to provide a vehicle for the management and orderly disposition of the silver positions and other investments contributed to the partnership by the Hunt brothers on a basis which affords Placid a satisfactory investment opportunity.' Even Placid wanted a few ounces of flesh.

The flesh was very substantial in form. The loan documents, which occupy 181 pages of a congressional report, offer conflicting evidence of the worth of Bunker and Herbert Hunt, but each version shows a breathtaking range of wealth. One version details the brothers' contribution to the partnership by beginning with 1.96 billion tons of coal reserves in North Dakota, whose value is estimated at $294 million. Then there are $100 million worth of South African gold shares spread prudently among thirty-nine mining companies. Bunker contributed gold coins, too. The silver still owned by the brothers was inexplicably undervalued at $645 million. (Lamar's contribution scarcely reflected even a 1 per cent share in the partnership. For some reason that was never explained, it was in cash; the exact sum was $1,044.94.) And besides the contribution of these assets, the brothers also had to mortgage everything they owned to Placid.

Under the heading of 'covenants' came the paragraph of the agreement that had most concerned Paul Volcker. Even in legal language it was explicit enough: 'The Hunt Brothers will not, and will not permit any person, trust or entity owned or controlled by them or any of them (or any of their descendants). . . to make any new investments in securities (other than appropriate money market instruments) to take any position in commodities or any other futures position, for any speculative purpose or otherwise except investments in commodities necessary for the prudent operation of the farm and ranching business included in the Hunt collateral and the sugar business owned by Hunt affiliates.'

As for the banks, they could hardly complain about a billion-dollar loan on which they were receiving interest of a bit more than one percentage point over the prime rate. This meant that when all the money had been drawn, and the prime rate was at 20 per cent – not an unusual occurrence in the coming months – their interest payments could be $232 million a year (or $635,000 a day). Bunker and Herbert might be wealthy beyond most people's dreams of avarice, but those interest payments were brutal. One more group had reason to feel content – the lawyers. The Dallas law firm of Shank, Irwin, Conant, Williamson and Grevelle had to increase its staff to cope with the extra business. When calculating who won and who lost in the great silver gamble, the quick answer is that the banks won, beating the lawyers by a short head.

Not all the players in the game acted like the Hunts, however. At least Bunker and Herbert Hunt raised a loan to pay their debts. Naji Nahas did not bother. The accounts opened by himself and his band of uncles, cousins, secretaries, and business associates at Conti Commodities showed losses of $51 million, which is not surprising seeing that Conti had paid Nahas's margin calls for no less than thirty days before the silver price collapsed. Conti managed to scrounge $3 million in cash from Nahas, who also gave Conti two ocean-going ships, at Nahas's optimistic valuation of $17 million. The deficit of $30 million was made to look more acceptable by perfectly legal, but nonetheless convenient bookkeeping that, by writing off $20 million as a tax loss, reduced the embarrassment to $10 million or so. Conti also demanded a contribution from its noisy man in the silver pit, Norton Waltuch, who had not waited for the price to fall before liquidating his silver position, and had emerged from the debacle a millionaire many times over.

Nahas and his Saudi friends were also in debt to ACLI, although the sums were relatively modest – a mere $20 million or so. ACLI took the loss as philosophically as it is possible to do, having learned a lesson expensively. Had it not been overshadowed by the size of Bunker and Herbert's debts, the default of Naji Nahas and his Saudi friends would have been one of the great financial scandals of the decade. As it was, hardly anyone outside Conti and ACLI even noticed.

Naji Nahas retired to his homes in São Paulo, Brazil, in Paris, and in Deauville, France, feeling that he was an injured party. He justified his default by persuading himself that he had been the victim of a conspiracy, and that Paul Volcker, of all people, had forced the market to change the rules. There was no evidence for this, but a man justifying a default of more than $50 million does not need evidence; chutzpah will do. Nahas was never short of that.

Naji Nahas never appeared before the congressional committees that investigated the silver market; their attention was fixed mainly on Bunker and Herbert Hunt. On the subject of the billion-dollar loan the last word was Bunker's, as it often is. When he finally showed up at a hearing on May 2, Congressman Rosenthal wanted to know how much he cared about the loan. Bunker replied that he would like to see it go through. Why? Rosenthal asked. 'It would make it more comfortable,' Bunker replied. For whom? 'Well, for myself . . .'

It did not help Paul Volcker's standing that Bunker now felt more comfortable.

Chapter 17

Cross-Examination

The billion-dollar loan had certainly made Bunker and Herbert Hunt more comfortable, since they could retain a substantial remnant of their silver collection and they would not have to reveal intimate details of their financial affairs in a public court during a bankruptcy hearing. But the brothers were not comfortable in the sense that their carefully preserved privacy had been successfully invaded, and members of Congress were insisting that they explain themselves, personally, before Senate and House committees. Their activities were now being scrutinized more carefully than ever before.

In the first week of April 1980 a thirty-three-year-old lawyer working for Congressman Rosenthal's subcommittee observed that the Hunts had brought not only themselves but commodities and the futures markets right onto the front pages of American newspapers, as they had in London and Paris, Zurich and Frankfurt. In the next few months, the attorney's own name, Barbara Timmer, was to appear in the newspapers, too.

Barbara Timmer is neat, lean, and eager; appointed a junior counsel, she had joined the staff of the Commerce, Consumer and Monetary Affairs Subcommittee of the House Government Operations Committee in the previous summer. It was her first job on Capitol Hill, and it was a good place to start, because the subcommittee has powers of oversight over all federal agencies, including the CFTC, the SEC, and the Federal Reserve Board.

During Barbara Timmer's first week on the job, Peter Barash, the staff director, told her to look at cattle-feed futures. Since her previous legal experience in her hometown, Muskegon, Michigan, had been largely confined to personal injury cases, she was forced to look through the financial pages of the *New York Times* to find out what a futures contract was; before long she had decided enthusiastically that the futures market was a hot topic. In December 1979 she began to keep a file on the silver market, after Barash had told her to do the research for some hearings on the CFTC in April 1980. By

Silver Thursday, she was in great demand; Barbara Timmer seemed to be the only person on Capitol Hill outside the agriculture committees who understood futures contracts. The following day she was discussing the crisis in the silver market over lunch with Barash, when they learned that Ben Rosenthal was looking for them. They found him eating a plate of macaroni in his office. 'I'd like a hearing on silver on Monday,' he told them.

'How about Thursday?' countered Barash.

'No, the topic is now,' Rosenthal replied. 'I want the CFTC and the SEC on Monday.'

'Ben,' said Barash, 'the chairmen of the CFTC and the SEC aren't going to come to a hearing if Barbara Timmer calls them.'

'Okay, I'll do it, then,' Rosenthal replied.

They came. Timmer was impressed. 'It was astonishing to me how people ascribe power to congressional committees,' she says.

They were, perhaps, more likely to come for Rosenthal than for others. He was thirty-third in seniority in the House of Representatives, an experienced man from Queens, and Timmer had already decided two things about her chairman: he had an uncanny instinct for the timing of a hearing, and he was honest. She had been particularly impressed by the absence of wealthy contributors from New York City when Rosenthal held a fund-raising party. 'If something is wrong, he smells it, and he's not averse to a little combat, either,' she observes.

Over the weekend Timmer prepared a list of eighteen questions for James Stone and seven more for Harold Williams, the SEC chairman. Stone's replies at the Monday hearing confirmed that there was a real possibility that an attempt had been made to corner the silver market, and that there was concern in the highest quarters in Washington that the attempt could lead to a financial panic.

Rosenthal thought Stone's replies justified the subcommittee's asking the Hunts to appear at a hearing. 'Send them a letter,' he told Timmer, who wrote to Bunker and Herbert on April 7, asking them to appear a week later. There followed much conversation between lawyers in Dallas and Timmer in Washington that ended with the issuance of a subpoena requiring the Hunts to appear on April 29. The Dallas lawyers then said that the Hunts had agreed to appear before the Senate Agriculture Committee on May 2, and asked if the House subcommittee members could not direct questions through their colleagues in the Senate. The lawyers who were paid to give Bunker and Herbert that advice might properly have lost their jobs, because nothing could have been better calculated to enrage a House subcommittee. The subpoena was not withdrawn, and Timmer, accustomed to the respect shown for subpoenas when she was in private practice, was sure the Hunts would turn up. She worked all weekend, the fourth in succession, to prepare the questions for Rosenthal. But the Hunts still found the timing of Rosenthal's hearing inconvenient; one of their lawyers was sent along instead. 'They really do seem to believe that the law does not apply to them,' said Elliott Levitas, one of the subcommittee's Democrats, angrily.

The lawyer sent by the Hunts to Washington, Roger Goldburg, seemed to have learned about arrogance from the Hunts themselves. Without quoting any relevant precedent, he simply insisted that the subpoena be quashed; though Goldburg quickly discovered that he would have to do better than that, which was difficult, since it soon became clear that the only reason for the non-appearance of the two brothers was that April 29 did not fit into their schedule. Once that was understood, Goldburg collapsed, like the school bully who is suddenly confronted by a real opponent. He confessed that he had inaccurately quoted conversations he had had with Barbara Timmer, and for all his pains was accused of being both contemptuous and deceitful. Goldburg had become noticeably more humble by the time the hearing concluded with the subcommittee's unanimously agreeing to ask the full Government Operations Committee to find the Hunts in contempt of Congress. That was not what Goldburg was paid for, and the enemies Bunker and Herbert made even before they appeared in Washington were to haunt them for months to come.

Rosenthal's anger on April 29 convinced Bunker and Herbert Hunt that the chairman was just another member of the conspiracy against them – he was Jewish and a New Yorker, so the brothers must have assumed that he must be a shill (a decoy) for the shorts on Wall Street. But they had understood that Rosenthal could not be ignored, and Goldburg reacted to the threat of a contempt action by asking if the brothers might appear on May 2 before they gave evidence to the Senate Agriculture Committee. That was agreed to, but relations between the Hunts and Rosenthal did not improve. Goldburg told Barbara Timmer that his clients were nervous about the press and worried about their security: could they, he asked, come in through the back door? When Rosenthal learned of the request, he exploded: 'Who do they think they are? Are they not citizens of the United States?'

Bunker and Herbert came in through the front door of the large hearing room in the Rayburn Building, which was crowded with television crews, photographers, and spectators. The brothers looked their best for the occasion. Herbert's steel-grey hair was carefully cut, and Bunker had put on his best blue suit. Both smiled graciously, but Bunker picked nervously at his nails, and compulsively adjusted his thick-rimmed spectacles when they slipped on the bridge of his nose. The Hunts were questioned for two and a half hours by the subcommittee members, and revealed more about themselves than about the great silver speculation. The listeners sensed that they were learning less than the truth, but it was not until the transcript was published that the full, gorgeous extent of the Hunts' prevarication, equivocation, fabrication, distortion, misstatement, and dissembling became apparent.

Although Herbert Hunt's role in the silver game had been shadowy – he did the sums while Bunker conceived the strategy – the roles were reversed when the Hunts appeared before Rosenthal's subcommittee. Bunker said as little as possible, and Herbert was made to appear the leader of the team. He looked so much more presentable. His suit fitted properly, and although Herbert has the distinctive Hunt jowls, he was not obviously overweight. Nor was it too early in the morning for Herbert; it was nine a.m., a time at which Herbert had customarily been at work for a couple of hours but Bunker liked still to be in bed. So it was Herbert who delivered the opening statement, reading from a text that blamed everyone and everything, but most especially Comex, for the collapse of the Hunts' silver fortunes; the fault was definitely not in themselves. Herbert sounded confident, like a man who has won a promising-businessman award from the Junior Chamber of Commerce. Had there been no questions afterward, Herbert might have returned to Dallas feeling that he had done his cause no harm. But when the questions started, Herbert's confidence began to crack. His manner occasionally appeared shifty, and his memory, which had seemed impeccable during his opening remarks, started to fail him. In reply to the very first question, Herbert said that he did not know how much silver he owned. 'My commitments in silver have varied up and down and I don't have with me today exactly what my positions were at any given time between 1973 and January of 1980.' He went on: 'I own no interest in Placid Oil Company.' Time for questioning was reduced while the subcommittee established that it was Herbert's and Bunker's *trusts* that owned the interest.

Next, Rosenthal wanted to know about the billion-dollar bailout loan to Placid. 'Is it something to benefit you individually?'

'No,' Herbert replied. 'Placid is making borrowings on their oil and gas properties for a loan.' The inference was that the billion dollars was intended to develop further oil and gas properties.

The questioning then alluded to fifty letters that had been sent by a brokerage house to Arabs in 1978 with a translation of a bullish report on silver from *Myers' Finance and Energy Report*. 'I don't know which letter you are talking about,' said Herbert. 'I wrote no letter to anyone,' said Bunker. He had not written it, merely asked that it be sent. But he was to become bolder than that. 'I have no interest in speculating at all,' said Bunker, the greatest single speculator in the history of commodity markets.

Herbert Hunt insisted, of course, that the two brothers always traded separately; but the suspicion that the two in fact acted together was the subject of precise questioning by Elliott Levitas, who began by repeating an assertion of Herbert's:

LEVITAS: Do I understand your testimony to be that you and your brother N. B. Hunt act totally independently of each other in making investment decisions with respect to silver and silver contracts?

HERBERT: Let me answer that by saying that I make all my own decisions as to whether I want to buy silver, sell silver, buy a futures contract, sell a futures contract, and as far as I know my brother Bunker Hunt does also. In fact, there have been cases I have found out where later he was a seller and I was a buyer, and I think we bought from each other.

LEVITAS: Do you share information about problems in the silver market or matters relating to investment decisions you make?

HERBERT: Well, we do office in the same building. We do eat lunch together very often. We do contact and discuss things, so, yes, in a general way we do express our feelings between each other.

LEVITAS: And concerns about the silver market?

HERBERT: Yes I have discussed the silver market with him.

LEVITAS: In some detail?

HERBERT: Yes, on numerous occasions.

LEVITAS: Mr N. B. Hunt, would you adopt that answer or make any changes that you would like to make?

BUNKER: I think that I can't argue with him on that one. We do see each other quite a bit. We talk to each other, and naturally I guess because our contact is close, we have similar views on the market, but Mr Herbert Hunt sometimes trades, does things quite differently.

LEVITAS: I want to make it clear I am not suggesting that you always make the same decisions. I am suggesting, however – and if either of you wish to contradict this, this is your opportunity to do so – that you work closely with each other on matters relating to the silver market, and sharing information about its potential and its problems, and that occurs almost routinely as between yourselves.

BUNKER: I think, Congressman Levitas, that that is a fair statement, yes.

Bunker was always more straightforward than Herbert; he was more confident or, perhaps more arrogant. Herbert would not even concede that the brothers had contributed to the remarkable rise in the silver price. 'I don't really think that we caused it; I really feel I am a victim,' he said. The price had risen, he argued, because of the seizure of the hostages in Tehran, the occupation of the Great

Mosque in Mecca, and the invasion of Afghanistan, not what was conceived in Dallas, Texas.

But it was their forgetfulness that almost got the brothers into real trouble. Elliott Levitas wanted to know whether there had been any undisclosed positions through foreign trading companies. 'I do not and have not owned any interest in any undisclosed foreign accounts,' said Herbert. Bunker said the same went for him. But Levitas would not let the question go: 'Do either of you make purchases of silver or silver contracts in the names of others, nominees, or other entities in which you are controlling persons?'

'No,' replied Herbert; but Bunker sensed the trap and mentioned IMIC, the offshore company in Bermuda, though he added: 'I don't know whether I am the controlling person in it. I am a stockholder.' Bunker and Herbert owned half of IMIC's shares between them, borrowed its capital, and dictated its market strategy.

Herbert blundered on. Rosenthal wanted to know if he had ever transported silver from the United States to Europe. 'The answer is no,' said Herbert; but 6 million ounces had been shipped to London in 1975.

And Herbert's memory kept on failing him. Asked whether the billion-dollar loan had a covenant preventing the Hunts from speculating in silver, he replied: 'I don't know.' He had signed a contract including that covenant only twenty-four hours earlier.

On the subject of their borrowing spree in February and March, Herbert's memory was still faulty. 'When the additional margin requirements were required we had to put up additional cash at that time. I did not borrow any additional sums. I had the funds, and I put them up.' Had there been representatives of Citibank, Crédit Lyonnais, the Swiss Bank Corporation, First National in Dallas, or First National of Chicago in the hearing room, they would have been startled. They had lent Herbert $175 million. So would his brokers, who had lent him $192,322,400. Bunker did recall some loans from banks, but he could not remember which. 'I don't have a list here,' he explained.

The one thing the Hunts were quite certain about was that they had not cornered or attempted to corner the market. Had they, they were asked, discussed it, even in jest? 'At no point was I ever in any position where I cornered anything, so there was no reason for any discussion,' answered Herbert. Bunker added: 'I do not really believe you can corner anything. I was just an investor.'

The performance did not please Ben Rosenthal. 'It is incredible,' he said angrily, 'how neither of you have any notion of how much you are worth, or the Hunts are worth, or anybody.'

BUNKER: No, I don't have any idea. A fellow asked me that once and I said I don't know, but I do know people who know how much they are worth generally aren't worth very much.

ROSENTHAL: You don't know how much silver you owned in March; you don't know how much silver you own today; you don't know how much you are worth; you don't know how much you owe. How do you operate?

BUNKER: I guess my operation can be a little unorthodox, yes, I will agree.

Bunker enjoyed the exchange considerably, and it put his face and his philosophy all over America on television network news. The audience was able to experience that strange combination of folksiness and arrogance that is so characteristic of his public appearances. But he did not mollify Ben Rosenthal or Barbara Timmer; they had seen the whole performance, not just a fifteen-second film clip.

The Hunts' next appointment, in the Senate, was with the Subcommittee on Agricultural Research and General Legislation of the Committee on Agriculture, Nutrition and Forestry. The subcommittee's chairman was the junior senator from Alabama, a Democrat named Donald Stewart. He was in his early forties, a lawyer by profession and a populist by nature. But Stewart was not an old-fashioned Southern demogogic populist. Rather, he had a seething distaste for the arrogance of wealth symbolized by the Hunts, and was quietly sarcastic about the ease with which they had been able to raise a billion-dollar loan while farmers and small businessmen in his home state left the banks empty-handed because of Volcker's policy on credit restrictions. Stewart described himself, with evident false modesty, as a simple country lawyer; in fact, he is a sophisticated man who subjected the players in the silver game to the kind of detailed scrutiny that was not possible in the House of Representatives, where each member of the subcommittee was rationed to a five-minute burst of questioning. Stewart mostly sat alone and had the time to press a consistent case.

Stewart's basic questions were researched by another lawyer, a man who was a perfect foil to Barbara Timmer on the House subcommittee. Stephen Storch is cautious, fond of playing devil's advocate with visitors like myself who sometimes develop theories built on evidence that might not be entirely convincing in a courtroom. Storch developed his case gradually, basing it on information he had received from the CFTC and from contacts he had in the Comex market in New York. As an agriculture specialist, Storch knew more than Barbara Timmer about the futures markets; he was less inclined to question whether they ought to exist, but he recognized that Bunker and Herbert had perfectly illustrated how vulnerable the markets were to ruthless speculation.

When Bunker and Herbert Hunt appeared before Senator Stewart they were no less forgetful than they had been a couple of hours earlier. For example, Stewart wanted to know more about IMIC: Had it made purchases after July 1979? 'I don't know. I'd have to go back and look at the records. They probably did,' replied Herbert, who must have known that IMIC made purchases *only* after July 1979. Stewart suggested a figure for the Hunts' silver holding that was closer to the truth than any that had so far been mentioned in public – anywhere between 200 and 250 million ounces of silver, he said. But he could not break them down. 'No, Senator, I don't have any figures and my memory is not perfect on that kind of thing. . . . I'm sorry, it would be speculation, and my lawyer tells me not to speculate,' said Bunker.

Stewart did, however, force out of Bunker concessions about his relationship with his Arab allies. He admitted: 'I know a lot of Arabs, and I'm not sure which ones are members of the royal family and which ones aren't. I do know I have met some of them. I have in the past when silver was reasonably priced like it is now, I have recommended silver.'

STEWART: Are you aware of the fact that some of them have or have not taken a position on the futures market during that particular period of time, as a result of your conversations with them?

BUNKER: I've heard rumours. I have no proof that they have bought any silver, but I have heard that they did; but it's just like hearing that board members were short in the silver market. I don't have any proof that they shorted the silver market, but I hear rumours.

STEWART: Did you have any conversations with Mr Naji Nahas of Brazil and urge him to buy silver as a wise investment during this particular period of time?

BUNKER: He's a friend of mine and I've talked to him many times. I see him in Europe from time to time, and I've always told him that at a cheap price . . . that I thought silver was an excellent buy.

That was the first mention of the friendship between Bunker and Nahas and members of the Saudi royal family, and it shocked the CFTC commissioners, who were listening. All the more so when Bunker admitted that he had bought $40 million worth of silver from Naji Nahas in January 1980. Bunker had always told the CFTC's Read Dunn that he did not know the other players in the game. But both brothers appeared quite unrepentant; indeed, they had admitted nothing that might make repentance necessary. Before they left, Bunker personally recommended silver to Senator Stewart as 'an excellent buy', charged that the markets had been guilty of manipulation, and added, in a remark that some listeners found slightly ominous, that 'the game is not over yet'.

Nor was it. Still, there were new players now, in Washington, and they had a different conception of the game. At the hearings on May 2 Bunker and Herbert said that, although their memories were faulty, they did have the information about their silver holdings, the debts, and the loans back home in Dallas. They offered to send it if necessary. By May 9 Barbara Timmer had prepared a four-page, single-spaced letter demanding an extensive trawl through the silver records of Bunker, Herbert, and IMIC. The sixteen-page reply, received from Roger Goldburg on June 9, 1980, incorporated all the figures that had been requested, and concluded hopefully: 'Please consider this information as confidential and intended solely for the purpose and use of your subcommittee.' But Rosenthal and Timmer did not regard themselves as bound by confidentiality at all, and the details of the Hunts' silver holdings and their debts were a feast for students of the silver game. When Timmer insisted on seeing the bank-loan documents, they, too, became part of the public record. It sometimes seemed as though the only statistics missing from the documentation were the brothers' medical records.

Timmer did not confine her interest to the Hunts. Earlier in 1980 she had been named in a court case brought by Commissioner David Gartner of the CFTC, because she had subpoenaed confidential records from the CFTC Gartner wanted the subpoena quashed, but he lost his case, and, following that, the CFTC's constitutional duty was clear: it had to provide whatever information the subcommittee asked for. Storch also forced the CFTC to disgorge copious records of the silver dealings of the Hunts and the Saudis. The documents, taken altogether, add up to a statistical refutation of most of the arguments Bunker and Herbert offered in their defence against the charge that they were in a position to manipulate the silver market. But statistics do not provide clinching evidence of intent.

Barbara Timmer thought the Hunts' performance on May 2 might provoke someone to provide that evidence, and, as she suspected, the hearing did prove to be a magnet that attracted more information. One of the numerous subsequent telephone calls was from a man who announced that he was a former employee of Bunker and Herbert Hunt's. He impressed her because, unlike the other callers, he sounded calm. His name was Bill Bledsoe, and Timmer asked if he could visit Washington to give a sworn statement on May 23. Bledsoe's evidence contradicted virtually every assertion Bunker and Herbert had made: he insisted that the brothers traded in concert and knew their daily positions by heart; that they were attempting to control the world's supply of silver; that they had shipped silver to Europe; and that Bunker was cavalier about the transfer of assets into the family trusts, which were used as tax shelters. After Bledsoe's visit, Timmer wrote letters that Rosenthal sent to the attorney-general asking that the Justice Department investigate the possibility of perjury, and to the commissioner of the Internal Revenue Service suggesting that it look into possible violation of federal tax laws.

Stephen Storch's concern was to establish links between the Hunts and the 'foreign investors' in Geneva. He provided Senator Stewart with enough information to enable him to give Norton Waltuch a tough time when he finally appeared as a witness on June 26, and the net around Bunker, Naji Nahas, and the Saudis was drawn a little tighter. Storch had hoped to persuade Nahas to give evidence, too, but his intention leaked to reporters, and Nahas shied away. This confirmed Storch's belief that circumspection was the best tactic when dealing with Arabs, so he approached the Saudi Embassy discreetly. But Storch learned very little when he finally was admitted to the diplomatic presence, and the reason for the embassy's reticence can best be inferred from an unusual interview that took place, a few weeks after the Senate hearings, between Storch's boss, Senator Stewart, and the Saudi ambassador to Washington.

Stewart recalls his surprise when the Saudi ambassador asked him for an interview. The senator was not a member of the Armed Services Committee, which was then engaged in tortuous discussions about the advisability of selling bomb racks and long-range fuel tanks for the F-15 jet fighters that Saudi Arabia was buying in the United States. The ambassador politely made his case for the additional defence equipment to a somewhat bemused junior senator from Alabama, until he said suddenly: 'By the way, the Saudi royal family was not involved in the silver market.' Stewart, suspecting the ambassador was trying to deliver a message, listened to more talk about F-15s; but again, just before he left the office, the ambassador added, 'The Saudi royal family did not lose any money in the silver market.' There was not necessarily a contradiction between those two statements, but Stewart suspected one, and speculated about the meaning of the interview for months afterward. (The probable truth, I learned from diplomats later, was that the ambassador had received instructions from the Foreign Ministry in Riyadh to deny the involvement of the royal family, and without having been given any detailed information, was doing so as best he could, which was not very convincingly.)

What the two subcommittees had achieved between them was the exposure of Bunker's and Herbert's performances at the hearings as farce. But there did not seem to be much more they could do, and the investigations petered out after the 1980 elections (which also meant the elevation of one of Bunker's friends, Senator Jesse Helms, to the chairmanship of the Agriculture Committee). Rosenthal co-sponsored legislation in the House of Representatives to outlaw the use of the futures markets as a vehicle for tax evasion – and this became a live issue when the Ways and Means Committee took it up in 1981. In the Senate, the Banking Committee (of which Donald Stewart was also a member) held hearings on a proposed law that would allow the Federal Reserve Board to intervene in commodity markets to establish margins. These hearings, held in late May 1980, were revelatory about the role of the banks in the silver affair – the First National of Chicago among them – but there was no great enthusiasm for the bill, least of all from the man who would be charged with the additional power, Paul Volcker. (One more committee held hearings – the House Agriculture Committee. Bunker and Herbert Hunt, returning to Washington for these, received an unusually friendly reception from a largely uncritical membership, who seemed not to have been briefed at all about the happenings in the silver market.)

In the offices of the Securities and Exchange Commission and the Commodity Futures Trading Commission, the enforcement divisions were able to use the evidence that had been prised out of Bunker and Herbert Hunt to aid their own investigations into the silver game, which was, indeed, not over yet. For the time being, the last word appeared to be Herbert's. Asked at the Rosenthal hearings: 'As a result of these events, in your opinion, who has been hurt the worst?' Herbert replied: 'Well, at the moment, I think you are looking at him.'

But it was always impossible to be sure with Herbert. His smile suggested that he might be joking.

Chapter 18

A World Without Secrets

At the beginning of May 1980, when the dreadful nature of their plight was finally revealed, the Hunts were not without sympathizers; there are still enough conservatives who believe in the rough-and-tumble of capitalism to ask whether they had done anything wrong. The brothers' orchestrated defence was that they were the victims, not the instigators, of the silver collapse, and that their misfortune was all the fault of the market professionals. As Bunker told Allen Pusey of the Dallas *Morning News* three months later: 'It was almost like the shorts had the power to manipulate the market, break the market, cost the longs a lot of money, and then turn the media – television, radio, newspapers – on the longs. I would have thought the media would have been more discerning, but apparently, the shorts had a lot of influence.'

Without ever having been manipulated by the shorts myself, I had found it difficult to sympathize with the Hunts, but when I eventually visited the second floor of the Dallas County Courthouse, a building a block away from the Texas School Book Depository, which overlooks the city's memorial to President John Kennedy, it was impossible not to feel a flicker of compassion. Among the voluminous mortgages that the brothers had had to file there, a single sheet marked 'Personal Things' had been contributed by Lamar. It listed his cars – a Cordoba, a Chrysler, and a Mercedes-Benz – a lady's diamond ring with two birds, a gold necklace with five gold medallions, a gold American coin bracelet, a charm bracelet, a blond mink coat, a lynx coat, an antique Chinese dress, a lady's diamond wristwatch . . . Poor Lamar had to hock everything he and his wife owned, right down to the Rolex watch on his wrist.

Between March and June 1980, Bunker, Herbert, and Lamar Hunt filed eighty-four separate mortgages in the Dallas courthouse. All three brothers filed as debtors on March 25; the secured creditor in each case was the Placid Oil Company. A second substantial batch of mortgages was filed on May 6 and 7, a pile three inches thick detailing the millions of acres of land owned by the Hunts, down to the finest detail – such as Herbert's 8,747.97 acres in Kleberg County, Texas. On May 28 the document transferring 20 per cent of their oil and gas leases in the Beaufort Sea to Engelhard Industries was deposited; and finally, on June 6, the last sheaf of papers listed the land not previously collateralized to Placid. Lamar's list of assets came in dribs and drabs during those months, as though he had not realized that to have Placid organize a billion-dollar loan on behalf of himself and his brothers, he personally would have to mortgage all he owned.

The mortgages are intriguing – revealing, for example, how early the brothers realized that Placid would have to help them out of their difficulties. The first big filing, on March 25, occurred twenty-four hours before Bunker's announcement of the silver-backed bond issue in Paris, and two days before Silver Thursday. In fact, Herbert must have signed the mortgage documents for himself and Bunker (Herbert signed for him in his absence) shortly before telephoning Bache to inform them that no more margin calls could or would be met.

A second revelation in the mortgages is the scale of Bunker's lending to members of his own family, obviously to meet margin calls. Bunker lent $23 million to Herbert in February and $11 million to Lamar in March. (Herbert made undated loans of $17.5 million to Lamar.) But Bunker's really big spending was lavished on members of his immediate family. His daughter Elizabeth Hunt Carnes was the largest beneficiary, having been lent $86.1 million between January 24 and March 17. Apparently Elizabeth, like Lamar, had bought when the silver price was near its peak. So had her brother-in-law, Albert Huddleston, who had had to borrow $33.3 million. His wife, Mary Hunt Huddleston, borrowed $12.6 million, and her brother, Houston Hunt, was lent $7.1 million in the middle of March. The silver game was more like the Chicago soybean business in 1977 (when many of the same family names surfaced) than anyone had suspected; except, of course, that the scale was even larger. His family's involvement cost Bunker $173 million.

The documents also disclose the caution of the First National Bank in Dallas, which had never wanted silver as collateral; rather, they grabbed Bunker's third share in the Dallas Bowling Center, plus all his cattle – and there were tens of thousands of those, which could readily be turned into cash.

The most interesting feature of the mortgages, however, is the insight they provide into the life-style of a family that had carefully preserved its privacy against those who like to pry into the lives of the very rich. Bunker, Herbert, and Lamar Hunt still have secrets after their great gamble, but many fewer than before.

Placid's summary of the estimated value of the collateral the three brothers put up to finance their partnership reflects part of their personal wealth; the collateral does not take account of their trusts' holdings in Placid itself, or in Penrod Drilling, or in Hunt International Resources, the successor to Great Western United. Without the inclusion of these properties, the brothers' fortune is mildly disappointing, amounting to $2.8 billion, of which 2.25 billion is attributed to the undeveloped concessions in the Beaufort Sea. Deduct this notional wealth in the Arctic, and that leaves them with a net worth of no more than $550 million; the brothers would now have to include the capital value of their trusts in order to describe themselves as billionaires.

Of the family fortune disclosed in the mortgages, Bunker's was the largest share, because in the courthouse files, Bunker's are the thickest by a few inches. There were the horses, for example, valued at $116 million, stabled in Kentucky, in France (at Maurice Zilber's stables, among others), in Ireland (with his trainer, Ted Curtin), and in Italy. Despite the court judgment in favour of British Petroleum that made Bunker's British assets vulnerable to legal action, he even had a few horses in England. The names of the best of these horses are familiar to anyone who studied racing form in the 1970s: Dahlia, Empery (which won the Epsom Derby in 1974), Vaguely Noble (for which Bunker paid a record price for a horse in training), Youth, and Exceller. The best horses of their generation, such as Brigadier Gerard in England, and Secretariat and Canonero II in the United States, had sired foals in which Bunker owned a share. Famous or not, every single one of Bunker's horses was mortgaged, including thoroughbreds with such irresistible names as Burn the Money, Charming Alibi, Goofed, and Coin Silver. The schedule of horses in the United States alone ran to twenty-one pages, and there were a further 133 racehorses in training abroad. The total was more than 500. Perhaps no one has ever owned as many racehorses as Bunker; certainly none of his contemporaries does. But it was a market he could never try to corner; racehorses are unpredictable beasts, and Bunker's horses could be, and were, beaten by rivals that cost their owners a fraction of what Bunker had paid for many of his. Other owners were suspicious, nonetheless, of Bunker's behaviour in the thoroughbred racehorse market.

The pattern of Bunker's horse sales was eccentric, and it deeply confused the professional horse traders, since many of the highest prices for horses Bunker sold were paid by friends of his with no previous form as racehorse owners. Some regular buyers suspected that Bunker's friends were raising the prices with money Bunker had lent them, a practice that might increase the value of a stallion's next crop of yearlings by making them appear more desirable than they really were. This could explain why Bunker's accounts receivable showed that he lent substantial sums to a number of his cronies who had recently become owners themselves; for instance, there were loans of $350,000 to each of five men, including names familiar from Bunker's activities off the track – Alvin Brodsky, the silver trader, and the two men who bought so heavily at Bunker's sale in Kentucky, in July 1979, the coin dealer Bruce McNall and the Hollywood producer Seymour Weintraub.

Another riddle concerns a Greek coin, minted in 460 B.C., listed in Bunker's collection as 'Attica Athens AR decadrachm, Seltman Col.' 'AR' is the symbol for silver, and 'Seltman Col' is the coin's provenance, meaning that its authenticity is guaranteed by the coin's having once belonged to one of the world's finest coin collections. That Athenian decadrachm is immediately recognizable to experts as one of the world's rarest coins, and it was included in the collection Bunker Hunt mortgaged in 1980. It is, therefore, particularly difficult to explain a transaction subsequently announced in 1981 by Bruce McNall, president of Numismatic Fine Arts of Beverly Hills, California. Almost a year after the mortgages had been filed, McNall stated that the same Athenian decadrachm had been sold for a world-record price, $1.5 million. According to *Coins* magazine, the seller was 'an unnamed Hollywood movie mogul' and the *buyer* was Nelson Bunker Hunt. The trade immediately identified the movie mogul as Seymour Weintraub. The transaction was certainly curious: Bunker buying from an old friend a coin that was already in his collection. (I met Weintraub, a tanned, handsome man in his early fifties, in New Orleans, but he was unhelpful, though impassively polite. The only advice he had for me was: 'Bunker is the fulcrum; he's ninety-nine per cent of the story.')

Including that expensive decadrachm, Bunker's coin and art collection was valued at $34 million, and the list of Greek and Roman coins alone covers eight single-spaced pages in the mortgages. Directors of a London auction house specializing in coins, to whom I showed the list, were excited by many items but not by the collection itself, which looked to them like a random accumulation. 'Most collectors know something about coins, but there is no evidence that Nelson Bunker Hunt does,' said the experts. But it is easy to imagine the charm that hundreds of aurei, didrachms and tetradrachms, staters, sigloi, and shekels held for Bunker: they were worth even more than their weight in either silver or gold. Sadly for him, the ancient-coin market had reached its peak in 1975. The year 1980 was the time he should have got out, but Bunker was as deeply in as anyone had been since the late nineteenth century, when an infamous collector named Hyman Montague almost cornered the market. That, the experts claim, is not possible any longer. . . .

Bunker Hunt paid less attention to his art collection, which takes a mere three pages to list, and consists mainly of porcelain models of birds by the American artist Edward Marshall Boehm. There are three paintings by distinguished eighteenth-century English artists (George Romney and Sir Joshua Reynolds), but Bunker probably preferred his contemporary portraits: pictures of Vaguely Noble, Dahlia, Empery, and Exceller, and one of father and son, himself and Houston.

At $37 million, Bunker's cattle were worth more than the coins, though less than his real estate – he had bought a quarter of a million square feet of building land in downtown Anchorage, Alaska, plantations in Mississippi, a forest in Florida, and the largest tract of land owned by an individual in northern Australia (students of that purchase surmised that he might want to be somewhere lonely if the Russians ever fulfill his expectations and take over the United States). The real estate, valued at $43 million, included the ranches, such as the Circle T outside Dallas, and the farmhouse at the Bluegrass Farm in Kentucky 'with all its furniture, antiques and paintings.' The ranch plant and equipment were worth another $9.7 million, and everything in them was added to the list – lawn mowers, roping saddle, bangs rocker, fans, tire changer, the 1967 Chevy pickup, and the five-ton scale.

There were a few mysterious entries in the four-page list of accounts receivable, because, for a man who is reputedly so mean, Bunker appears to have been unusually generous. On one occasion, in October 1978, he lent twenty-four separate individuals a total of $180,000 (to buy a horse, maybe); a lady with the beguiling name of Anita Arbour owed $220,000; and there was also a more familiar name on the list. Scott McFarland, Bunker's San Francisco broker, borrowed $1 million on January 18, 1980, the day the silver price was at its record level. The single most baffling entry is to be found among his art objects: 'English Batchelor Ghost,' it reads.

On the evidence of his mortgaged property, Herbert Hunt is a man of simpler tastes than either Bunker or Lamar. True, he had a pleasing collection of nineteen Greek and Roman statues – the oldest being a Grecian sphinx dating from 530 B.C.; there was a Greek Venus, a bronze dancing girl, a young Dionysus, and a statue of a young man who might have been Alexander. There were some Viking silver ornaments, too, and a coin collection, but not in the same class as Bunker's. The good coins were Roman, but Herbert seemed to like bulk purchases: he had literally thousands (8,400, to be exact) of Byzantine gold, silver, and bronze coins. The fact that his assets were now mortgaged did not prevent him from adding to that collection: on April 30, 1980, Bruce McNall sent him a bill of $2.4 million for the purchase of 4,200 more Byzantine coins from the Greenleaf Collection. (Presumably, the terms of the loan do not define coin purchases as speculation.) Herbert emerges from his mortgages as a rather dull dog, which cannot be said of Lamar.

Lamar Hunt is a shadowy figure in our silver story. He had started to buy heavily in January 1980, just when the price was about to fall. It is possible that he chose such an inopportune moment because it coincided with the end of the football season. He lost a great deal of money in February and March and, thus, had to be included in the partnership with Placid. Although his share of the partnership was only 1 per cent, it did not excuse him from the self-revelation of the mortgages: Lamar's were the most detailed of the three. So we learn that, despite his insistence that sports should be a profitable investment, Lamar was owed money by all his sporting interests except his football team in Kansas City. His tennis circuit, World Championship Tennis, had to borrow $4.8 million just when Lamar needed cash most, in February 1980; and his soccer team, the Dallas Tornado, which had never quite lived up to the ferocity of its name, drew $1.8 million between November 1979 and March 1980. His investment in sports had turned out rather expensive.

The pages of Lamar Hunt's mortgages headed 'Miscellaneous Personalty' showed that there was some real variety to his tastes. He had a good collection of American art, centred on thirty-five paintings by the nineteenth-century Lancashire-born landscape artist Thomas Moran, a famous painter of the Western states. Other works in Lamar's house in the Dallas suburb of Graywood include an *Adoration of the Magi* by Brueghel, a Rubens portrait, four Aubusson tapestries, a pair of Della Robbia busts, and much good seventeenth- and eighteenth-century European furniture. The most suggestive acquisitions of all, however, reflect Lamar's interest in Napoleon: a watercolour portrait by the French painter David; an anonymous drawing entitled *Napoleon Triumphant*; and a bronze statue of Napoleon seated in a chair.

Lamar Hunt was alone among the three brothers in hinting that the mortgages had caused him distress. He told the *Wall Street Journal* that 'if what we own becomes public we're going to have to hire a lot more police protection.' But that was about all he said. 'This is a private matter,' he added, 'and I don't consider it good taste to talk about it.' Lamar could not have been more wrong. The Hunts' possessions were no longer a private matter; the lists were available for all to see in the Dallas County Courthouse. It was a consequence the brothers had not foreseen when they started to buy silver. Acquaintances reported that the brothers were in a state of shock, but Bunker Hunt denied that. When he interviewed Bunker for the Dallas *Morning News*, Allen Pusey asked if the disclosure in the mortgages had upset him. 'Naw, it didn't bother me none. Actually there's no secrets in the world, anyway. This is an age of informants that we live in. The Internal Revenue Service has got their informers. The FBI has got their informers. The police have got their informers. This is an age of informers, the CIA and so forth. A person is just kidding himself if he thinks he's got any secrets.' Apparently the only thing that had really shaken Bunker was that he – a man with such a wealth of possessions – should have run out of ready cash.

But that was not the only indignity Bunker experienced in the months after his gamble failed. He became a public figure, instantly recognizable when he went out to a restaurant or a racetrack. For years Bunker has resolutely refused to tip any of his own horses; he just tipped silver instead. One day in the fall of 1980, at the private Turf and Field Club at Belmont racetrack on Long Island, one of the racing men who had taken that advice and lost more than he could afford, grasped Bunker Hunt by the throat as though to strangle him. And the racetrack was one of the few places where Bunker had friends.

Chapter 19

Winners and Losers

If the Hunts and their Arab friends were losers in the silver market, the logic of futures trading dictates that there must have been winners. Since such a great deal of money was lost, someone among the short sellers of silver must surely have made a great deal. Bunker was convinced that the winners were among the board members who changed the rules on Comex and the Board of Trade, but all stoutly denied the charge. Only one man boasted that he had made money in the silver market, and he was not a bullion dealer or commodities broker at all. Actually, he was an oil man, an old rival of Bunker's: Dr Armand Hammer, chairman of Occidental Petroleum. At the age of eighty-one, Hammer had trumped Bunker, just as he had done in Libya eight years earlier when he had made a deal with Colonel Qaddafi that allowed Occidental to keep a 49 per cent share of its Libyan oil. Bunker Hunt might have thought that alone enough to condemn his rival, but there was worse; Hammer actually felt cozy with the leading politicians in the Soviet Union. He had known them all since the 1920s, and he can also trump Brezhnev by telling him what Lenin said to him when they met. (Bunker's prejudice was in no way mitigated by the fact that Hammer is also a friend of Queen Elizabeth the Queen Mother.)

Armand Hammer has never hidden his light under a bushel, and on March 28, 1980, Occidental called a press conference to announce the chairman's latest coup. By going short in the silver market, Hammer had made a windfall profit of $119.6 million. It was a pile of money, even for him, but in the excitement of the moment no one thought to ask *why* Hammer had been in the silver market or how his transactions had been done. There is more to the tale of Armand Hammer's adroitness than meets the eye.

In the mid-1970s Occidental had been determined to diversify its interests, using the profits from oil, and in 1976 the company formed a partnership, known as Candelaria, with a Denver company named Congdon and Carey No. 4. The Denver partners owned mining properties in Nevada with promising reserves of silver, and exchanged a 60 per cent share of the mine in return for Occidental's agreeing to finance the pilot study of the mine's commercial viability. By November 1979 mining engineers had decided that Candelaria's mine was capable of producing 2.5 million ounces of silver a year, at a cost of between $8 and $9 an ounce. Had the report been completed a year earlier, Hammer might have been less enthusiastic, but by November 1979 the silver price was double those production costs. The mine was an admirable prospect, and work began immediately. Production was scheduled to start in the early winter of 1980.

Occidental entered the silver futures market on January 8, 1980. As explained by the president of Occidental's Minerals Corporation, Paul Bailly, this was an exercise in business prudence. He wrote to Occidental's partners the following day: 'This hedging action represented by the contracts was taken by us in order to protect the Partnership against a deterioration in the price of silver, from that of its current record levels, until the time the production would be ready for sale in normal commercial transactions.' Bailly added that such costs as margin payments would be met by the partnership.

But Paul Bailly omitted to say that in three weeks Occidental's short position in the silver market had grown to 6.2 million ounces, enough to hedge Candelaria's production well into 1983, assuming that the mine opened on time. What happened was that Hammer had decided that, with silver at $30 an ounce, he could not lose: if the price fell, he could cover his short contracts, and if it rose, he could eventually deliver the silver with production from the mine. The mine had another great advantage: Occidental was eligible for hedging margins, which are a privilege awarded by the markets to bona fide producers or users of silver. Hedgers differ from speculators in the initial margins they have to put up, and in January 1980 there was a palpable advantage in being liable for hedging margins of $20,000 for a Comex silver contract, rather than the $75,000 paid by speculators. So Hammer, as a legitimate hedger, went short, and the consequence was that $119.6-million windfall when he covered his short position with long contracts bought at bargain-basement prices at the end of March.

That Hammer's dealing had been more complex than it appeared did not become clear until later in the year. Since most losers feel that they have been either cheated or manipulated by the winners, they often take to the law for redress of their grievances. After the collapse of the silver market, one such court action was initiated by Congdon and Carey No. 4, Hammer's partners in Candelaria.

Documents filed in Jefferson County Courthouse in Colorado

charged Occidental with breach of fiduciary interest and misrepresentation. The claim was based on conversations held between Thomas Congdon, of the Denver partners, and Armand Hammer himself in Los Angeles on March 4, 1980. The crux of the dispute is whether Occidental speculated on its own account or whether it hedged on behalf of Candelaria. Congdon understood that Occidental was *speculating* in silver on its own account, and that any profits would go to Occidental, not Candelaria. It was when he discovered that any losses would be attributed to the partnership that he became suspicious. Hammer seemed to have made an offer Congdon could not accept; and Congdon formally stated that Congdon and Carey wanted nothing to do with the futures market for the time being.

Thomas Congdon was surprised, therefore, to read the March 28 announcement that Hammer had made $119.6 million, not by speculating but by *hedging* Candelaria's future production. He felt, frankly, that he had been conned on March 4: if it really was Candelaria's production that had been hedged, his side of the partnership should be due its share of the profit. In May 1980 Congdon and Carey No. 4 made a legal claim for 40 per cent of the $119.6 million, and demanded that the issue be settled by arbitration; Occidental's response was that there had been no misrepresentation, and no breach of fiduciary responsibility, and thus there was no dispute to arbitrate. Some of the windfall profit was consumed by lawyers, but an unworried Armand Hammer went on travelling the world, meeting innumerable heads of state, purchasing a unique collection of Leonardo da Vinci's drawings from the collection of the Earl of Leicester at Holkham Hall, Norfolk, known as the Codex Leicester (he renamed it the Codex Hammer). Speculator or hedger, he was still the big winner.

Despite their reticence, there were winners on Wall Street, too. Bunker was sure they were the large holders of short positions, and later these were specifically identified by the Commodity Futures Trading Commission. Precious-metals dealers such as Engelhard, Mocatta, Sharps Pixley, and J. Aron were short by 40 million ounces in mid-March 1980, but most if not all these positions had been acquired to hedge the bullion they owned, and they made no profit because as the price of silver futures contracts fell, so did the value of their bullion. The other large short position was owned by Continental Grain, which was 11.3 million ounces short in mid-March; but if Michel Fribourg, the head of that massive and discreet private company, made a fortune by speculating, he was certainly not going to call a press conference to boast about it.

Nonetheless, Bunker Hunt was right in thinking that the precious-metals dealers had profited from the silver collapse, but he adduced the wrong reason. They had, in fact, made money mostly by dealing, not by speculating.

When prices are moving quickly, the futures market becomes an adventure playground for arbitrageurs – men like Theo Hook, who make money whether the price is rising or falling. The most reliable public indication of their success was the financial report of the largest trader of all, Engelhard. Its interim report for the first three months of 1980 revealed singularly satisfying profits, and Engelhard noted: 'The precious metals operations turned in a strong performance. Its earnings considerably exceeded those of the comparable 1979 period. It is gratifying to report that the Division's U.S. refinery registered very satisfactory operating profits in the quarter.' Engelhard's trading division, Philipp Brothers, had done even better, dealing in silver, among other commodities. During that quarter Engelhard's net sales and operating revenues were up from the same period in 1979 by almost $3 billion, to nearly $6 billion; as for profits, they trippled, to $141 million. Engelhard had done better even than Hammer, and theirs was not entirely a windfall profit. Henry Jarecki announced record profits, too, and Theo Hook's company was particularly proud of its year-end results; even Bache made money in 1980. So, either directly or indirectly, there was a transfer of substantial sums of money from the Hunt brothers and the Saudis to the bullion dealers and some of the brokerage houses in New York. These winners were disinclined, however, to attribute their good fortune to the Hunts in case it provoked retaliation. The market participants were fairly sure they would win any lawsuit, but were apprehensive about the time it would take, and about the cost.

The Hunts were not the only losers who believed that they had been victims of a conspiracy by the shorts on Comex and the Board of Trade. Their allegations were repeated by a man who appointed himself the representative of the small traders at various congressional hearings. His name was Brian Walsh, and he was an orchardist from Salem, Massachusetts. By his own description, Walsh was a fairly typical follower of Jerome Smith's (to the extent of farming two crops that Smith thought an excellent investment – jojoba and macadamia nuts), and he had sought to convert hard-earned dollars into a hedge against inflation by buying two silver futures contracts. After the rules were changed in January, Walsh lost, by his standards, a substantial sum, and in his anxiety he advertised in the *Wall Street Journal*, asking to hear from investors in a similar plight. By the time Walsh gave a statement to Senator Donald Stewart's subcommittee early in May, he had heard from eighty small investors who had lost a total of more than $80 million. 'Many of the people who have contacted me – small businessmen and homeowners – have now incurred severe financial problems; they are also at present unable to borrow money at the banks to tide them over these hard times.' Their trouble, it would seem, was that they had not lost *enough* money, for Bunker and Herbert experienced no such difficulties.

Walsh made a further statement to the Senate Banking Committee a month later, and by then the toll had risen to eight hundred small investors with losses in excess of $150 million. The harrowing consequences were spelled out. 'A member of the group who lost $40,000 suffered an attack of high blood pressure, now resulting in complete loss of sight. Others have also suffered emotional traumas – some unable to mortgage their homes, or pay off their losses.' The natural response of the free market to these misfortunes is to murmur *caveat emptor*, but Walsh was convinced that the market had not been free: there was, he said, 'a serious question of impropriety in the actions of the exchanges'. Most small investors agreed with him.

The allegation was serious enough to merit an investigation by the CFTC, and the commission reported its conclusions to Congress in May 1981. But they offered only momentary consolation to Walsh's sad band of speculators. The rule changes in January 1980, the report stated, 'after a period of time, appeared to contribute to reversing the upward price movement'; and the report further conceded that 'those exchange board members holding physical silver hedged by futures positions could have gained from reversing the rapid rise in silver prices because of the adverse cash flow and interest costs associated with maintaining their hedges.' But the report concluded that there was no evidence suggesting that board members acted in their own interest, rather than to maintain an orderly silver futures market. Only in a footnote did the authors point out that their investigation had not drawn on information being collected by the enforcement divisions of the CFTC and the SEC. 'This information may not support, and indeed may be inconsistent with, the statement in this report,' the note said, perhaps ominously. The inference of the CFTC's report is that one or two individuals might have benefited by the rule changes (and the name of one Chicago dealer was mentioned with uncommon regularity), but that there had been no conspiracy. (The SEC was not so sure; in October 1981, one of the SEC's commissioners, Philip Loomis, told the House Agriculture Committee: 'We continue to believe that the silver report may not attach sufficient significance to the regulatory actions of the boards of trade.'

After all, Loomis added, the price did fall all of $10 in the twenty-four hours after the rules were changed.)

The bitterness of small investors is easy enough to understand; they had learned a harsh lesson in the perils of speculation, and the evidence suggests that they were victims of the clash between professional market participants and huge speculators like Bunker, in which the cost of defeat would have been immense to whoever lost. But the small traders who were long in silver were bound to lose after liquidation-only trading was introduced on January 22, because they had no one to sell to. The irony is that, early in 1980, small speculators would actually have made money by buying Treasury bills, or just by putting their savings in the bank – though that was not what the gurus like Jerome Smith had advised.

The Saudis were no less resentful than the small investors. At first it seemed as if their disenchantment with silver speculation was directed at Bunker, for having sold them the idea, and at the futures markets, for having changed the rules of the game. More than a year after Silver Thursday, it became evident that their anger was infinitely fiercer than had been supposed, and that it was directed specifically at the dealers who had managed their accounts during the great speculation. Saudis do not like to sue in Western courts; they dislike their affairs coming under public scrutiny. This was the exception. The most sensational case in the aftermath of the affair was brought by Mahmoud Fustok against the Banque Populaire Suisse and others. Fustok's charge was that the fourth-largest bank in Switzerland had been deeply involved in 'a scheme to cheat and defraud the plaintiff and other customers of hundreds of millions of dollars.' Presumably, the 'other customers' were members of the Saudi royal family, but they remained discreetly silent. Fustok's claim for damages of $387.5 million was made entirely on his own behalf.

Fustok's list of defendants was remarkable. The Banque Populaire was represented by Alain Brussard, a senior vice-president and the manager of its Geneva office. Two other bank officials were named – Michel Blattman, co-manager of the Geneva office, and Roger Guex, head of the trading department. Brussard was a director of Advicorp Advisory and Financial Corporation (the firm, you might remember, with offices overlooking the pleasant cobbled Place du Molard in Geneva), and all his co-directors there were named as co-defendants – Pierre Alain Hirschy, Jean Jacques Bally, Antoine Asfour, and Paul Bisoffi. The list cuts a small swath through the Geneva banking community, especially as all the Advicorp directors except Brussard had worked until fairly recently for Chase Manhattan's Geneva branch. None could be described as a small-time operator.

The complaint, which was filed in federal court in New York on June 29, 1981, outlined the alleged scheme to defraud in fascinating detail, as follows. Fustok's personal account with the Banque Populaire Suisse was placed in an omnibus account along with those of 'other customers', and none of the names was disclosed to the brokers with whom the Banque and Advicorp dealt in New York. The effect of this secrecy was that no single customer had any way of knowing which transactions were executed for his account, except through the Banque, on whose honesty, accuracy, and promptness the customer had to rely. The Banque, through its own involvement in Advicorp, then 'induced' Fustok and other customers to authorize Advicorp to manage the accounts on a discretionary basis. This meant the Banque did not have to consult the customers about trades made on their behalf.

The language of the complaint explains clearly how the Banque and Advicorp were accused of having used this power. The basic charge was that, having executed silver transactions on Comex, 'the Banque Populaire Suisse did not immediately enter the transaction on its books and records for the account of specific customers. After a lapse of time which permitted the defendants to evaluate whether the transactions would be profitable or unprofitable, the Banque assigned unprofitable transactions to its customers, and profitable transactions to accounts maintained under code names, maintained for the defendants and persons acting in concert with them. Sometimes, even after transactions were assigned to specific accounts, they were retroactively reassigned when they subsequently became profitable' – and vice versa.

That was merely the beginning. The next trick, it was alleged, was to execute wholly fictitious transactions at prices that were unfavourable to Fustok and his friends; on the *profitable* side of the deal, said Fustok, were none other than the directors of Advicorp. A further charge was that the Banque used money owed to Fustok and others to pay margin calls on its own accounts.

These were not generalized charges; the details were cruelly specific. Take, for example, the case of the fictitious purchase of 200 silver futures contracts.

> On 21 January 1980, the Comex silver market was open for only 45 minutes, from 1:30 p.m. to 2:15 p.m., and the trading volume for all delivery months was only 210 contracts. During this 45-minute period, the silver contract for January 1980 traded at a high of $49.00 per ounce, and settled at $44.00 per ounce.
>
> It was in this context that Banque Populaire Suisse purported to have purchased 200 January 1980 Comex silver contracts of 21 January for 15 of its discretionary

account customers at a price of $49.00 per ounce – one million ounces at an aggregate price of $49 million.

No such purchases were made on the floor of Comex. In fact, the only 'purchases' of January silver that the Banque Populaire made on 21 January were fictitious purchases that took place solely on the books of the Banque. Entries on its books were made to indicate that 15 of its customers had purchased 200 contracts at $49.00 per ounce and that five of its accounts had sold 200 contracts at $49.00 per ounce. The accounts which were indicated as sellers were identified by code names 'Flamant', 'Loukoum', 'Muscade', 'Dattier' and 'Ryan'. The code name accounts, which benefited from the artificial profits derived from those fictitious sales, were accounts maintained for the benefit of one or more of the defendants and persons acting in concert with them.

The customers lost $38 million on that deal, the complaint alleged. That episode would have been stunning in its simplicity, for no knowledge of the market would have been needed to carry it out. Others were more complicated, and would have demanded more dexterity than a mere bookkeeping entry. There was, for instance, the inside deal between Advicorp and two employees of Conti Commodities, both dealing on their own account. One employee was Norton Waltuch, the great bull of the silver pit, and the second was Thomas Waldeck, who worked in Conti's Geneva office, just around the corner from the Place du Molard. In an exchange of futures for physicals, Waltuch and Waldeck sold 1.75 million ounces of silver, valued at $53.5 million (roughly $30 an ounce), to Fustok, cancelling 350 contracts that were valued on the market at $39 an ounce. Fustok claimed the Banque Populaire did not tell him of the transaction; instead, he was told that the contracts had been cashed in, for $15.5 million less than their market price. Fustok declared he was finally informed about his acquisition of 1.75 million ounces of silver by courtesy of Waltuch and Waldeck in May 1980, when it was worth less than $13 an ounce. 'In this instance alone,' said the complaint, 'the plaintiff was cheated and defrauded out of $50 million.'

Fustok claimed his income was further reduced, by $900,000, when the profitable sale of 25 contracts in his account was reassigned to the code-named accounts. And the last example quoted in the complaint was equally straightforward: Fustok alleged that Advicorp had bought 200,000 ounces of silver from Conti to be deposited in his account at the Swiss Bank Corporation. But when the receipts arrived in Switzerland, they were placed instead in the accounts of 'persons unknown to the plaintiff but believed to be one or more of the defendants'. Fustok stated that he had lost the original $80 million he had deposited with the Banque Populaire Suisse; calculated that his total losses by means of the alleged fraud were in excess of $250 million; and asked for damages of $387.5 million.

The Banque Populaire's response to this astonishing catalogue of charges was tight-lipped. All its spokesman said was that a counter-suit had been filed against Mahmoud Fustok in Geneva, claiming that it was he who owed the Banque money, not the other way around. The details of the Banque's case were not publicly available, however, as were those of the case against it in New York: the Swiss are more circumspect about such embarrassments. But before any legal judgment could be reached on either case, it was easy to draw one conclusion from the claim and counterclaim. If Mahmoud Fustok and the Banque's other anonymous customers had not felt so strongly that their substantial presence in the silver market should be secret, none of the alleged frauds would have been possible. But secrecy was an essential part of their plan, so Fustok and his angered co-conspirators were vulnerable.

Fustok's case was the first public indication of how much the Saudis had lost in the silver market. But high as they are on the list of losers, the biggest of all was still Bunker, for he was potentially the chief beneficiary of his gargantuan gamble. I had sought an epitaph for Bunker's defeat from the moment I began this story, and I came across it by chance one evening in Washington during one of those idle conversations with which reporters pass much time. A colleague, most expert in the grain trade, was recalling Bunker's foray into the soybean market in Chicago in 1977. Bunker, Herbert, and their families had bought more than one-third of the soybean contracts in the market, and the largest short seller was a grain trader named Cook Industries. The size of that short position bankrupted the company, and on June 1, 1977, its chairman, a man named Ned Cook, asked that trading in the company's shares be suspended while he organized 'an orderly repayment of its debts.'

A reporter telephoned Bunker in Dallas to ask what he thought of Ned Cook's plight.

'Is this on or off the record?' Bunker inquired.

'On the record, please, Mr Hunt,' said the reporter.

'Well,' replied Bunker, 'I think Ned Cook's a fine gentleman, and I'm real sorry this has happened to him.'

'Off the record, Mr Hunt, how do you feel about Ned Cook?'

'Tough shit,' said Bunker.

That remark serves as a satisfactory preliminary judgment on the failure of Bunker's silver gamble.

Chapter 20

'Tough Shit'

'Tough shit' is not merely invective; the phrase has recently been elevated into a political and economic principle. Although many of its practitioners express it more delicately, the principle is a fundamental premise of libertarianism, a system that has its own political party – the Libertarian party in the United States – and its own presidential candidate (a California lawyer named Ed Clark, in 1980). The principle has also deeply tinged the New Conservatism of President Ronald Reagan and Margaret Thatcher. The phrase would, no doubt, never pass the lips of either of them, but their economic policies bear harshly on the least privileged members of society: the poor, the ill-educated ethnic minorities, and the unemployed. Theoretically, these groups should be grateful for the economic liberty imposed by the New Conservatism and pull themselves up by their bootstraps; if they cannot do so . . . well, tough shit. As a principle, then, it is not wholly out of tune with our times.

The Libertarian party stands for what its name implies: it condemns all forms of state intervention, from literary censorship to taxation. But the emphasis always seems to be on taxation rather than censorship, and the Libertarian with whom I have discussed the subject at some length – an associate of Jerome Smith's named Robert Meier – admits that the party's basic economic philosophy differs little from Bunker Hunt's. Meier explains the Libertarian position as follows: 'Consensual economic activities are a civil liberty, and, as long as people do not use force or fraud, the state should not tell them what to do.' Applied to a speculator who tries to corner the market, the Libertarian philosophy is 'Why not?' More sophisticated party members will add there is nothing in economic history to suggest that a market corner will work. Meier declares: 'If someone is attempting to corner the market, they become a component, an integral part, of the market itself.' About Bunker's silver gamble, he concludes: 'There was an attempted corner, and the banks, the brokers, and the Hunts should have had to live with the consequences.' Which means that if any of them had gone bankrupt, that would have been tough shit. But they did not; so, no matter how satisfying a preliminary judgment that was, it will not do.

Before drawing any conclusions, however, it is worth recalling what Bunker Hunt, his friends, and his relations did, and why, and how it fits into context. So we should start with the fact that their game was not unique. It had been played almost one hundred years before in Paris, when a group of bankers (led by Denfert Rochereau of the Comptoir d'Escompte) and some industrialists formed a ring in 1888 with the intention of establishing a cartel to control the copper price. The outcome of that operation is described in the principal text on the subject, *Manias, Panics, and Crashes* by Charles P. Kindleberger, a distinguished economist at the Massachusetts Institute of Technology. 'By 1890 the French syndicate held 160,000 tons of high-priced copper, plus contracts to buy more, with old mines being reworked, scrap processing being initiated everywhere, and the price sinking like a stone. From £80 a ton at the top to £38, the collapse almost took with it in 1889 the Comptoir d'Escompte, which was saved by an advance of 140 million francs from the Bank of France, guaranteed by the Paris banks.' The two major differences between the two episodes are, first, that Denfert Rochereau (like Chunilal Saraya of the Indian Specie Bank) afterward committed suicide; the other difference is of scale. A crisis in late-twentieth-century markets spreads faster and affects more people.

As Denfert Rochereau had failed in the copper market, Bunker and his syndicate failed to corner silver. A realistic description of what they actually achieved is contained in one of the classic legal definitions of 'market manipulation': 'the creation of an artificial price by planned action, whether by one man or a group of men.' If there was ever any doubt that this is what did happen, it was dispelled by the final report to Congress of the Commodity Futures Trading Commission in May 1981, which expressed it this way: by the end of October 1979, the Hunts, their interests, and the investors operating through Conti Commodities controlled more than 20 per cent of the estimated worldwide commercial demand for silver. Add to that the prospect of the conversion of 140 million ounces of silver futures positions into delivered bullion, and there was a demand for silver that could not be met from available supplies. This alone led to price increases; furthermore, the report said, the expectations of substantial continuing increases in the silver price may have exacerbated the initial price increases. 'This resulted in a situation in which the price of silver temporarily rose far above the level which has subsequently been sufficient to balance silver's supply and demand.' This is a cautious man's way of saying that the price was artificial, or, as James Stone was to describe it, 'a temporary flirtation with fantasy.' Bunker's fantasy was that the gold/silver ratio would fall to 1:5, and that a new ratio would indicate a silver price of at least $85 an ounce.

But his gamble did not lead to a 'crash', and although it contained all the ingredients of a 'panic', things never became quite that bad. But it was definitely a 'mania', a condition that Kindleberger compares to a 'bubble'. This was also the description given to the affair at a hearing of the Senate Banking Committee, when Comptroller of the Currency John Heimann and the SEC's chairman, Harold Williams, were among the witnesses:

> HEIMANN: It looks like a bubble, it smells like a bubble, it feels like a bubble.
> SENATOR [ADLAI] STEVENSON: It walks like one.
> HEIMANN: It's awful darn close to being one.
> WILLIAMS: Yes. It's a bubble.

There were precedents for a bubble, too, in the eighteenth century. There were the Mississippi Scheme, and – the best known so far – the South Sea Bubble. Like those, Bunker's bubble burst.

And who blew the bubble in the first place? Bunker, obviously; but he could not have done it without forming the alliance between Texas and Saudi Arabia. In Paris I asked him why the Arabs had joined it. He hesitated before asking: 'What's the word you have in England . . . "flutter"?' I said it was. 'Well, that's what it was, a flutter, a gamble.' Some flutter.

Bunker Hunt, who applied his intellect to the mechanics, was probably unaware of the implications of the gamble. But there are consquences that no one would have considered before the Yom Kippur War in 1973, when the OPEC cartel, prompted by the Shah of Iran and by a distaste for the swollen profits of the Seven Sisters, quadrupled the price of oil. That allowed a few men in the Middle East, and in the United States, too, to accumulate more money than King Midas ever dreamed of. At first, public attention was drawn to the extravagance with which it was spent: the casino losses, the magnums of Dom Pérignon every evening (outside the kingdom, of course), the mansions, the apartments, the girl friends and Rolls-Royces. A few politicians and bankers worried about the accumulated reserves of the Arabs, but their concern was the money markets. They never really considered the commodity futures market as a target for this cornucopia of new wealth. That idea was so foreign to the politicians and bankers (outside Switzerland, at least) that they were taken by surprise. After all, a gamble on such a scale for such high stakes was not what the commodity markets were supposed to be for.

The markets themselves were surprised, and although there were a few greedy professionals with inside knowledge who took advantage of the new money, most of the dealers and brokers were too slow to comprehend what was happening to them, right under their noses. They were probably too busy making money. But the episode demonstrated that the contention of Milton Friedman, the guru of the New Conservative economics – that markets are rational, and that whatever goes wrong can be blamed on government interference – is, frankly, bunk.

Friedman further argues that as the de-stabilizing speculator will fail to survive, there can be no de-stabilizing speculator. This is a semantic exercise by a man whose theorizing failed to take account of de-stabilizing speculators like Bunker, Herbert, and the Arabs. They did fail to survive, but not before they had almost destroyed the markets that Friedman describes as such perfect economic instruments. Maybe they were, once, but the futures markets have become less a medium for identifying a world price and absorbing the risk of price changes; in highly taxed societies they are as much a means of dodging taxes and making money out of arbitrage as anything else. Greed is a perfectly tolerable goal in the commodities futures markets.

Nonetheless, it would be idle to suggest that the gamble was an isolated event, that the bubble formed in a vacuum, because no bubble can. A friend of mine in New York, a sagacious investment banker, dates the origin of Bunker's gamble as the late spring of 1977, when Western leaders met at the 'Downing Street summit' in London. On that occasion, President Jimmy Carter was persuaded by James Callaghan, against the advice of Chancellor Helmut Schmidt, that more government spending to reduce unemployment had a higher priority than the fight against inflation, which would cause governments to spend less. The principle, though socially admirable, was economically disastrous and signalled the beginning of an unprecedented American inflation, an inflation which was certainly one factor that drove Bunker Hunt into his great silver speculation. (Greed and a delight at the prospect of being the richest man of all were two others.) Bunker wanted assets that came from the earth and were needed by industry, rather than a paper fortune that was steadily depreciating under the weight of dollar bills flowing from the printing presses of the U.S. Treasury. A similar motive impelled the Saudis (though they were greedy, too), who were particularly conscious of American inflation because their oil sales were linked to the U.S. dollar.

This second cause of the bubble does not necessarily contradict the first – that a few rich men had more money than was good for them. And once this syndicate of opulent men used their economic power on an unprecedented scale, two of the basic elements of a mania, as defined by Professor Kindleberger, helped them along. The first was the foolishness of the speculators, whose expectation, fuelled by Bunker Hunt's unwavering optimism, was that the silver price would never fall. This condition had been observed during the South Sea Bubble by no less a personage than the man who discovered the law of gravity, Sir Isaac Newton. 'I can calculate the motions of heavenly bodies, but not the madness of people,' said Sir Isaac, whose own law of gravity might have had something to teach speculators – it being also true in markets that what goes up will eventually come down. (His wisdom was of little use to Sir Isaac, however, because he bought shares at the height of the South Sea Bubble, and lost £20,000.)

The second element in the formation of a bubble is the rapid expansion of credit and money, and that condition was clearly present, even after Paul Volcker became chairman of the Federal Reserve Board. Despite his first warning against speculation, banks like the First National of Chicago and brokerage houses like Bache could hardly contain their eagerness to finance the game. Jonathan Swift was inspired by the earlier bubble to produce a couplet that aptly describes their haste:

> Get money, money still
> And let virtue follow, if she will.

When Western banks are made to count the cost of exotic activities such as Bunker's silver bubble, they will rue the extravagant years of the 1970s when they lent money as though there were no tomorrow. Bunker Hunt and his pals, and the speculators in the market, were not the only greedy ones.

What happens when the bubble bursts depends, of course, on the circumstances, and in March 1980 they could hardly have been worse. Throughout the 1970s the orderly international economic system created at Bretton Woods in 1944 by skilful men who admired stability and continuity had begun to crack up. One outcome was inflation on a scale unknown since the 1920s. When inflation was eventually identified as the chief problem, its cure in the most profligate economies – Britain's particularly, with America catching up fast – was so harsh as to create unemployment worse than most

Western countries have known since the Great Depression. There is an aeronautical analogy that describes this condition: if the economy were an aircraft, it would now be flying so slowly as to be in danger of a fatal stall.

It would be overdramatic to suggest that the Hunts almost triggered the events that stalled the American economy, but it is quite realistic to conceive that they might have done. By blundering through the institutions of capitalism, they nearly brought some of them tumbling down. The fear of a crash lasted for five full days in March 1980. Wall Street brokers were threatened; if they had collapsed, the crisis would have spread to the clearinghouse and the stock exchange, and from there to the banks. A slump could have become a recession. This did not happen because the mess created when the bubble burst was hurriedly cleared up – largely, it can reasonably be said, by sweeping it under the carpet. Honoré de Balzac described such an exercise in his novel *La Maison Nucingen*: 'The most virtuous merchants tell you with the most candid air this *mot* of the most unrestrained immorality: "One gets out of a bad affair as one can."'

Had the United States been the great imperial economy of a generation ago, Paul Volcker and John Heimann could have allowed the Hunts to forage for themselves; if the consequence of their speculation was that they went belly up, too bad. By 1980 the bank regulators had to adhere to one of the more sophisticated concepts of central banking, first conceived in London after a panic in 1825: there are times when rules and precedents cannot safely be broken; others, when they cannot be adhered to with safety. This means that if the consequences of the greed and impropriety of Bunker and Herbert Hunt were likely to inflict serious injury on innocent bystanders, they had to be bailed out. In other words, the 'tough shit' principle, in which Bunker believes so firmly, could not be allowed to operate in his case. Many innocent bystanders criticized the central bankers for their unwillingness to punish the Hunts; they might have been equally critical if they themselves had been hurt.

The 1970s were littered with other examples of central bankers getting out of bad affairs as best they could. In 1973 and early 1974 the governor of the Bank of England, Gordon Richardson, launched what he described as a lifeboat operation when the collapse of a number of fringe banks, to whose malfeasance the central bank had turned a blind eye, endangered the whole British banking system. The Bank of England was forced to dirty its hands in order to avert the threat to the stability of the City of London. As for the Federal Reserve Board, during the 1970s it had grown accustomed to dealing with impending bankruptcy or collapse. The list included Penn Central, Lockheed, Chrysler, the Franklin National Bank, and the international fallout from the crash of the Herstatt Bank of Cologne. The lender of last resort had rarely been resorted to so regularly. In fact, there is now a danger of the bailout's becoming a first rather than a last resort.

The last question raised by this story is: will it happen again? In theory there is no doubt that it will, because Professor Kindleberger's text admirably demonstrates the repetitive nature of manias, panics, and crashes. The Commodity Futures Trading Commission also thought a recurrence quite possible, and its report to Congress stated that 'events similar to those in the silver market could be repeated in silver or another commodity.' The ingredients still exist: stupendously wealthy individuals and corporations, and foreign-nominee accounts like those of the Banque Populaire Suisse. The CFTC report actually identified the most likely candidates for a corner or squeeze: the financial futures markets in Chicago, particularly the ninety-day Treasury bill market at the Mercantile Exchange, and the long-term Treasury bond market at the Board of Trade. And one man who had lived through the silver crisis – Chairman James Stone of the CFTC – went a step further: 'With no further change in regulation, I believe that the formation of another bubble some day in some commodity can be predicted with near certainty. It is only a matter of time.'

The CFTC did propose some rule changes: there would be position limits, foreign traders would be identified, and brokers would be stopped paying a customer's margin calls. They were proposed, but eighteen months after Silver Thursday, the new regulations were still on the drawing board. Stone was not satisfied that these new rules, if they were eventually implemented, would be enough, and proposed further that federal agencies be allowed to fix margins. Moreover, he wanted the holders of large positions to be identified publicly. 'I cannot say that disclosure would have prevented the silver bubble,' he wrote. 'I can say . . . public policy should follow the advice of Justice Louis Brandeis who told us years ago that "sunlight is the most powerful of all disinfectants".'

But even if Stone's reforms had been accepted by Congress, which seemed dubious after the election of President Reagan, his own experience ought to have led him to confess that a silver bubble could still occur. Bunker's silver gamble gives us no reason to believe that regulatory agencies will necessarily perform more effectively if the laws they administer are made tougher.

So, it seems likely that the last of these questions was wrongly phrased. Instead of: will it happen again?, the question should read:

when will it happen, and where? Whom will the lender of the last resort have to bail out (or allow to be bailed out) next? It is a pessimistic conclusion, but the problem is that our economic system, far from defending itself against gamblers, actually encourages them, for capitalism needs gamblers in all their varieties. Indeed, the next candidate could still be Bunker Hunt. He can speculate again when the billion-dollar loan is paid off by 1990, and it is difficult to imagine his not trying. Speculation, like oil, is in the blood.

Chapter 21

Postscript

There remains the task of collecting together the threads of this narrative – although they cannot yet be tied together in a neat knot because, as Bunker said, the game is not over. But a year later it had already had a profound effect on the lives of some of the participants; others, it seemed to have left almost unmoved.

When last heard of, there was only good news of Naji Robert Nahas. He spent but a short time licking his wounds. Within a year of his disaster in New York, Naji had announced that he believed 1 million per cent in Brazil, and that as a mark of his confidence he hoped to invest $100 million in the country's future. The first indication that Naji Nahas might be as good as his word was his purchase of a stake in the Banco do Comércio e Indústria in São Paulo; to add to the gaiety of the nation, Naji also financed the smartest new nightclub in Rio de Janeiro, opened late in May 1981, in the presence of the most elevated politicians in the land. Naji Nahas's relations who stayed on in Beirut had reason to remember him, too; every time their accommodation was shelled during the war in Lebanon, a cheque would arrive from Brazil to help them out.

Mahmoud Fustok went on racing his horses in France and gathering information for his lawsuit against the Banque Populaire Suisse – a step he was unlikely to have taken without first referring to his liege lord, Prince Abdullah Ibn Abdul-Aziz al Saud, whose position in the hierarchy of the kingdom of Saudi Arabia was, if anything, more secure than before. Crown Prince Fahd grew increasingly confident of his succession to the ageing King Khalid, and seemed to have begun to understand that the security of the Saudi regime – especially after the shocking invasion of the Great Mosque in Mecca – would be helped by a lessening of the appearance of greed among members of the royal family. By 1981, the really outrageous commissions on government contracts were no longer thought expedient. As for Khalid bin Mahfouz, the word in Jeddah was that the loss of $600 million had had a detrimental effect on his health. Gaith Pharaon went on borrowing large sums of money from banks, whose vocabulary seemed not to include the word 'no', to extend his share in the Hyatt International hotel chain.

Jerome Smith retired to his mountaintop in Costa Rica and wrote a best-selling book. During a season in which books about bad news in the American economy were good news in the book trade, Smith's opus suited the mood perfectly. Entitled *The Coming Currency Collapse; And What You Can Do About It*, the book was dedicated to Henry David Thoreau 'and kindred noble spirits everywhere'. The book jacket indicated what could be done about the coming currency collapse: the reader could subscribe to *World Market Perspective* and receive a special bonus offer worth up to $60.

Harry Jacobs, chairman of Bache, had done neither himself nor his company a good turn by persuading Bunker and Herbert Hunt to become shareholders. A year after its indecent exposure in the silver market, Bache was taken over by an insurance company, the Prudential, and before that indignity, there had been another. The Hunt brothers sold some of their shares in Bache to the same Belzberg brothers in Vancouver from whom their shareholding had originally been supposed to protect Bache. (And there was a curiosity about that transaction: the agent for the sale was Andrew Racz, the man who had claimed that the Hunts, Michael Boswell of Sunshine Mining, and his Arab colleagues had intended to create a silver cartel. Racz fell quite silent after Bunker Hunt's share deal had been consummated.)

Robert Abboud left the First National Bank of Chicago, and was hired on the turn by the wily old fox of Western capitalism, Armand Hammer of Occidental Petroleum. Hammer had been one of Abboud's best clients at First National – along with Bunker and Herbert Hunt – but Abboud quickly discovered that Hammer was not an easy man to work for. It was rumoured that the first task Hammer set Abboud when he sat at the chairman's right hand in the boardroom was to fetch him a cup of tea.

In the futures market in 1981, Norton Waltuch was creating less of a stir. A compulsive gambler, he apparently played the sugar futures market with such dire results that he was forced to sell one of his two seats on Comex. There was not a great deal of sympathy for him among the dealers. Dr Henry Jarecki went on energetically expanding Mocatta Metals, and affected total indifference to the crisis through which he had passed in September 1979. His name was more widely known, however; as august a figure as Paul Volcker asked a bank chairman one day: 'Just who *is* Henry Jarecki?' Theo Hook went on making money, but for the first time he spoke of the strain of dealing in silver and gold without a lapse of concentration from breakfast time to mid-afternoon each day, and even thought of taking a break. In the silver market, business was rotten; speculators, large and small, preferred not to play in a casino where the rules could be changed in the middle of the game. The men in the markets did not entirely lose their sense of humour, however. The menu at the annual dinner of the London Metal Exchange in the winter of 1980 began with suprême de saumon poché Bunker, and ended with tranche d'ananas et pêche impériale Hunt.

As the whole world knew, Paul Volcker had become a figure to be reckoned with. His preoccupation with inflation was criticized at home and abroad, because the consequence of it was record interest rates. The new president in the White House did not mind at first; but the new president of France, François Mitterrand, and the chancellor of West Germany Helmut Schmidt, were not at all pleased by the tall, stubborn man at the Federal Reserve. Volcker had established the independence he sought, and was disinclined to alter his policy to suit presidents, chancellors, or prime ministers; though when it was pointed out to him by impatient congressmen that the Hunts had still not begun to 'liquidate their silver in an orderly manner', there seemed to be nothing he could do about that.

The Swiss banks that had played the game most boldly – the Swiss Bank Corporation and the Banque Populaire Suisse – reported substantial losses because of their speculation in silver and received a severe ticking off from their country's Federal Banking Commission, which punished them by lifting a corner of the veil of secrecy behind which they had previously been able to play the commodity markets. In New York, Philipp Brothers, the Engelhard subsidiary, which had been renamed Phibro Corporation, spent some of its profits purchasing Salomon Brothers, the largest private investment banking company in the United States.

Of James Stone, it can only be said that he still had a position, but one much diminished in status. After the inauguration of President Ronald Reagan, the administration looked urgently for a new chairman of the Commodity Futures Trading Commission, and eventually appointed a Chicago lawyer named Philip Johnson, who had worked for the Board of Trade. Stone stayed on as a commissioner, becoming a more radical and still more isolated figure; he could actually be overheard speculating about whether there was much purpose to the futures market at all.

On Capitol Hill there was no justice. Senator Donald Stewart, having lost the Democratic primary in Alabama, went back home to teach a course at the university and practise some law, not at all comforted by the fact that the Democrat who had beaten him was himself beaten by a Republican opponent in the November election. The result of that election also promoted a right-wing Southerner, Jesse Helms, to the chairmanship of the Senate Agriculture Committee; Stephen Storch decided that it was the moment to quit the committee's staff, and took a lobbying job in the Washington office of the New York Stock Exchange.

Barbara Timmer stayed put on the House Subcommittee on Commerce, Consumer and Monetary Affairs. Although her duties increased in number, her interest in the affairs of the Hunt brothers never diminished, and she remained a thorn in their sides. Congressman Ben Rosenthal kept on trying to have commodity straddles bought for tax purposes declared illegal, and finally had his wish fulfilled in August 1981.

All was not well for Bill Bledsoe in Dallas. Bledsoe's oil business was doing fine, but his ex-employers harried him ruthlessly, and eventually he was indicted by a federal grand jury for alleged misrepresentation in land deals in Oklahoma that he had negotiated for Bunker Hunt. Bledsoe remained cheerful and confidently swore that he was innocent.

And what of our heroes – or, if you prefer, our anti-heroes – Bunker, Herbert, and Lamar Hunt? Truth to tell, their outward behaviour gave hardly any hint that something had happened. In January 1981, the three of them cheekily bought a 50 per cent share in a western Canadian silver-mining company, Terra Mining, for $35 million, with the acquiescence of their bankers, who saw no contradiction between this purchase and the loan conditions. Admittedly, they had to sell stocks worth $200 million in June 1981 to finance their share in the partnership with Placid Oil. But, that little local difficulty apart, Lamar announced a new bid to become the Napoleon of professional tennis; Herbert continued to work away at the sums in Dallas; and Bunker went on making public appearances so that he could spread his own eccentric version of the gospel. He appeared in Washington at a dinner organized by one of the newly influential right-wing pressure groups, the Council for National Policy; and in June 1981 he made a succinct statement of his beliefs at an investment seminar in Anaheim, California. 'The most important thing to have is a spiritual environment in this country which will mean we can keep the money we make. Just making money doesn't mean much when the system is going to collapse,' he said.

Bunker Hunt did not address himself to the question of what – or who – was most likely to be responsible for the collapse of the system. His own dealings had made him a serious candidate for that dubious honour in the first four months of 1980. But Bunker appeared not to have noticed it; he is, perhaps, too obstinate to learn from experience. If he had a regret, it was possibly that he had not succeeded in becoming the richest man in the world again, as he had been in 1967. Because that is still the way he keeps the score.

Notes on Sources

Evidently, no footnotes have been included in this story. It would be quite wrong, however, not to detail the sources of much of the information, not as an academic rite but out of gratitude. I say 'much' because not all the information can be directly attributed. I realize that a standard of journalism is to be able to confirm the authenticity of information with two separate sources. In this case, had that standard been required, the story could not have been told, since many of the participants declined to be sources at all – understandably, because much of their activity could involve breaches of the law. Others wished to speak only off the record, for use but not for direct attribution. Although I prefer not to accept this limitation on an interview, I regard it, on the whole, as preferable to having no interview at all. But, with a single exception – in Chapter 12 – I have not speculated myself. What follows, then, is a partial record of the interviews I conducted, but I believe it is a complete list of the published sources I used. Publishing details of books are in the Bibliography.

CHAPTER 1: The Libyan story is taken from contemporary reports in the London *Financial Times*; Anthony Sampson's *The Seven Sisters*; and from conversations with two employees of Bunker Hunt who wish to remain anonymous. I interviewed Bill Bledsoe, Phillip Hirschkop, and Gordon McLendon, but the most complete source on the Hunt family is Harry Hunt III, whose book, *Texas Rich*, was published in 1981, after invaluable excerpts had appeared in *Texas Monthly* (April 1978) and *Playboy* (August 1980). *The Review of the News*, published by the John Birch Society, is assiduously collected by the Public Affairs Press in Washington; the interview referred to appeared on December 12, 1979. I also made use of articles in the British press: by Charles Foley in *The Observer* (March 27 and December 12, 1974), Brian Hitchen in the *Daily Mirror* (March 20, 1968), and Max Hastings in the *Evening Standard* (May 13, 1968).

CHAPTER 2: The primary source is Jerome Smith's *Silver Profits in the Seventies*, a copy of which he generously gave to me. I interviewed Scott Dial and Gordon McLendon, and much of my knowledge of the history of silver comes from *The Book of Old Silver*.

CHAPTER 3: Glenn W. Clark, a lawyer specializing in commodity markets in Washington, guided me through the history of the futures markets. My first glimmerings of how they work were provided by Stephen Greenburg in New York, Leo Malamud in Chicago, and Peter Robbins in London. That educational process was carried on by Theo Hook, in whose dealing room I spent many hours, and whose own dealers were just as helpful. If I did not learn well enough, it is not the fault of Theo Hook and his colleagues. Russell Baker gave me his copy of *Extraordinary Popular Delusions and the Madness of Crowds*, signed by Bernard Baruch himself. Dr Henry Jarecki of Mocatta Metals Corporation kindly made contemporary accounts of the collapse of the Indian Specie Bank available to me. Both Comex and the Chicago Board of Trade publish guides to the markets, which describe how they ought to work.

CHAPTER 4: Interviews with Haji Ashraf in Dubai, Bill Bledsoe in Dallas, and George Lamborn in New York; the legal opinion commissioned by the Hunts to establish their relationship with Great Western United came from a commodities lawyer in New York who, like the original author of the opinion, wishes to remain anonymous. Details of the soybean case brought by the CFTC against the Hunts are drawn from *Commodity Futures Law Reports* (October 1974 and January 1979). Information about Nasrullah Khan's bouncing cheque came from the CFTC's ensuing indictment, released on April 24, 1980.

CHAPTER 5: My introduction to the politics of Saudi Arabia was given by Richard Johns of the *Financial Times* and by his colleague, James Buchan, though neither is responsible for my conclusions. The *Financial Times* is also the source of published information about the Eurosystem Hospitalier bankruptcy. In no other area of this story, however, did more people request anonymity; journalists, bankers, businessmen, and diplomats in London, Paris, Jeddah, and Washington prefer not to have their views identified. It is bad for business with the kingdom. The best depository of published information about Saudi Arabian private investment overseas is produced by the Chase Manhattan Bank. The *Sunday Times* correspondent in Bermuda, Brenda Roulston, kindly provided me with details of the company registration of IMIC. Norton Waltuch's evidence to the Senate Agriculture Committee was published in Part II of its *Hearings*. The court documents in the case of *Mahmoud Fustok* v. *Banque Populaire Suisse and others* is file number 81 Civ. 4139 in Federal Court, Southern District of New York. I spoke to Haji Ashraf and Abdul Wahab Galadari in Dubai; and Bill Bledsoe in Dallas. Brough Scott, racing correspondent of the *Sunday Times*, looked after me at Longchamp.

CHAPTER 6: Henry Jarecki's article was published in *Euromoney* in March 1980. The rest of the guide was constructed with help from various dealers who regarded it as an interesting exercise, but not one on which they would like to base their public reputations.

CHAPTER 7: I relied heavily on interviews with each of the four commissioners of the CFTC. All were unfailingly courteous and helpful. The transcript of the surveillance meeting in July was published by the House committee. The annual reports of the CFTC and the comptroller general's *Report to Congress*: *Regulation of the Commodity Futures Markets* contained documentary material. Much of the documentation was made available to me by the commission's obliging director of public affairs, Randall Moore.

CHAPTER 8: Both Comex and the Chicago Board of Trade produced voluminous evidence about the silver market for congressional committees. The CFTC's confidential trading records were released by both House and Senate committees, as were the accounts of Read Dunn's conversations with Bunker and Herbert Hunt. I interviewed Robert Wilmouth, Henry Jarecki, and George Lamborn. *Fortune* magazine was a useful source of the version according to the Hunts, in an article entitled 'A Talkfest with the Hunts', published on August 11, 1980. Allen Pusey of the Dallas *Morning News* very generously allowed me to use the unedited transcript of his own long and expert interview with Bunker Hunt, which took place in August 1980.

CHAPTER 9: Interviews with Dr Andrew Brimmer, CFTC commissioners, and an anonymous executive of Engelhard. Comex's evidence to Congress was particularly helpful. Martin Meredith of the *Sunday Times* helped me in Beirut, and Nicholas Asheshov, that newspaper's correspondent in Lima, provided much of the information from Peru.

CHAPTER 10: Interviews with Walter Hoving and Walter Frankland. Read Dunn gave me a copy of Henry Jarecki's letter to him, which was sent on August 27, 1980. Much of the statistical information about the economic impact of the silver bubble is taken from James Stone's postscript to the CFTC's *Report to Congress*; both became available in June 1981. Some of the information about Ilford comes from Thames TV's *Inside Business* programme, transmitted on May 15, 1980.

CHAPTER 11: Chris Welles's article on Bache in the *Institutional Investor*, September 1980, is invaluable to a student of that company. *Saudi Business*, published bimonthly, is a most useful source of information. My information about the First National Bank of Chicago came from employees who were determined to remain anonymous. The president of the bank, Richard Thomas, was on the record, however, during his appearance before the Senate Banking Committee; the transcript is in its published *Hearings*. On the subject of Swiss banks, my *cher collègue*, Nicholas Faith, is expert. Details of the loans made to the Hunts are contained in the House committee's published *Hearings*. The Federal Reserve Board's *Interim Report on the Silver Situation* was published in the *Hearings* of each of the committees that investigated silver.

CHAPTER 12: Interviews with Chris Anderson and Andrew Racz, whose detailed allegations were published in the Senate Banking Committee's *Hearings*. *Forbes* magazine (January 21, 1980) published a profile of Michael Boswell, which was reprinted in the House committee's *Hearings*, along with many other newspaper and magazine articles on silver.

CHAPTER 13: Interviews with Carl Gewirtz, Jack Aboaf, and David Pearson; Robert Carswell, George Lamborn, Jerome Katz. Harry Jacobs was quoted in *Fortune* magazine (May 5, 1980). The CFTC's *Report to Congress* contained details of the course of events in the last week of March 1980. The Placid mortgages are to be found in the Dallas County Courthouse.

CHAPTER 14: Interviews with Carl Gewirtz, Henry Jarecki, George Lamborn, Stuart Eizenstat, Andrew Brimmer, Robert Carswell, Gerald Corrigan. *Fortune* magazine published an article entitled 'Engelhard's Not So Sterling Deal with the Hunts' on May 19, 1980. Engelhard's financial reports for 1979 and the first quarter of 1980 were obtained from the company. Both the Senate Agriculture Committee and the House committee discussed the events at Boca Raton exhaustively.

CHAPTER 16: The terms of the Hunt loan were published in full in the House committee *Hearings*. Elvis Mason's evidence is contained in the Senate Banking Commitee *Hearings*.

CHAPTER 17: Interviews with Barbara Timmer and Stephen Storch were more helpful than any others I had throughout my inquiries. Keven Putt, Senator Donald Stewart's administrative assistant, and Connie Gleason, on the staff of the Senate Agriculture Committee, helped me find obscure documents. I interviewed Senator Stewart. The transcripts of the appearance of Bunker and Herbert Hunt are published in the Senate Agriculture Committee and the House committee's *Hearings*. The House committee's *Hearings* also reprint Bill Bledsoe's statement.

CHAPTER 18: The Dallas County Courthouse is the repository of the Hunt mortgages. Allen Pusey guided me to them.

CHAPTER 19: Documents in the case of *Congdon and Carey* v. *Occidental Minerals* are filed in the Jefferson County Courthouse, Colorado. Brian Walsh's statements are in the Senate Agriculture and the Senate Banking Committee *Hearings*. Mahmoud Fustok's allegations are, as already mentioned, filed in New York City, and the CFTC's *Report to Congress* discusses the position of the short traders.

CHAPTER 20: The inspiration for this chapter is Professor Charles Kindleberger's *Manias, Panics, and Crashes*. I interviewed Robert Meier. The best discussion of the possibility of a recurrence of the bubble is contained in the CFTC's *Report to Congress*, and James Stone's memorandum written as a postscript to the *Report.* The excerpt from the evidence to the Senate Banking Committee is from its published *Hearings*.

Finally, I should like to thank the editor of the *Sunday Times* at the time I began to work on this story, Harold Evans, and his successor, Frank Giles, for allowing me the luxury of time to conduct the research. In the newspaper's London office, John Barry, Peter Watson, and Peter Roberts each encouraged me in his own way. In the New York and Washington offices of Times Newspapers, Robert Ducas, Therese Stanton, Patrick Brogan, and Frank Vogl were remarkably patient and helpful.

I owe an unquantifiable debt to Peter Pringle and Eleanor Randolph, and to Russell and Mimi Banker for both putting me up and putting up with me. The enthusiasm of Elisabeth Sifton at The Viking Press helped me to retain my own.

Bibliography

Blandford, Linda. *Oil Sheiks*. London: Weidenfeld and Nicolson, 1977.
Carswell, John. *The South Sea Bubble*. London: The Crescent Press, 1960.
Commodity Futures Trading Commission. *Annual Reports, 1976–1980: Report to Congress in Response to Section 21 of the Commodity Exchange Act*. Washington, D.C., May 29, 1981.
Comptroller General of the United States. *Report to Congress: Regulation of the Commodity Futures Markets – What Needs to Be Done*. Washington, D.C., May 17, 1978.
Duncan, Andrew. *Money Rush*. London: Hutchinson, 1979.
Fowler, William Worthington. *20 Years of Inside Life in Wall Street*. New York: Orange, Judd and Co., 1880.
Hunt, Harry, III. *Texas Rich: The Hunt Dynasty from the Early Oil Days Through the Silver Crash*. New York: W. W. Norton and Co., 1981.
Kindleberger, Charles. *Manias, Panics, and Crashes*. New York: Basic Books, 1978.
MacKay, Charles. *Extraordinary Popular Delusions and the Madness of Crowds*. Boston: L. C. Page, 1932.
Morgan, Dan. *Merchants of Grain*. New York: The Viking Press, 1979.
Rees, Graham L. *Britain's Commodity Markets*. London: Paul Elek Books, 1972.
Robbins, Peter. *A Guide to Precious Metals*. London: Kogan Page, 1980.
Sampson, Anthony. *The Seven Sisters*. London: Hodder & Stoughton, 1975.
Sarnoff, Paul. *The Silver Bulls*. Westport, Conn.: Arlington House, 1980.
Smith, Jerome F. *The Coming Currency Collapse; And What You Can Do About It*. New York: Books in Focus, 1980.
———. *Silver Profits in the Seventies*. Vancouver, B.C.: ERC Publishing Co. 1972.
Sobel, Robert. *Panic on Wall Street*. New York: Macmillan, 1968.
Soda, Ralph. *Silver! The Story Behind the Hunts' Raid on the Market*. Washington: Gannett News Service, 1981.
Teweles, Richard J.; Harlow, Charles V.; and Stone, Herbert L. *The Commodity Futures Game: Who Wins? Who Loses? Why?* New York: McGraw-Hill Book Co., 1977.
Thesiger, Wilfred. *Arabian Sands*. London: Penguin Books, 1979.
U.S., Congress, House, Committee on Government Operations, Subcom-

mittee on Commerce, Consumer and Monetary Affairs. *Silver Prices and the Adequacy of Federal Actions in the Marketplace, 1979–80. Hearings*, March 31, April 14, 15, 29, and 30, and May 2 and 22, 1980.

U.S., Congress, Senate, Committee on Agriculture, Nutrition and Forestry. *Price Volatility in the Silver Futures Market. Hearings*, Part 1, May 1 and 2, 1980: Part II, June 26, 1980.

———. *To Prohibit Futures Trading of Potatoes on Commodity Exchanges. Hearings*, November 15, 1979.

———. *Report of the Commodity Futures Trading Commission on Recent Developments in the Silver Futures Market.* Washington, D.C., 1980.

U.S., Congress, Senate, Committee on Banking, Housing and Urban Affairs. *Margin Requirements for Transactions in Financial Instruments. Hearings*, May 29 and 30, 1980.

———. *Information Related to Futures Contracts in Financial Instruments.* (Part I includes positions of exchange directors in silver futures; Part II includes positions of exchange directors in gold futures.) Washington, D.C., July 1980.

Wyler, Seymour B. *The Book of Old Silver.* New York: Crown Publishers, 1937.

Index